THE BOOK OF LIES

THE BOOK OF LIES

Schemes, Scams, Fakes, and Frauds
That Have Changed the Course of
History and Affect Our Daily Lives

M. HIRSH GOLDBERG

Illustrations by Ray Driver

William Morrow and Company, Inc.
New York

Library of Congress Cataloging-in-Publication Data

Goldberg, M. Hirsh.
The book of lies : schemes, scams, fakes, and frauds that have
changed the course of history and affect our daily lives / M. Hirsh
Goldberg ; illustrations by Ray Driver.
p. cm.
Includes bibliographical references.
ISBN 0-688-08443-5
1. Truthfulness and falsehood. I. Title.
BJ1421.G64   1990
177'.3—dc20   89-29099
                                                                        CIP

Printed in the United States of America

2 3 4 5 6 7 8 9 10

BOOK DESIGN BY ARLENE GOLDBERG

To the memory of
my beloved father
Herman Goldberg
(1911–1986)
who was
honest and honorable
in everything he did

Lying is such a central characteristic that better understanding of it is relevant to almost all human affairs.

—Dr. Paul Ekman
Telling Lies (Norton, 1985)

According to one psychologist, lying is so much a part of our lives that the average American tells some 200 lies a day. This includes "white" lies, false excuses, lying by omission, and so on.

—Dr. Joyce Brothers
Cosmopolitan Magazine

If your mother says she loves you, check it out.

—*Advice for cub reporters*
pinned to the wall at the
City News Bureau of Chicago

CONTENTS

CONTENTS

CONTENTS

A NOTE TO THE READER

Why the Type on This Book Was Set Q to M

The manuscript for this book was first typed on a Smith-Corona SC110 electric typewriter, then retyped on an IBM-PC before being sent to the publisher, where it was set for printing on Linotron 202N phototypesetting equipment. The keyboards for these different pieces of typing equipment were the same—they all had that strange distribution of the alphabet that looks like this:

QWERTYUIOP
ASDFGHJKL
ZXCVBNM

Why, you might ask, are the keys on all typewriters, computers, and typesetting equipment the same? And why are they not in alphabetical order? And if not, why are they in such a jumbled order without any seeming rhyme or reason?

These questions are even more bewildering when one realizes that the very first typewriter, developed by Christopher Latham Sholes, the American inventor of the world's first commercially produced typewriter in 1873, had the keys in perfect alphabetical order.

What happened? Why do we have keyboards that all begin with . . . with . . . QWERTY?

The answer is that after Sholes developed his typewriter, he found to his amazement that the keys jammed when struck by a typist of any speed. To solve this problem, he turned to his brother-in-law, a mathematician and schoolteacher, who devised a plan: he separated on the keyboard the letters most often used together in the English language. In this way, the slight but added delay in striking the letters one after another would prevent jamming.

Sholes readily adopted his brother-in-law's solution—even though that solution wound up with the letters in a weird QWERTY order. But Sholes, possibly too embarrassed to let the public know that such a jumble of letters was necessary to keep his invention from jamming, hit on a promotional gimmick that also involved a heavy dose of deceit. He said that the letter configuration on his typewriter had been scientifically arrived at as the fastest way to type. No mention was made publicly of the jamming, of the brother-in-law sent out to keep common letter combinations apart—so far apart, in fact, that it has been found that a typist's fingers have to travel more, not less, than necessary to type almost any word in the English language on the QWERTY arrangement.

In fact Sholes's promotion of his typewriter's keyboard arrangement as being scientific and adding speed and efficiency has been labeled by a British authority on the history of the typewriter as "probably one of the biggest confidence tricks of all time." Wilfred A. Beeching, director of the British Typewriter Museum and author of *Century of the Typewriter* (St. Martin's Press, 1974), declared that while Sholes's particular machine gained added speed from his keyboard, "the idea that the so-called 'scientific arrangement' of the keys was designed to give the minimum movement of the hands was, in fact, completely false!"

Beeching further points out that "any haphazard arrangement of letters would be mathematically better than the existing one."

Sholes's QWERTY keyboard, however, became firmly established, and no one—not even rival companies—questioned the validity of Sholes's statements about his grouping of the alphabet (note that less-used numbers, unlike letters, are in order on the Sholes keyboard). What makes this an even more surprising development in our competitive world is that those companies that did not go along with the arrangement sank out of sight. And no variations have ever gained acceptance, even though studies have shown that much greater speeds can be achieved on typewriters with a different, more scientifically designed keyboard.

But no matter. The lie has stuck. And we are stuck with a strange typewriter alphabet.

A NOTE TO THE READER

What follows are a host of other lies that have, in one way or another, changed our history and shaped our lives. And, appropriately enough, you will learn all this in a book composed on typewriting and typesetting equipment that is itself affected by a lie.

A few in the cast of characters from *The Book of Lies*.

INTRODUCTION

"This book is free!" (and other great lies)

The preacher concluded the services by announcing that the following Sunday he would deliver a sermon about liars, and in preparation for that sermon he wanted everyone in the congregation to read the 155th psalm in the Book of Psalms.

At the services the next Sunday the preacher began his sermon by asking those in the congregation who had read the 155th psalm to raise their hands. All of the congregants raised their hands.

"You are the very audience I want to talk to," roared the preacher. "There is *no* one hundred fifty-fifth psalm!"

The purpose of this book is not to glorify lies and liars, however clever, charming or eloquent many of them may be. Mark Twain once said, "When in doubt, tell the truth"—and he wasn't lying. The truth is obviously more accurate, usually easier to remember, often kinder, and ultimately more healthful to mind and soul. I therefore recommend it.

Why, then, write a book about lies and liars? Because it is amusing, interesting, surprising? Yes, of course. But it is also revealing, in a rarely explored way, of human nature.

Lying is such a part of the fabric of our lives that even the Bible story of the beginning of humanity is filled with lies told by its three protagonists. Amid the splendor of the Garden of Eden, the serpent lies to Eve about her right to eat from the Tree of Knowledge, Eve in turn lies to Adam to get him to eat also of the fruit, and Adam later lies to God about his own role in the violation of God's commandment.

Today, the same widespread condition of telling falsehoods persists. A nationally syndicated newspaper article recently reported that a human-resources consulting company, hired to investigate the truth about the backgrounds of job applicants, found "outright lies on more than 30 percent of résumés today."

Consider these news stories of recent years: A U.S. senator who is also a candidate for president—Joseph Biden—is found to be lying about the origin of language and ideas in some of his campaign speeches, after it is revealed he also lied and cheated in college . . . another presidential candidate—Gary Hart—is finally forced to confess in public he lied about his private life . . . Lt. Col. Oliver North, testifying in the Iran-Contra affair (itself a cover-up operation based on deceptions), points proudly to his lying as an act of patriotism . . . a young *Washington Post* reporter, after lying on her résumé to get her job, fakes a story about an eight-year-old drug addict and wins the Pulitzer Prize before being discovered. (Of course, none of these people may be as potentially harmful to society as the man with only a high school diploma who several years ago lied his way to a job as a safety engineer at a nuclear power plant.)

Yet, little has been written about lying, this most prevalent of human practices. How common is it today? How pervasive has it been and what effect has it had on history? Who have been its most potent practitioners? Has any good ever emerged from this attempt to change reality?

The answers to these questions will be presented in the pages that follow—through news articles, facts, statistics, studies, essays, quotes, and anecdotes. The approach will be both light and serious, depending upon the material and in keeping with the subject itself. For lying, while it does have the potential to destroy others and oneself, can be at the same time comical—since it reveals us in our all-too-human human condition.

In these pages will be found the truth about the lies told by such historic figures as Christopher Columbus and J. Edgar Hoover, by Pharaohs and Führers, by common people and Presidents.

I am reminded of the axiom that without lying, there would be no truth. Indeed, an exploration of lies is, ultimately, a celebration of truth. And that's no lie.

THE BOOK OF LIES

Everyday lines for everyday lies.

CHAPTER I

"Trust me."

READING BETWEEN THE LIES

. . . How Lies Shape Our Everyday Lives

Half the people in America are faking it.
—Robert Mitchum

We begin our excursion into the world of untruth and truth by sampling in this chapter some of the oddities and surprises connected with lying.

Let us start with a definition of the word *lie*.

DEFINITIONS, PLEASE

> *lie* (lī) n. **1.** A false statement or piece of information deliberately presented as being true; a falsehood.
>
> **2.** Anything meant to deceive or give a wrong impression.
>
> —*The American Heritage Dictionary of the English Language*

A lie, as noted here, has two definitions—a lie can be a verbal or written untruth; it can also mean an activity undertaken by one human being to dupe or defraud another.

The Book of Lies explores the full range of lies in our lives—whether the lie be a statement or an act . . . spoken, written, or

19

implied . . . a frivolous fib or a serious scam. The goal is to see and understand what human beings try to do surreptitiously to one another before they are discovered doing it. It is hoped such understanding can help all of us better cope with and protect ourselves against the liars and cheats of this world. This book's advice to you is to follow what Goodman Ace, the creator of many of TV's most successful shows, once said: "I keep reading between the lies."

THERE'S A WHOLE LOT OF LYING GOING ON: EXHIBIT A—WORDS

In *Roget's Thesaurus,* in its division on "Communication of Ideas," the section presenting synonyms for *truth,* labeled "Veracity," lists only enough words for four small paragraphs. However, words that deal with various forms of lying and deception fill six sections covering three and a half pages.

While many of the words presented are familiar everyday words or expressions, the thesaurus shows how varied are the nuances for this aspect of human behavior by also listing the following words, now somewhat obscure, for various shades of lies and lying:

Nouns

Coggery	A cheat or deceiver
Gudgeon	Someone who is easily duped; a gullible person
Gullery	Trickery, deception
Subreption	A secret, underhanded, unlawful, or unfair representation through suppression or fraudulent concealment of facts.
Tarradiddle	A petty falsehood; fib
Thimblerig	A swindle gambling game

Verbs

Bam	Fool, hoax (may be short for *bamboozle*)
Benet	Ensnare

Blaque	Talk pretentiously; lie boastfully
Chouse	Cheat, trick, defraud
Cully	Trick, cheat, deceive
Gudgeon	Dupe
Illaqueste	Trick, enmesh, ensnare
Palter	Act insincerely or deceitfully

EXHIBIT B—EXPRESSIONS

Plus, there are expressions that imply deception, duping, or untruth, such as these that can also be found in the thesaurus:

- "Keep the word of promise to the ear and break it to the hope"
- "Draw a herring across the trail"
- "Varnish right and puzzle wrong"
- "Catch a Tartar"
- "False as dicers' oaths"

EXHIBIT C—NAMES THAT GIVE THE LIE

Here are names, places, and things that have provided our language with words to characterize various forms of lying:

Brummagem	(n.) Something cheap or inferior; counterfeit. Named after Birmingham, England, because of seventeenth-century counterfeit groats coined there.
Charlatan	(n.) A person who claims to possess knowledge or skill that he does not have; a quack. It is a French word, derived from the Italian *ciarlatario,* variant of *cerretano,* an inhabitant of Cerreto, a village near Spoleto, Italy, famous for its quacks.

Janus-faced	(adj.) Two-faced, deceiving. The word is based on the god in Roman mythology who was the patron of beginnings and endings and had two faces, one in the front and one in the back of his head.
Machiavellianism	(n.) The political doctrine that rejects morality in politics and endorses the use of wiles and deceit in securing and employing political power. The concept is based on the writings of Niccolò Machiavelli, an Italian statesman of the late fifteenth and early sixteenth centuries.
Mountebank	(n.) a hawker of quack medicines who entices buyers with stories and tricks. The word comes from the Italian *montambanco,* "one who climbs on a bench."
Pecksniffian	(adj.) Hypocritical, insincere, falsely moralistic. Named after the character Pecksniff in Charles Dickens's novel *Martin Chuzzlewit.*
Pinchbeck	(n.) Something that is counterfeit. Named after Christopher Pinchbeck, an eighteenth-century English watchmaker who invented use of copper and zinc alloy to imitate gold in cheap jewelry.
Tartuffe	(n.) A religious hypocrite. Derived from the character Tartuffe in Molière's satirical comedy about a religious hypocrite.

THE DAY SET ASIDE FOR LYING

Lying is so prevalent that it has its own day—April Fools' Day. Also known as All-Fools' Day, it occurs on the first day of April. At that time, according to custom, practical jokes and outrageous lies are played on others (the victim is called an April fool in English, but in France the victim is called an April fish and in Scotland an April gowk, which means a cuckoo).

The origin of the day comes from a practice started in France when that country became the first to adopt the reformed calendar of Charles IX, which in 1564 shifted the New Year from April 1 to January 1. Until then the New Year celebration actually started at the time of the vernal equinox on March 21 and concluded April 1. Those who continued to celebrate the New Year on April 1 were called April fools and, starting in France, the custom developed to fool friends on that day. (Of course, if the trickery was nasty enough, the victim became a former friend.)*

MAYBE PINOCCHIO'S NOSE WAS DUE TO THE MUNCHAUSEN SYNDROME?

Lying also has its own fairy tale and figure—Pinocchio—and its own medical condition—the Munchausen syndrome.

Pinocchio

Pinocchio, the puppet who becomes a boy with a nose that grows when he tells a lie, is considered one of the most enduring of children's stories. A philosopher, Benedetto Croce, said of the tale that "the wood out of which Pinocchio is carved is humanity itself."

The story, first published in Italy in 1883 as *The Adventures of Pinocchio,* has by now been translated into almost every living language and into at least one dead language—Latin.

The author is listed as Carlo Collodi, but that was a pseudonym (which is a nice way of saying an author lied about his name). One can only wonder at the irony of the creator of a fairy tale against lying who hides behind a false name. His real name was Carlo Lorenzini (1826–1890). A lifelong bachelor, he left the study of the priesthood to enter journalism, from which he eventually

---

*Interestingly in India, at the feast of Huli, the last day of which is March 31, the custom is to fool people by telling them to go on fruitless or ridiculous errands.

turned to the writing of children's stories (in 1875 he wrote to a friend that he was now going to devote himself to "writing only for children. Grown-ups are too hard to satisfy; they are not for me.").

The moral of the boy-puppet who learned never to tell a lie eventually entered the modern consciousness when Walt Disney turned the fable into a full-color animated motion picture.

The Munchausen Syndrome

The Munchausen syndrome is a term given to a condition in which patients lie about their medical condition, invariably providing more dramatic symptoms and ills than are warranted or truthful. Unlike the hypochondriac who sincerely believes he or she is ill (even if such might not be the case), those who exhibit the Munchausen syndrome know they are not ill but wish, for various psychological reasons, to make the doctor or hospital believe they are sick.

Usually these people complain of acute abdominal pain or bleeding and they can easily produce hemoptysis or hematuria. They often subject themselves to many painful and dangerous diagnostic procedures and numerous hospitalizations. They seem especially prone to undergoing abdominal surgery. There are even cases of parents giving false symptoms about their children (such was reported in the *Medical Journal of Australia* in 1986 in a case of child abuse said to be in the category of Munchausen syndrome by proxy).

The cause of the Munchausen syndrome is not known. Patients who exhibit it are often labeled schizophrenic or psychopathic, but no specific diagnosis appears to match all cases.

Interestingly, the naming of the syndrome reveals other aspects about the colorful history of lying and liars.

The term Munchausen syndrome is named after a semifictional character who was based on Baron Karl Friedrich Hieronymus von Münchhausen (1720–1797). A German who lived in Hanover, he had fought in the Russian cavalry against the Turks from 1737 to 1739. When he retired in 1760, he regaled his friends back in Germany with what were regarded as exaggerated stories of his exploits.

In 1785 Rudolph Erich Raspe (1737–1794), an unsavory German

mineralogist who had fled to England, published a book mocking the Baron as a teller of tall tales. Raspe changed the main character's name to Munchausen (without the umlaut and with only one *h* to make the name easier for English readers) and *Baron Munchausen's Narrative of His Marvellous Travels and Campaigns in Russia* became highly successful and was widely translated.

Raspe himself was considered a scoundrel who owed large debts, embezzled metals from a collection under his care, fled to England to stay ahead of his creditors, wrote the book with as one of his goals the humiliation of his German friends, became involved in a mining swindle, and then fled once more—this time to Ireland, where he died of scarlet fever.

In many ways Raspe and not Münchhausen should have had his name associated with a syndrome that denotes deception.*

MAYBE THEY JUST FORGOT TO RENEW THEIR LITERARY LICENSE

Many of our greatest authors have led less than truthful lives. Consider this sampling:

Daniel Defoe

Daniel Defoe's greatest novels—*Robinson Crusoe* (1719) and *Moll Flanders* (1721)—as well as *Roxana, The History of Colonel Jack,* and *The Journal of the Plague Year*—were all written by Defoe (1660–1731) during a five-year period after the English novelist and journalist had turned sixty. Until that time he had experienced bankruptcy as a businessman, his political career as a journalist was a disaster, and his reputation when he finally turned to novel writing was in ruins.

He was also known as someone who was an "inventor of news," according to novelist V. S. Pritchett in a biographical sketch in

---

*Unlike those with the Munchausen syndrome, the true hypochondriac is not a liar, as can be seen in the classic story of the tombstone erected above a hypochondriac's grave. It read, "I told you I was sick."

Brief Lives. Furthermore, Pritchett called Defoe "a born impersonator and dedicated liar."

And yet Defoe is often called the father of the English novel, for he is the one, notes Pritchett, who "laid the foundation of realistic narrative in the English novel."

Miguel de Cervantes

The Spanish novelist is the author of *Don Quixote*, considered among the greatest works of fiction in history. Written nearly 385 years ago, it was a highly popular book during Cervantes's time and has persisted in its worldwide popularity throughout the four centuries of its existence. It is all the more interesting, then, that Cervantes, who worked as a tax collector, began *Don Quixote*, which is about trying to right the world's wrongs, while he was in prison in Spain accused of fraud in his tax collecting.

Hans Christian Andersen

The famed Danish writer of fairy tales said that he was born and grew up in poverty and was so ugly as a child that he had no friends. Recent research now reveals that Hans might have looked like an ugly duckling, but he was worth a princely sum. The truth is that Andersen lied about his parentage. He was really the illegitimate son of a prince who later became King Christian VIII of Denmark.

"No one is more dishonest than authors—except publishers."

—Gaston Gallimard (1881–1975),
   founder and head of the most
   prestigious and influential
   publishing house in France

THE LIES ON OUR MAP

Those Vikings must have been very interesting people. They certainly knew how to lie. In fact, two of their lies are now a permanent part of our world's map.

Greenland is the largest island in the world. It is also one of the coldest, being basically a frozen land mass in the Arctic Circle. Viking explorers, however, who had come upon the island in the late ninth century, wanted to attract settlers, so they called it Greenland to purposely mislead people into believing it had greenery. The truth is that only the coastal areas turn green, and even this greening takes place just during Greenland's brief summer. In fact, most of Greenland lies above the Arctic Circle, and thick ice covers 85 percent of it. But even though the truth was later learned, the trickery remained and the inappropriate name Greenland has stuck.

About the same time in the ninth century another group of Vikings discovered another island. This one they wanted to keep to themselves. So they gave it the most unappealing name they could think of. They gave it a name to fool people into thinking it was a forbidding, cold place. They called it Iceland.

But Iceland is hardly just a land of ice. Although located at latitude 66 degrees North, it has lush green forests, beaches that have both black and white sands, mountains ringed with flowers, and underground forces that create not only fiery volcanoes but also geothermal steam and superheated water. In fact Iceland has more hot springs and sulfur steam areas than any other country. The word *geyser* actually comes from the most famous hot spring in Iceland—Geysir, which when active spouted hot water 195 feet high.

Yes, there are also glaciers and snow here and just two seasons—with either much light or much dark. But in the lowlands, summers are cool and winters mild. Ports are free of ice all year. Something must be right about the living. Here is a thriving democracy, with many cultural offerings. Icelandic women have the longest life expectancy in the world (79.5 years) and the men also lead long lives (73.9 years). And even in the dead of winter, its capital city, Reykjavík, can experience warmer temperatures than New York City.

Most if not all of this is generally unknown to the world at large. The name Iceland has done its job. It has fooled mankind for over a thousand years.

Those Vikings were very good explorers—and liars.

THEY TAKE LYING ON THE JOB

One profession that has made a living out of other people's lying has been investigative reporting. The reporter is paid to ferret out the untruths, find the truth, and expose the liar and his lie in public print. Isn't that what the First Amendment, concerning freedom of the press, is all about?

In any event, all this concentration on lying does some peculiar things to an investigative reporter, as Leonard Downie, Jr., an investigative reporter himself, writes in *The New Muckrakers,* a book about the breed. The reporter must learn to "recognize and disregard more lies than are told to a police detective in an entire career on the homicide squad," Downie says.

And who are the ones telling these lies? According to Downie, "Many of these lies come from very respectable people—government officials, top business executives, judges, and lawyers—people who would never be suspected of such duplicity."

In fact, Downie quotes a *New York Times* investigative reporter, Robert M. Smith, about what this does to a journalist's attitude toward what other people say: "Being lied to becomes so much a part of the investigative reporter's life that once or twice a year he asks himself, 'Why is this guy telling me the truth?' "

Who Said It?

Who said the following? (One hint: it was said in 1930.)

> Lying increases the creative faculties, expands the ego, lessens the friction of social contacts. . . . It is only in lies, wholeheartedly and bravely told, that human nature attains through words and speech the forbearance, the nobility, the romance, the idealism, that—being what it is—it falls so short of in fact and in deed.

Did you guess Adolf Hitler? Or Mussolini? Or maybe Stalin (although it does seem a little too high-blown for Stalin)?

The answer is none of the above. The statement, appearing in the October 1930 issue of *Vanity Fair,* was made by Clare Boothe Luce, wife of Henry Luce, the publisher of *Time* magazine.

HERE'S THE ONLY PLACE IN THE UNITED STATES WHERE LYING IS LEGALLY PROTECTED

There is one place where it is perfectly legal to say any lie you want, to slander or libel anybody you wish, to utter the most outrageous untruth—and you will never face prosecution. In fact, you are protected by Congress, by the courts, by the Constitution.

The place?

Why, Congress itself.

All members of Congress have immunity from prosecution for libel and slander. This safeguard is in the United States Constitution, which states that "for any speech or debate in either House, they [members of Congress] shall not be questioned in any other place."

In challenges to the provision, the courts have interpreted this congressional privilege liberally. The concept behind it is that members of Congress should be free to carry out their discussions without fear of prosecution. As a result, a U.S. senator or representative—unlike any other American—has the absolute protection to say anything he or she wants in a speech or debate in the Senate or the House, to insert in the *Congressional Record* any material so desired, even if it might not have been said on the floor of either chamber, and to make any statement in committee while the committee is acting within its authority.

The member of Congress can even take the *Congressional Record* in which the statement was made and distribute it or reprints of it and not face prosecution (provided that the distribution or reprinting is not done for malicious purposes).

The U.S. Supreme Court has even upheld the right of a member of Congress to deliver in Congress a speech containing falsehoods uttered as part of a larger conspiracy. In *United States* v. *Johnson,* two House members were charged under federal conspiracy and conflict-of-interest statutes with allegedly accepting payoffs to try to influence U.S. Justice Department personnel in connection with an investigation into certain savings-and-loan practices. As part of the conspiracy, one of the two congressmen gave a speech on the floor of the Congress to foster confidence in the Maryland savings-and-loan industry. He was convicted, with this speech cited as evidence of his participation in the scheme, but the Supreme Court overturned the conviction based upon its broad interpretation of the constitutional protection each member of Congress has to say anything he or she wants in either House "and not be questioned in any other place."

NOW YOU CAN'T EVEN TRUST A DYING MAN'S WORD

An axiom in the legal profession is that one can rely on the truthfulness of a deathbed confession. The logic here is not hard to see: A person about to meet his Maker is not likely to commit the sin of lying. Neither does such a person have much if anything to gain by lying at a time when he or she will be leaving this earth.

Well, now even this maxim about honesty has to be revised because of an incident in October 1988 in which Georgia and federal officials disproved the confession of a dying man who declared he had participated in a notorious bombing of a black church in 1963 that had killed four black girls.

As reported in *The New York Times* of October 22, 1988, Gary A. Tucker, who was then a fifty-four-year-old cancer patient with not much time to live, had told authorities that he and another person had placed the bomb at the Sixteenth Street Baptist Church in Birmingham, Alabama. The bomb exploded on Sunday, September 15, 1963, killing the four girls, who were in a lounge preparing for a youth program. The bombing aroused national outrage, coming as it did during the height of the civil rights movement. It marked a turning point in the struggle to end segregationist policies in the Deep South.

In 1977 Robert Chambliss, who was connected with the Ku Klux Klan, was tried and found guilty of the bombing and sentenced to life imprisonment, but police officials long believed that two other individuals were also involved. Chambliss died in 1985, and the case had remained open when Tucker gave his deathbed confession.

At first his statements seemed to be accurate. "He really knew his dates and his places, and he knew the players in the bombing," said a Justice Department official. "He did have information that wasn't commonplace." And hospital officials, who at Tucker's request had called federal investigators, found that Tucker "was in touch with reality, had a good memory and was lucid."

Tucker first told his story to the local district attorney, David Barber. "His explanation to us was that he realized he was dying and he wanted to get this off his conscience," Barber said.

But subsequent investigation showed that Tucker's story was a fake. He did not seem to know the location of the church, gave three different descriptions of the car in which he said he brought the dynamite to the church, and said that his accomplice was a boyhood friend, who, it was subsequently determined, had been in prison at the time of the bombing.

Relatives speculated that Tucker was hallucinating when he made his confession, while law enforcement officials felt that Tucker, who may have been indirectly involved in the bombing, had, because of his physical and mental condition, believed himself actually responsible.

In any case efforts were made to corroborate Tucker's statements. This could not be done. In fact, said one investigator, "they were disproved."

As District Attorney David Barber concluded, this bizarre case had resulted in a dying man being "a confessor to a crime that he did not commit."

AMERICA'S MOST POPULAR CRIME

Tax fraud is said to be the most popular crime in America. Not even drug abuse is as popular or as profitable, according to *Louis Rukeyser's Business Almanac* (Simon and Schuster, 1988). IRS surveys have revealed that nearly 25 percent of all Americans admit underreporting their taxable income. In 1981, for instance, a year closely studied, it was estimated that American taxpayers did not report $260 billion in income—which meant the government, saddled with a growing budget deficit and increasing debt, lost $75 billion in revenue that year. By 1988, the "tax gap," as it is called—the difference between what is actually owed Uncle Sam and what is actually paid (on legal incomes only)—reached $87.1 billion.

TAX CHEATER, OBSERVE THYSELF

What kind of person lies on his tax return? The latest research has uncovered a fascinating portrait of those who cheat a lot on their taxes.

According to this profile, the more a person cheats on taxes, the more likely he or she . . .

- is greatly concerned with financial success

- is unhappy with the present and gloomy about the future

- thinks the legal system is unfair

- has a tendency to manipulate people

- enjoys taking risks (they have more speeding tickets, twice as many traffic accidents, are more likely to drive while drunk, and commit adultery more than the average population)

But the people who cheat the most are those with the most opportunity. While a 1983 Internal Revenue Service study found that general taxpayers reported 94 percent of their true income, only 47 percent of income was reported by the self-employed, by professionals, and by small-business owners, who have more chance to cheat.

All in all the IRS has found in its research that of those who filed their tax returns, 43 percent did not pay their correct share—costing the treasury $64 billion in 1987.* While some or many of

---

*Interestingly the IRS studies also found that 8 percent of taxpayers paid too much tax.

these people may have honestly misunderstood or miscalculated on their returns, researchers using confidential surveys have found one-fourth of taxpayers admitting to lying about their taxes.

In a front-page article on these findings, *The New York Times* reported that the figures are "alarming, even to experts who expected to find some evasion." The data, along with the psychological findings, "raise questions about ethical decision making in general." *

The new profile of the large tax cheater shows that the previously accepted economic models of tax evasion are wrong. It had been assumed that all taxpayers are equally likely to lie about their taxes, but those models incorrectly assumed that people act out of purely rational reasons—assessing the saving of money for taxes against the punishment for being caught.

Now, not only personality but attitudes have been found to play a key role in tax cheating. One key is whether a person thinks it is all right to cheat—whether it be on taxes or on padding deductions or underreporting income—especially if otherwise the individual is a law-abiding citizen.

Fewer than 10 percent of taxpayers have been found to admit to strongly holding such feelings about taxes. Those who agree the most, say researchers, are those who tend to be male, young, and living in the suburbs in the Northeast, the Sun Belt, or the West.

But most troubling is the finding that those who cheat are not troubled by cheating. For many people, according to the head of the American Psychiatric Association, success—whether in the form of money, fame, or prestige—is what counts today more for most people, rather than morality. It is a success-at-any-price mentality.

And yet there are many people for whom such an attitude is wrong, who have such values that they do not break the rules or cheat, or who do so in only one small aspect of their lives.

But for those who cheat in a large way on their taxes, the studies show that these people have an ability to have a Jekyll and Hyde mentality about morality. Although many normal people can be more ethical in certain areas than in others, there are those

---

*Daniel Goleman, "The Tax Cheats: Selfish to the Bottom Line," *The New York Times,* April 11, 1988, p. A1.

who can compartmentalize their ethical behavior to such a degree that it can become pathological.

Thus within one person the good citizen and the cheat are so separated that lying about large sums on a tax return provokes no guilt. The normal person with the normal morality is not able to make such a division in his or her thoughts. The individual with the normal morality still wants to be admired for doing good.

NOW, IS THIS YOUR TYPICAL TAX CHEATER?

Among the many tax cheaters brought to justice, one surely stands out.

It wasn't so much that he was found guilty in federal district court in Manhattan in 1988 for failure to file income tax returns for three years.

It also wasn't so much that he owed $210,000 in taxes.

It was more that he held a very interesting position in the community.

To be more precise, this tax cheat was an assistant United States attorney for nearly six years and then served as head of the federal strike forces prosecuting organized crime in Manhattan and Brooklyn.

ARE THEY COUNTERFEITERS OR LAUNDERERS?

The best counterfeiters of U.S. money are now said to be found in Italy. They appear to have overcome one of the problems in counterfeiting U.S. currency—and that is duplicating the paper. Counterfeiters operating out of Milan, Italy, simply take a one-dollar bill, bleach it, and then print a one-hundred-dollar bill on it.

The next problem facing the U.S. Treasury Department: office copier machines that can duplicate in color.

PERJURY IS A HARD RAP TO PROVE

In *The Prosecutors,* (Simon and Schuster, 1987), which deals with several recent highly publicized criminal proceedings conducted by U.S. government prosecutors, James B. Stewart wrote about why the government's most powerful lawyers find perjury difficult to prove.

"Perjury is probably the most underprosecuted of all crimes. The offense itself is rampant, occurring during the course of most investigations and trials. But prosecutors rarely seek indictments," Stewart reports.

"It is, for one thing, a derivative crime, one that usually occurs as an outgrowth of another offense. If it is the suspect or defendant who lies, a perjury case distracts from the principal, usually more important case. Only when the chief case is weak, as has been the case with some prominent organized-crime figures and labor leaders, does a perjury indictment sometimes serve as a substitute. And even in those cases, convictions are far from certain—probably because juries suspect that the perjury case is a surrogate for other charges that the prosecution can't prove."

Or as a president of the United States, Richard Nixon said, consoling one of his worried aides at the height of the Watergate controversy (as heard on the White House tapes): "Perjury is a hard rap to prove."

Everyday Lines with Everyday Lies: A Sampling

How much lying are you exposed to? Consider how many of the following statements you have heard in the last twenty-four hours:

"I'll just be a minute."

"Let's get together for lunch. I'll give you a call."

"Everything's fixed."

"The check is in the mail."

"I'll return your book as soon as I finish reading it."

"The doctor will be with you shortly."

"This will only hurt a little."

"The check will be in the mail tonight."

"I just love your new _____." (hairdo, dress, coat, carpet, etc.)

"Remember—there's absolutely no obligation on your part."

"Honey, I had a little accident with the car, but there's nothing to worry about."

"This insurance policy is comprehensive."

"What? The check was in the mail two weeks ago."

"You've made yourself a great deal on that car."

"And if elected, I will . . ."

THE QUIZ SHOW SCANDALS—AND HOW THEY AFFECTED THE CAREER OF AN HONEST MAN

In the late 1950s, the big ratings success on television was the quiz shows. It had started with *The $64,000 Question* on CBS-TV and had continued with another big-money quiz show on NBC-TV called *Twenty-One.*

With such large sums involved and with high ratings at stake, the quiz shows relied on a carefully crafted aura of honesty. In both shows the contestants were placed in soundproof isolation booths to protect against their receiving help with the answers during the show.

The problem was that the producers of *Twenty-One,* in their pursuit of the big ratings, had helped rig the answers with some of the contestants. The one who aroused the interest of the TV audience the most was Charles Van Doren, a young, handsome, Columbia University professor and a member of the famed literary Van Doren family. Living in the shadow of his more illustrious uncle and father, Charles was enticed into going along with the charade because, as he said later, it all seemed harmless and he was beguiled by the possibilities for fame and fortune. He was carefully coached before the shows—not only with the answers but in how to fake the agonizing and careful deliberating he was to go into before coming up with the right answers. The dramatics, it was felt, would enhance the show's impact—and ratings.

It did, and with the vast TV audience watching, Van Doren earned $129,000 over a period of six weeks, before he was finally defeated by Vivian Nearing. But soon, a losing contestant tipped some reporters off that the show was rigged. With headlines blaring, an investigation was begun in late 1959 into not only *Twenty-One,* but the other big quiz shows of the time. This included the original *$64,000 Question* and a spin-off, *The $64,000 Challenge.*

It was then found out that the producers of *The $64,000 Challenge* had also been rigging the show.

Enter the name of Louis G. Cowan. As told about by his son, Paul Cowan, in *An Orphan in History* (Doubleday, 1982), Louis Cowan had been the original producer of the first of the big quiz shows, *The $64,000 Question.* Cowan had gone on to become president of CBS-TV, divesting himself of any ownership in *The $64,000 Question,* let alone *The $64,000 Challenge,* which was developed after he had left for what was then a vice-presidency at CBS.

But when the quiz-show scandals hit, to protect itself, the CBS hierarchy asked Louis Cowan to resign. "There was no investigation. There were no allegations of impropriety," writes Paul Cowan. "The company's officials simply asserted that he was a poor administrator. But the code was clear. Most people assumed that Lou had been fired because his role as the creator of the biggest quiz show of them all made him an embarrassment to the network."

Cowan was asked to resign in November 1959. As his son remembers it, while in previous years the front hall closet in their home filled up to overflowing with Christmas gifts from people in the television industry, that year "no one in the industry sent a Christmas gift." The closet "remained a clothes closet throughout the winter."

And when Louis Cowan died, *Newsweek* magazine mistakenly wrote that he had produced the rigged quiz show *Twenty-One.*

Thus the ultimate power of lies—they can sully not only the guilty but the innocent as well.

IS MAN ALONE OR CAN ANIMALS LIE, TOO?

Mankind may be singularly alone in its capacity to dissemble, deceive, cheat, fabricate, distort, hoodwink, hoax, snooker, prevaricate—in short, lie.

Experiments conducted with apes have demonstrated that in the controlled environment of the laboratory, apes can be shown to lie—but only in the lab. In *The Mind of an Ape* (Norton, 1983), authors David Premack and Ann James Premack told of four young chimpanzees tested by means of being tempted to help or hinder a friendly and an unfriendly trainer with either direction or misdirection concerning covered containers that held food. Although all four chimpanzees eventually misdirected the unfriendly trainer, only one wound up clearly showing that he understood what was involved. This chimpanzee demonstrated his *intention* to lie to the unfriendly trainer, while telling the truth to the friendly trainer.

But such behavior as the chimpanzee pointing to the wrong container so as to misdirect—and thereby lie—to the unfriendly trainer was not seen outside the lab. Animals do not normally point nor understand pointing, looking at the end of the extended finger rather than what the finger is indicating in the distance. Pointing, however, essential in the experiment to show lying, was developed by the chimpanzees in the test space, but outside in the compound with other animals, the chimpanzees never once used pointing, even when it would have proven helpful to them (as for instance securing food for themselves) or enabled them to misdirect and therefore lie to another animal or to the hostile trainer.

So although lying in a basic sense can be shown in animals, lying that involves intention and willful duping of another is, in its wide range of emotions, highly peculiar to humanity. It seems as though it could be said that we are human, therefore we lie; it can also be said that we lie, therefore we are human.

Thus, add the ability to differentiate between lying and telling the truth as another possible difference separating man from beast. To be able to choose to be honest rather than dishonest is a way in which we as humans come nearer to the divine.

Which Source Is Telling the Truth About Lying?

"A liar should have a good memory."
                    —Quintillian,
                        as quoted in *Public Speaker's
                        Treasure Chest*

"He who is not strong in memory should not meddle with lying."
                    —Michel de Montaigne, in
                        Bartlett's Famous Quotations

"A liar should have a good memory."
                    —Folklore advice, as quoted in
                        A Treasury of Jewish Folklore

ARE WHITE LIES RIGHT LIES?

Not all lying at all times is harmful. Doctors are often faced with easing a patient's worriment and pain by downplaying—even lying—about symptoms or possible pain from impending surgery. Nurses, too, often rely on half-truths and even full lies to comfort a patient worried about the safety of a treatment. In fact, a study conducted in the United States found that the trainee nurses who got the best grades were also the ones who were the most skilled at deceiving patients.

Indeed, in dealing with Alzheimer patients, an assistant professor of medicine at the Johns Hopkins University School of Medicine, writing in a newspaper column on aging, said that instead of answering a patient's questions that surface and are repeated about people who are deceased, the best tactic is to evade the question and distract the patient. The result of these "evasions" for the Alzheimer victim is "much less frustration and anxiety than those fruitless attempts to explain the truth."

As for dealing with difficult ethical decisions, most doctors have found themselves fibbing to patients. A survey of 211 physicians by Brown University and published in the *Journal of the Ameri-*

can *Medical Association,* discovered that 70 percent would fib about the reason for a mammogram so that the patient would be eligible for medical insurance coverage. If it meant saving a marriage, 50 percent said they would lie to a spouse to hide a husband's venereal disease. Forty percent of physicians would not tell the truth if an overdose of medication led to a patient's death.

The survey found, however, that when it came to a teenager's pregnancy, only a small percentage of doctors—fewer than 10 percent—would lie to parents to avoid revealing their daughter's condition.

But 80 percent of doctors responding to the survey said they "rarely or never" use deception.

A doctor who was not involved in the study but is a director of an institute that studies ethical problems in medicine noted that expectations of strict physician honesty are a recent development. "It was common up until twenty or twenty-five years ago for physicians generally not to tell the truth to patients," he noted.

But white lies may be appropriate not only in medical settings.

In *The Eighth Day,* Thornton Wilder wrote, "It is the duty of old men to lie to the young. Let these encounter their own delusions. We strengthen our souls, when young, on hope; the strength we acquire enables us later to endure despair as a Roman would."

Indeed, white lies are often acts of grace, providing the other person with time- or face-saving moments with which to regroup the inner strength to face the world and to proceed onward and, it is hoped, upward.

"Telling a young actor that he gave a credible performance, when he actually gave a substandard one, gives him time to develop his talents," observed Dr. Erving Goffman, a sociologist, in a *New York Times Magazine* article, "How Black Is the 'White Lie'?" "You don't have to enthuse over a mediocre performance, but you don't have to dash all of his hopes, either."

As Dr. Goffman noted, in most cases it does no harm to let someone feel he is thought of more highly than he is. "We get more than enough knocks to counterbalance this."

From this debate we can see just how variegated, subtle, and important to the human condition is an understanding of lying and of how lying affects our world. Indeed, if the psychologist who said we lie on the average about 200 times a day is correct, then next to breathing, lying is our most common activity.

What Do We Lie Most About?

According to those who have studied lying, we humans lie most about the Big Three—age, income, and sex.

"The Sudetenland is the last territorial claim I have to make in Europe. Right, Benito?"

CHAPTER II

"We are the Super Race."

HISTORY AS A PACK OF LIES

. . . How Lies Have Affected History

> The victor will never be asked if he told the truth.
>
> —Adolf Hitler

History is in large part shaped by war, and war is waged in large part by deception. "All is fair in love and war," goes the old adage, and generals and lovers have pretty much shown an ability to tamper with the truth to gain their ends.

We need go back only to the partly true, partly legendary story of Troy and the Trojan War—which interestingly began over a love affair—to find one of the classic uses of deceit in history. The war started when Paris, son of the king of Troy, and Helen, the beautiful wife of the king of Sparta, fell in love. Paris took her—or kidnapped her—to Troy. The Greek states then united in a war to bring Helen back to Greece.

After ten years of fighting and laying siege to Troy, the Greeks found they could not penetrate the walls of the city. It was then that Ulysses, the Greek hero, devised a plan to fool the Trojans. He had the Greeks build a giant wooden horse, hid soldiers inside, and brought it up to the gates of Troy. He announced to the Trojans in the city that the horse was a gift for the goddess Athena. Then the Greek army pretended to sail away.

Interestingly a Trojan priest warned that the gift was a trick. But even though a spear he threw against the horse made a hollow sound, the Trojans believed a Greek prisoner who said the gift was real and that it had been built large so that the people of Troy would not bring it into the city.

The Trojans thereupon pulled the horse into the city. That night the Greek soldiers crept out of the horse, opened the gates to the returning Greek army, and together massacred the inhabitants of Troy. The Greeks then burned the city.

Although the tale is largely the stuff of legends, the Trojan-horse story has lingered as a vivid symbol of treachery and trickery in the annals of history.

What follows are other examples—all true and not the stuff of legends—of how lies have shaped our history.

COLUMBUS KEPT TWO SETS OF BOOKS: HOW A LIE HELPED DISCOVER THE NEW WORLD

One use of lying that may have changed history occurred during Columbus's voyage of 1492. The major problem Columbus faced on his journey of discovery was keeping his crew from falling into depression and mutinying because of the length of time it was taking to reach land. While Columbus understood the world is round, as did many of the scientists of the day, members of the crew had no such perceptions. They truly feared that either they would drop off the end of the earth if the voyage went long enough or that with too long a journey they would be unable to return to port.

So Columbus hit on an ingenious idea—or actually an ingenious lie. He kept two logs of the expedition's sailing distance. In one log, which he made available to the crew, he recorded a less-than-truthful distance covered each day. In this way he placated his sailors with the belief that they were not so far from home. But in another, secret log, he recorded the real distance traversed by the ships so that he, and he alone, knew the awful truth of how far they had traveled without sighting land.

The story of Columbus's deception can be found in a biography of the admiral written by his natural son, Ferdinand. Noting that once the crew lost sight of land, "many sighed and wept for fear that they would not see it again for a long time," Ferdinand writes that Columbus "comforted them with great promises of lands and riches,'' and then also pacified the crew with his scheme of two sets of statistics.

"To sustain their hope and dispel their fears of a long voyage, he decided to reckon less leagues than they actually made, telling them they had covered only fifteen leagues that day when they had actually covered eighteen. He did this that they might not think themselves so great a distance from Spain as they really were, but for himself he kept a secret accurate reckoning,'' Ferdinand states.

The ploy worked, with little to spare. The crew came close to mutinying, but Columbus was able to extract an agreement to travel for another three days, citing the log to show they could still sail onward and yet return to Spain. Land was finally encountered with one day to go.*

We should not be too surprised at Columbus's little act of deceit. The rulers of Spain had offered a reward of an annuity of 10,000 maravedis to the first person who sighted land. A sailor on watch on that fateful night yelled out a sighting that proved true in the morning. When he came forward for his prize, Columbus denied the request, saying that he himself had really made the first sighting earlier in the evening. Columbus later demanded—and was given—the reward money.

AMERIGO'S LIE PUT HIM ON THE MAP

The most cunning—and productive—use of lying may belong to Amerigo Vespucci, the Italian merchant-explorer after whom not

---

*Actually, because of a navigational error, Columbus's phony log was closer to the truth than the one he kept for his own eyes. Columbus estimated his speed in Roman miles per hour and his distance in leagues of 4 Roman miles each (the league was equivalent to 3.18 nautical miles). But Columbus, with no way of checking, was not accurate. Samuel Eliot Morison, the famed biographer of Columbus, retraced some of the voyages and found that "a careful plotting of his ocean crossing in 1492 proves that he overestimated the distance run at sea on the average 9 per cent." Columbus credited the *Santa Maria* with too much speed, which meant that the league he used really measured only 2.89 nautical miles. Thus, comments Morison on Columbus's attempt to deceive his crew, "owing to his overestimate of distance, the 'phony' reckoning was nearer the truth than the 'accurate' day's work!" (See Samuel Eliot Morison, *Admiral of the Ocean Sea: A Life of Christopher Columbus* [Little, Brown and Company, 1942], pp. 190–91.)

one but two continents—North America and South America—are named.

Vespucci (1451–1512) claimed to have discovered the continent of America in 1497. He also claimed to have made voyages in 1499, 1501, and 1503. In a letter printed in 1503 or 1504 under the title *Mundus Novus* ("Our New World"), he declared that the South American coasts that he had traveled to in 1501 "we may rightly call a new world because our ancestors had no knowledge of them, and it will be a matter wholly new to all those who hear about them."

Christopher Columbus never disputed Vespucci's claims of discovering a new continent and a new world, because in 1492 Columbus did not realize he had reached the Western Hemisphere. He believed the land he encountered were islands that were part of the Indies.

In 1507, when a mapmaker needed a name for the new continent, which was actually South America, he named it *America* "because Amerigo discovered it." Prompting such a decision was the publication of Vespucci's letters describing his discovery. Eventually North America was named in his honor as well.

The problem with all this is that scholars no longer believe our Amerigo was the actual discoverer of a new continent because he did not make the 1497 voyage he claimed to have made. Vespucci's correspondence about his supposed involvement in the 1497 voyage is tentative and lacking in conviction. As to his third voyage, Vespucci gave two accounts that differed markedly, with discrepancies in such important details as dates and distances. Historians now generally agree that Vespucci had nothing to do with the first discovery of the American continent.

As for the voyages he was on, Vespucci did not take a leading role, as he implied. He was only an astronomer, then called a pilot, on the ships, but did not captain them.

But Amerigo certainly did well for himself. While Columbus missed out on having even one continent named for him, Amerigo Vespucci had two out of the world's seven continents named in his honor. He certainly put lying on the map.*

---

*It should be noted that a defense of Vespucci can be found in *Amerigo and the New World* (Knopf, 1955) by Germán Arciniegas, who served at various times as Colombian Vice-Consul in London and twice as Colombian Minister of Edu-

A PHARAOH'S FALLACY

For over 3,000 years Pharaoh Ramses II was credited by history with a military victory over the Hittites, then the leading power in the Mideast, during the Battle of Kadesh about 1285 B.C. Such credit was based upon a monument, erected by Ramses following the battle, in which he spelled out his glorious victory. Archaeologists have now unearthed evidence that instead of triumphing, Ramses barely escaped with his life. The battle, which took place at Kadesh on the Orontes River, north of Palestine, and was one of the greatest of ancient times, ended indecisively. A pharaoh had tried to alter history with a monumental lie.

PTOLEMY: THE MOST SUCCESSFUL FRAUD IN THE HISTORY OF SCIENCE?

Claudius Ptolemy is often referred to as the greatest astronomer of antiquity. Little is known about him except that he made astronomical observations in Alexandria, Egypt, around the year 30 and wrote about his observations and theories in a thirteen-volume work that he called *Mathematike Syntaxis* (*Mathematical Composition*). His observations and theories about astronomy, the stars, and Earth's place in the heavens ruled for 1500 years—until many of his theories were supplanted by Copernicus.

But not only has Ptolemy been proven wrong about his key theory (he declared the earth stood at the center of the solar system and the sun and the planets revolved around it). Evidence

---

cation. He cites a series of scholars who "have taken up the cudgels in Amerigo's defense," but he also acknowledges that "they have been unable to erase the widespread, conventional impression" that Vespucci lied. What seems to stand is the sentiment of people like Ralph Waldo Emerson, whom Arciniegas also quotes: "Strange . . . that broad America must wear the name of a thief. Amerigo Vespucci, the pickle dealer at Seville . . . managed in this lying world to supplant Columbus and baptize half of the earth with his own dishonest name." Interestingly, Arciniegas points out that although Vespucci had a hemisphere named for him, "yet in this whole hemisphere, from Alaska to Tierra del Fuego, not one statue has been erected to him."

has emerged that he plagiarized much of the findings of a Greek astronomer and lied about the basis for some of his work.

The first indication that Ptolemy played fast and loose with his data came in the nineteenth century when scientists reviewing Ptolemy's original work noted that using the position of the planets and calculating back to Ptolemy's time showed major mistakes. In the 1980s, Dennis Rawlins, an astronomer at the University of California, San Diego, propounded the theory that Ptolemy lied about making the observations on his own, that he actually took them en masse from Hipparchus of Rhodes, a pre-Ptolemy astronomer who had compiled a widely followed star catalog. When Ptolemy's references to stars and working out of spherical astronomy problems are checked, the latitude given is consistent with that of Rhodes but not of Alexandria, five degrees of latitude south of where Ptolemy lived.

As for his theories about the earth's position relative to the other planets and to the sun—theories that affected thinking for centuries and established what was called the Ptolemaic system that went unchallenged for 1500 years—there is now evidence that Ptolemy used deceit to come up with supporting data. Robert Newton, of the Johns Hopkins University Applied Physics Laboratory, wrote a book presenting such findings—*The Crime of Claudius Ptolemy* (The Johns Hopkins University Press, 1977). In it, he shows the dozens of times that Ptolemy's observations differed from what he should have observed. One example: Ptolemy claimed to have observed an autumnal equinox on September 25 in the year 132 at 2 P.M., but using modern tables and calculating backward reveals that an observer in Alexandria should have witnessed the equinox more than a day earlier.

Ptolemy's work, *The Syntaxis,* was referred to by Islamic astronomers as *Almagest,* which means "the Greatest." But even defenders of Ptolemy today say that the *Almagest* has "some remarkably fishy numbers." And Robert Newton is so incensed about the widespread fraud and deception he finds in the work that he refuses to refer to Ptolemy's writings as the *Almagest* but uses the original *Syntaxis.* His conclusion: "All of his own observations that Ptolemy uses in the *Syntaxis* are fraudulent so far as we can test them. Many of the observations that he attributes to others are also frauds that he committed. . . . Thus Ptolemy is not the greatest astronomer of antiquity, but he is something still more unusual: He is the most successful fraud in the history of science."

WAS THAT FUDGE THAT FELL FROM THE TREE?

In 1973, in an issue of *Science* magazine, an article by historian Richard S. Westfall appeared entitled "Newton and the Fudge Factor." The gist of Westfall's piece was that the great scientist Sir Isaac Newton, in his monumental work *Principia* issued in 1687, had fudged his data to support some of his preexisting theories—and had used the deception to quiet his opponents.

Newton (1642–1727) is considered the founder of physics and possibly the greatest scientist in history. But when his *Principia* was published, its theory of universal gravitation was the subject of controversy. In later editions, Newton therefore presented supporting measurements that seemed irrefutable, going so far in his last edition of the *Principia* to offer data with a precision of better than one part in a thousand. Among the adjusted calculations he offered were those on the velocity of sound and on the procession of the equinoxes. He also altered the correlation of a variable in his theory of gravitation so that data and theory agreed totally.

The ploy worked and Newton's critics—especially his arch rival the German Leibniz—were quieted. In fact, they were stilled for nearly 300 years before Newton's deceit was uncovered. Writes historian Westfall: "Not the least part of the *Principia*'s persuasiveness was its deliberate pretense to a degree of precision quite beyond its legitimate claim." *The Principia,* he points out, showed that "no one can manipulate the fudge factor so effectively as the master mathematician himself."

Newton not only resorted to falsifying data, it seems he also played games with reality. To advance his claim to having invented calculus and combat Leibniz's claim to the same honor, Newton had the Royal Society, England's major scientific club, study the matter. The eventual report, issued in 1712 by what was said to be a committee of impartial scientists, supported Newton and accused Leibniz of plagiarism. Although the preface to the report stressed the impartiality of the process, the report itself—

and the preface—were actually written by Newton—who also happened to be the president of the Royal Society.*

How Prevalent Is Fraud in Science?

In *Betrayers of the Truth: Fraud and Deceit in the Halls of Science* (Simon and Schuster, 1982), William Broad and Nicholas Wade not only present evidence of deceit by Ptolemy and Newton, but cast doubt that Galileo actually performed some of his experiments and show how Gregor Mendel, the monk who founded the science of genetics, offered statistics supporting his theories that are "too good to be true." Reviewing the history of science, the authors picture a world in which frauds range from manipulating statistics to "cleaning up" data in experiments to unconscious and conscious finagling of results. While the feeling is that the complete fabrication of an experiment is probably rare, minor cheating "could well be just as common as scientific gossip assumes it to be." And for every major fraud that is uncovered the estimate is that throughout history some 100,000 others, major and minor, "lie concealed in the marshy wastes of the scientific literature."

As for science today, the authors find that fraud continues to occur "at a far from negligible rate." The inducement to fraud is caused by careerism, a system that rewards publication, large research grants, and the presence of money. Fraud is allowed to flourish because of the looseness of the self-policing system and the tendency of colleagues not to impute the work or motives of fellow scientists.

There is even an expression for the phenomenon of scientists faking their data, knowing that their chances of being caught are slim. Those who derive their data from their imagination rather than their laboratory are said to be "dry-labbing it." Conclude authors Broad and Wade, "The self-serving manipulation of data is endemic to modern science."

---

*Historians now credit both Newton and Leibniz, working independently of the other, with the invention of calculus.

WAR IS HELL—AND LIES

The Spanish-American War had its origins in lies concocted and spread by a publisher—William Randolph Hearst.

Intent on building circulation for his newspapers and a political future for himself (he even harbored ideas of running for president), Hearst tried to provoke a war between the United States and Spain over Cuba. In 1896 he sent the painter Frederic Remington to Cuba with instructions to draw Spanish atrocities and send them back as soon as possible for use in Hearst's chain of newspapers.

After a period of time in Cuba, Remington found it hard to find such atrocities. He wired Hearst: "Everything is quiet. There is no trouble here. There will be no war. I wish to return."

Hearst would have none of this. He fired back a message of his own: "Please remain. You furnish pictures. I'll furnish the war."

Finally Remington did furnish the pictures, but unbeknown to him his drawings were based largely on fabrications—such as his sketch showing a naked Cuban girl, on an American ship about to leave Havana for New York, being searched for documents and leered at by Spanish secret police. (She and two other young women had actually been searched by women matrons in a stateroom, with policemen waiting outside.) These and other pictures in Hearst's papers fanned the flames of hatred among Americans toward Spain, and when the U.S. warship *Maine* was blown up in Havana harbor, America readily plunged into war with Spain to free Cuba.

Hearst did the same thing with Mexico. In 1913 a photo splashed across Hearst papers showed Mexican children, in water up to their waist, their hands raised. The caption said how they had been herded into the ocean by Mexican *féderales* before being shot. Only later was it discovered that the photo, taken by a tourist, was of bathing children in British Honduras.

When the Spanish Civil War broke out, Hearst once again jumped into the fray. He ran photos showing atrocities supposedly being committed by the Loyalists against followers of Franco. The truth was just the reverse—the pictures were of Franco's men committing atrocities against the Loyalists.

OH, SAY, CAN'T YOU SEE?—THE TOWN THAT FOOLED THE BRITISH

The War of 1812 is noted for, among other things, the writing of "The Star-Spangled Banner," which occurred when Francis Scott Key witnessed the British navy's unsuccessful day-long shelling of Fort McHenry at the mouth of Baltimore's harbor.

But the War of 1812 is also notable for an episode in which a small Maryland town used the first blackout in recorded history to trick the British navy and to escape unscathed from another shelling.

St. Michaels is the oldest town in Maryland's Talbot County, an eastern-shore county with a history that predates colonial Maryland. Surrounded by water and heavily wooded forest, St. Michaels was a natural site for shipbuilding in early America, and in both the Revolutionary War and the War of 1812, the town became a vital center for building such ships as privateers and blockade runners. During the War of 1812 the British were compelled to strike back and destroy the St. Michaels shipyards because ships constructed there had been used by the Americans to capture or sink over 500 British merchant ships.

Shortly before dawn on a foggy August 10, 1813, the British mounted an artillery attack on a small fort in the harbor. But after prolonged shelling, the British realized they were not hitting any targets. They eventually departed, frustrated at their inability to damage the fog-enshrouded fort or town. What the English did not know was that during the night the citizens of St. Michaels had darkened the town to prevent a shelling and then, in the early-morning fog, had placed lanterns in the tops of trees to trick British gunners into aiming their fire high.

The deception was nearly perfect. Only one house was hit (it came to be known as Cannonball House), and St. Michaels became dubbed "The Town That Fooled the British."

HOW THE WEST WAS STOLEN—ER, WON

The American Indians were once the rulers of the 2.3 billion acres that make up the continental United States. The transfer of much of this land from Indian tribes to the United States government came as the result of 245 treaties executed between 1789 and 1850. The agreements brought about the purchase of land at a price of twenty cents an acre (450 million acres for $90 million)—probably a bigger bargain than the famed steal of Manhattan Island from the Indians for a basket of beads.

The treaties negotiated between the United States and the Indians invariably had one thing in common—a solemn promise by the whites not to make any additional demands for Indian territory. But the United States government just went on breaking treaties. George Washington, himself, openly said of one such treaty, "I can never look upon that proclamation other than as a temporary expedient to quiet the minds of Indians."

Eventually, after years of broken treaties, the Indians were left with the least desirable land—least desirable on the surface, that is. For it has been found that under present Indian territory sit large deposits of the nation's oil and coal—and half of the country's uranium.

I have Indian blood in me. Just enough white blood to make my honesty questionable.

—Will Rogers

Great Moments in the History of Lies

The following statements represent interesting attempts to alter reality through the spoken word:

"The Sudetenland is the last territorial claim I have to make in Europe."

—Adolf Hitler

"I have here in my hand a list of Communists . . ."

—Senator Joseph McCarthy

"Peace is at hand."

—Henry Kissinger, during the Vietnam War

> "I'm not a crook."
> —President Richard M. Nixon
>
> "Lying does not come easy to me. But we had to weigh in the balance the difference between lives and lies."
> —Lt. Col. Oliver North
>
> "Gaiety is the most outstanding feature of the Soviet Union."
> —Joseph Stalin

ADOLF HITLER AND THE BIG LIE

Adolf Hitler, the inventor of the Big Lie, spelled out his ideas on lying in *Mein Kampf.* His basic point was that for a government or its leaders, the bigger the lie the better: He taught that the populace is easier led, or misled, by the dramatic lie.

"The size of the lie is a definite factor in causing it to be believed," Hitler says in *Mein Kampf,* "for the vast masses of a nation are in the depths of their hearts more easily deceived than they are consciously and intentionally bad."

To Hitler, "the primitive simplicity" of the mind of the masses rendered them easier prey to a big lie than a small one because "they themselves often tell little lies but would be ashamed to tell big ones."

Interestingly *Mein Kampf* is itself one of Hitler's big lies. The book was composed in prison in 1923 with the help of Rudolf Hess, Hermann Rauschning, and others. Hitler used their ideas and their sentences, incorporating them often and without change. As a result, *Mein Kampf,* which means "My Struggle," was largely ghostwritten. The byline of "by Adolf Hitler" without reference to his sizable help is a lie.

WHY POLAND LOST IN TWENTY-SEVEN DAYS

The Nazis used a lie to help defeat, in record time, the first country they went to war against.

Poland in September 1939 was not necessarily the best fighting country to resist the Germans, but in 1939 the Poles were ready for a German onslaught, yet capitulated in just twenty-seven days.

What helped the Nazis rout the Poles?

One significant factor that did not become apparent until long after World War II was a brazen lie that enabled the Nazis to conduct extensive spying on Poland before the war.

Prior to hostilities between Germany and Poland, the Ufa film company in Germany asked for permission to make a movie in Poland. They told Polish authorities they wanted to make a movie called *Poland's Glorious Achievements.*

The subterfuge worked. Polish authorities allowed the German film company to send in several production units and spend four months filming extensively throughout Poland. The movie company eventually shot a million feet of film, a good portion of which happened to be inside Polish army fortifications, munitions dumps, and war plants.

By the time the war came, in September 1939, the Nazis had an inside look at Poland—and as a result, a field day on the battlefield against their first adversary.

"A lie travels round the world while Truth is putting on her boots."

> —often ascribed to Winston
> Churchill but originally stated
> by Charles Haddon Spurgeon
> (1834–1892), an English Baptist
> minister, in *Truth and Falsehood*

CHURCHILL USED A STAND-IN TO STAND UP FOR ENGLAND

The rescue of British and French troops at Dunkirk is one of the great stirring stories of war. It also may have been a turning point in World War II. With 300,000 soldiers trapped in Europe at the coast of the English Channel in May 1940, the Germans seemed poised to strike and deal a fatal blow to the British and French armies. But Hitler inexplicably delayed the attack, ordering his

tanks to halt their advance on Dunkirk. The British used the opportunity to mount a massive rescue operation, involving the use
of even small civilian boats, to evacuate the troops to safety in
England.

The date of the rescue operation was May 26, 1940, and on
June 4, Prime Minister Winston Churchill went on radio to address the British people. His speech that day captivated the English nation and gave them a great morale boost for the continued
waging of the war against Germany.

Declared an energized-sounding Churchill, "We shall fight in
France, we shall fight on the seas and oceans, we shall fight with
growing confidence and growing strength in the air, we shall defend our island, whatever the cost may be, we shall fight on the
beaches, we shall fight on the landing grounds, we shall fight in
the fields and in the streets, we shall fight in the hills; we shall
never surrender."

The speech was great, the words were great—but it was not
Winston Churchill who that day addressed the British people with
those words. It was an actor named Norman Shelley. He had per-
fected the Churchillian delivery to such a degree that few people
could pick which voice was Shelley's and which was Churchill's.

Too busy that day to appear on radio, Churchill had asked Shelley to make the speech. Afterward Churchill showed his pleasure
with the results: "Very nice," the Prime Minister remarked. "He's
even got my teeth right."

D-DAY WAS ALSO DECEIT DAY

While Adolf Hitler was a master of deceit, he was ultimately mas-
tered by deceit. D-Day, the Allied invasion of Europe on June 6,
1944, was the beginning of the end for Hitler. But the massive
force unleashed by the Free World against the Nazis that day may
not have been successful without the Allies' elaborate deception
that kept fifteen of eighteen of Hitler's best divisions 100 miles
away on the other side of the Seine River in France, waiting for
an invasion that never came by a phantom army that did not exist.

The invasion, targeted by the Allies to take place on the beaches
of Normandy, involved the massing of 5,000 ships, 9,000 planes,
23,000 parachutists, 176,000 assault troops, and 20,000 vehicles.

But to keep the Nazis off-guard, an elaborate ruse was worked out, over a period of months, in which the Allies led Hitler to believe that a large Allied army was poised in England ready to plunge across the English Channel into the Pas de Calais in France. Hitler therefore beefed up that area with added troops, and even when the Normandy invasion began, he thought that that was just a feint and that the true invasion was still to come at Pas de Calais. Thus of fifty-nine German divisions in France at the time, only six were in Normandy, but eighteen were across the Seine in the Pas de Calais, where the infantry divisions were two deep.

One of the ways in which the deception was carried out was based on the ideas of Dr. R. V. Jones, a physicist attached to MI-6, a section of British Intelligence, who had early learned how to defeat German air defenses by using radio waves and the reflection of tiny metal strips attached to balloons to confuse German radar. For D-Day, the Allies knocked out German radar except along the Pas de Calais. The radar screens there were then filled with the false impressions of approaching planes and ships—all created by R. V. Jones and his assistants with tiny strips of foil.

On the morning of June 6, D-Day actually began at 3 A.M., when the Allies "attacked" at Isigny at the southeastern corner of Cherbourg peninsula with an airborne assault that "consisted of three British paratroopers, hundreds of exploding dummies, a chemical preparation exuding smoke, and a battery of Victrolas amplifying recordings of gunfire, soldier talk, and troop movements."* The ruse worked. It diverted the 916th infantry regiment of the German 352nd Division from its position behind Omaha Beach. By the time the German troops returned to their previous position in Normandy, the U.S. 1st Division was firmly established on the Normandy beach.

But all avenues were used to reinforce the ruse that the real invasion was to come at Pas de Calais. Thus, along with the invasion, the story was propagated that the thrust at Normandy was being contained by the Germans so General Eisenhower was forced to divert to Normandy some of the forces intended for the Pas de Calais invasion, but those forces were being replaced by fresh troops from the United States. The Pas de Calais forces still stood

*See William Casey, *The Secret War Against Hitler* (Regnery Gateway, 1988), p. 102.

poised to invade and only awaited the diversion of enough Nazi troops to Normandy and the setting of the actual invasion date by General Eisenhower.

This message went out by BBC and wireless to the resistance in northern France and Belgium. Double agents also relayed the message back to Germany. One British agent, code-named Garbo, was even allowed to give the Germans, four hours before the Normandy assault, some of the information about the pending attack, but he was to indicate that such an attack was only a diversion for the later attack coming at Pas de Calais. After the war it was learned that Garbo's message was eventually seen by Hitler, who on June 10 countermanded his own orders of June 9, thereby keeping the 15th Army in Pas de Calais and away from Normandy.

In addition to the messages, the Allies took diversionary actions. Submarines, minesweepers, and torpedo boats began appearing in the waters near the Pas de Calais coast. Soon planes began bombarding the beaches there. The message was clear: The phantom army, believed now by Hitler to number up to ninety divisions on the British coast, was getting ready to invade.

The Origin of "Bodyguard of Lies"

In wartime, truth is so precious that she should always be attended by a bodyguard of lies.

— Winston Churchill

This is one of the famous quotes from World War II. In fact, the phrase "bodyguard of lies" provided the label "Bodyguard" for the secret deceptive operation mounted by the Allies to tie in with "Overlord," the name for their D-Day invasion of Europe.

But Churchill did not originate the phrase. He told one of his private secretaries that Stalin himself had provided Churchill with the quote. It was, said Stalin, a Russian proverb. The secretary later speculated that Churchill may have used the phrase to please Stalin "by quoting his own phrase back at him."

Indeed, Stalin had told Churchill and Roosevelt that he

> fully supported a deceptive campaign against the Germans and told how the Russians had "made considerable use" of dummy tanks, aircraft, and airfields and that "radio deception had also proved effective."

These actions proved highly effective in preventing thousands of German troops from rushing to Normandy and repulsing the Allied invasion. Eisenhower had hoped to keep the German 15th Army away from Normandy for forty-eight hours. But the Germans were hoodwinked enough that, even after the Allies had landed, Nazi troops stayed tied up elsewhere in France for several weeks. In fact, so successful was the Allied campaign of deceit that instead of the 20,000 dead that Churchill had feared it might take to storm the beaches at Normandy on the first day (the COSSAC—Chief of Staff to the Supreme Allied Commander—had estimated it would take 75,000 casualties if surprise was not achieved), the Allies lost 2,500 men, with another 9,000 to 10,000 wounded or missing by the end of the day after D-Day. The invasion was a success, and within less than a year World War II in Europe was over.

Thus Hitler, the master of the Big Lie, was eventually made a victim of the biggest subterfuge of the war.

IL DUCE'S LIES EVENTUALLY MADE IL DUCE VERY ILL

Benito Mussolini (1883–1945), Fascist leader of Italy for twenty-three years, loved to posture—which means he loved to play with the truth—which means he loved to lie. Il Duce, as he was called, felt that propaganda was the most vital aspect of policy. He had a Propaganda Ministry (which he changed in name to Popular Culture in 1937 when he realized the pejorative connotations of *propaganda*), and his press officials knew that if any crowd listening to Mussolini was unresponsive, they had to compensate by reporting "wild enthusiasm" in their dispatches. But, of course, Mussolini had a way of preventing problems: The police and the party usually mobilized an "applause squad" to make any such eventuality unnecessary.

Mussolini's problem, however, was that he let propaganda replace reality. This was nowhere more apparent—with ultimately devastating results—than when it came to preparing for Italy's entry into World War II. Mussolini played havoc with the truth. He had his spokesman, Virginio Gayda, announce on April 21, 1940, that "the whole Mediterranean was under the control of Italian naval and air forces and if Britain dared to fight them, she would at once be driven out." (Gayda later privately confided he did not believe it.) And on May 14, Mussolini's official newspaper warned that at any moment Italian forces might land on English soil.

As Denis Mack Smith relates in *Mussolini's Roman Empire* (Longman, 1976), Mussolini told Hitler in 1940 that over 8 million soldiers and seventy divisions were available if needed and that Italy would produce twice this number if Germany could help equip them.

The facts, as Mussolini knew, were far different. He had fewer than twenty divisions ready for battle and he could only muster about one million men—there were not enough uniforms, barracks, and weapons for any more fighters.

There had been other lies throughout the years. For example, in October 1936, Mussolini spoke of having 8 million bayonets, but by 1939 Italy still did not have sufficient bayonets for its 1.3 million rifles then available to the army. (These rifles utilized a design introduced in 1891. Most of the artillery Italy used during the war dated back to World War I.)

In August 1936, Mussolini declared he could mobilize eight million men in a few hours. Over the next several years this figure went from 9 million to 10 million to, by 1939, 12 million. As a result, Fascist writers declared that Italy had one of the most formidable armies in Europe, with a navy and air force of perfection, and the nation had "little or nothing to learn" from Germany—or anyone else for that matter.

Mussolini implied that he had three armored divisions that included twenty-five-ton tanks with the most advanced equipment anywhere. These armored divisions, however, existed in only two places—on paper and in Mussolini's mind. The Italians had nothing larger than a 3.5-ton armored car copied from the British that had only machine guns, no radio, poor visibility, and a susceptibility to penetration by small-arms fire.

When World War II started, Italy issued figures saying it had 8,530 planes, but the accurate numbers came out to be 454 bombers and 129 fighters—most of which were said to be outclassed by the Royal Air Force planes. Mussolini told the Nazis he was producing 500 planes a month, but at no time during the war did Italy's production exceed 300 per month. Actually, under Mussolini Italy manufactured fewer planes in the Second World War than it did in the First.

The Italian navy was said to be the best equipped of the military services, with eight battleships either completed or near completion by 1939 and a submarine fleet larger than any other country's at the time. But the Italian navy had been built for speed (the world records made Mussolini and Fascism look good), and speed was achieved at the expense of armor protection and range of operation (the ships could not function more than 500 miles from their base). Only two of the battleships saw any battle during the war. The engagement—off the coast of Calabria on July 9, 1940—lasted all of a few minutes, but this was enough time for Mussolini to boast to the Germans that Italy had destroyed half the British navy in the Mediterranean, but the Germans knew that little damage had been done by either side. Later the heads of the Italian air force, ever the rivals of the navy, claimed that "not a single shot fired from these vastly expensive battleships ever hit an enemy vessel during the entire war."*

As for submarines, Italy did have far more submarines than anyone else, and Mussolini believed this would enable him to paralyze England and rule the seas. But the Italian subs were overly slow in submerging and had too limited an offensive capability. As a result, within the first three weeks of the war in 1940, Italy lost a tenth of her operational submarines.

At a meeting with German Foreign Minister Joachim von Ribbentrop in Rome on March 10, 1940, Mussolini declared that "almost the entire civilian life of the Italian people had been sacrificed

---

*Conspicuously missing from the Italian navy were any aircraft carriers. This was because Mussolini made the decision back in the 1920s that aircraft carriers in a future war would be useless against bombing planes and that the Italian airforce, using land-based planes, could cover the Mediterranean. Mussolini resisted all efforts over the years to promote aircraft carriers and smugly believed he was ahead of other leaders in his theories about the death knell for aircraft carriers.

to the production of armaments"—when in fact "not one major decision was taken during these months of nonbelligerence to increase the strength and the provision of the army." At that time Italy had seventy light-to-medium tanks, no heavy tanks, World War I artillery, and only enough antiaircraft ammunition to deal with twenty enemy air raids.

However, while Il Duce was duping the Fuhrer, the Fuhrer was duping Il Duce. To solidify Italy as a future ally, Hitler informed Mussolini early in 1940 before Italy entered the war that Germany was ready to attack in the west with over two hundred fully equipped divisions and that they intended to win the war during the summer. Hitler's bright picture of Germany's preparedness and his prognosis for early victory—all delectable to a Mussolini who knew his own army could fight a war of only several months' duration—was a deliberate deception. The Germany dictator knew that Mussolini had no way to check the validity of what he was being told.

An ill-prepared Italy eventually lost the war, and the Fascist dictator Mussolini lost his life, strung up by Italian partisans infuriated with his rule.

A liar had lied to the one person he should never lie to—himself.

THE LIE TO END ALL LIES

WORK SHALL MAKE YOU FREE.

This sign, arched across the entrance of Auschwitz, could rank as the most murderous lie of all. Through its gates and beneath that sign went nearly 3 million Jews to their deaths—almost half of the Jews who perished in the Holocaust.

But that devilish Nazi sign—almost gleeful in its deception—was simply the last in a long line of lies that the Nazis had seized on as a way of fooling an unsuspecting people. The mass killings were facilitated by an elaborate ruse, carried out with guile and deception from beginning to end. Indeed, it was the deceptions that made the Holocaust possible.

Consider how the Holocaust was carried out. The Jews were often placed in ghettos as the first staging area for eventual shipment by train to the death camps. But to round up the Jews in the ghettos, the Germans often announced that the Jews were being sent out on work details or were being transported to areas of Europe where they were needed for labor purposes. This is why whole families of Jews did not try to avoid the roundups, but showed up at the railway terminals with bags packed.

The lie had another purpose: The Germans used it to smoke out the valuables and money of the Jews, knowing that with only a suitcase or two permitted to be taken, the victims would opt to take with them their money and most precious jewelry in hopes of preserving whatever wealth they had or using it later to barter for food or freedom. But this only ensured that the Nazi storehouses at the death camps eventually bulged with enormous sums of valuables taken from millions of victims.

The actual transportation of Jews to the death camps was carried out under the greatest guile of all. The Nazis, to assure the Jews that they were being sent away to work or were being resettled, encouraged them to bring not only their valuables but their work tools as well. Doctors therefore went to the trains with their instruments, musicians took their violins, dentists even brought their chairs. Greek Jews signed contracts with German authorities for shops in the Ukraine.

Once on the trains, the Jews encountered further deceptions. The Germans made an elaborate display of counting the people in each boxcar, telling them that if anyone was missing at the end of the trip, a person from the car would be shot. But it was a ruse. The Nazis, who were inveterate record keepers, did not count the arriving death trains by individual boxcar.

When they arrived at the extermination camps, the Jews were exposed to a number of deceptive schemes to ease their entry. Jewish musicians were often forced to play music for the arriving trainloads. Flowers could be seen growing in the camp grounds. And to get the victims to proceed peaceably to the gas chambers, the Nazis told the Jews that as a health measure to prevent the spread of disease they would have to take a shower in the camp's bathhouse and be disinfected. The Nazis gave them bars of soap, told them to take off their clothing, and even pointed out that they should fold their clothes neatly and leave identification on them so that the clothing could be returned. The rooms the victims entered had false shower nozzles and false drains to simulate bathhouses and hide the fact that these were diabolical gas chambers.

At the Treblinka death camp, most of those arriving were gassed the same day. Yet the Germans presented Treblinka as a transit camp. A large sign, printed in Polish and German, greeted arrivals with the following message:

> Jews of Warsaw, Attention!
> You are in a transit camp from which you will be sent to a labor camp. In order to avoid epidemics, you must present your clothing and belongings for immediate disinfection. Gold, money, foreign currency, and jewelry should be deposited with the cashiers in return for a receipt. They will be returned to you later when you present the receipt. Bodily cleanliness requires that everyone bathe before continuing the journey.

Later, to add to the lie, Treblinka camp commander Staugl ordered that the platform be constructed to resemble a train station. Adjacent to the platform was a barrack that actually served as a storage shed where the belongings of the murdered Jews were stored. Staugl had the front of the barracks altered dramatically. He had fake doors and windows installed, along with signs that read TICKET COUNTER, WAITING ROOM, INFORMATION, TELEGRAPH OFFICE, STATION MANAGER, REST ROOM, and so on. A train schedule was posted, with signs and arrows directing passengers TO THE BIALYSTOK TRAIN or TO THE VOLKOVYSK TRAIN. A dummy clock was affixed to the building.

To add to the deception, the SS even arranged for a group of Jewish inmates to play as the unsuspecting victims were led to the "showers," which were actually gas chambers of sixteen square meters where as many as 250 people could be killed at one time.

And as the victims proceeded, according to Abraham Goldfarb, who was one of the few to survive Treblinka, the German guards urged the victims to hurry: "Faster, faster, the water's getting cold, and others have to use the showers too."

Thus, when questions arise about why didn't the Jews fight back, why did they go seemingly like sheep to the slaughter, the answer resides in the overwhelming Nazi use of lies and deceit. We tend to talk of Nazi terror in the telling of the Holocaust, but it was Nazi guile that lessened Jewish reaction and reduced Jewish rebellion. The Nazis did not openly glory in their extermination of the Jews but saw fit to hide it under euphemisms about "final solutions" and gas chambers camouflaged as shower rooms.

THE HOLOCAUST: DID IT HAPPEN?

And yet, there are those who have said that the Holocaust is a lie, that it never happened—or that if it did, far fewer than 6 million Jews were murdered.

For instance, Paul Rassinier, a French author, has written about what he calls "the lie of Auschwitz." Arthur Butz, a Northwestern University professor, has termed the Holocaust "the hoax of the century." A Sorbonne professor, Robert Fausisson, once declared that the Nazis never gassed any Jews.

Such statements are ludicrous in the face of the fact that as a result of the Nuremberg War Crime Trials and the documentation amassed and maintained in the National Archives of the United States and the Library of Congress, the Holocaust has been called one of the most documented of all crimes. Plus there are the documents, records, films, and photographs produced and maintained by the Nazis themselves, as well as the materials assembled by the record-keeping center of the Holocaust at Yad Vashem in Israel. In fact, it has been estimated that German and Jewish documentation alone runs to 15 million pages.

The conclusion from all this evidence and research is that at least 4,194,000 and as many as 5,721,000 Jews were murdered during the Holocaust—conclusions that can be found in such an authoritative non-Jewish source as *Documents on Nazism 1919–1945* (Viking Press, 1975), edited by Jeremy Noakes and Geoffrey Pridham.

And then there is the personal eyewitness testimony of the head of the Allied armies and a future president of the United States. Writing in *Crusade in Europe* (Doubleday, 1948), Dwight D. Eisenhower told of how on April 12, 1945, he "saw my first horror camp." Located near the town of Hotha, it thrust upon Eisenhower "indisputable evidence of Nazi brutality and ruthless disregard of every shred of decency." He declared that "I have never at any other time experienced an equal sense of shock."

Eisenhower went on the describe his outrage and, in an almost prophetic statement, his desire to forestall any doubts that might be raised in the future about the veracity of the Nazi horrors. Wrote Eisenhower:

I visited every nook and cranny of the camp because I felt it my duty to be in a position from then on to testify at first hand about these things in case there ever grew up at home the belief or assumption that "the stories of Nazi brutality were just propaganda." Some members of the visiting party were unable to go through the ordeal. I not only did so but as soon as I returned to General Patton's headquarters that evening I sent communications to both Washington and London, urging the two governments to send instantly to Germany a random group of newspaper editors and representative groups from the national legislatures. I felt that the evidence should be immediately placed before the American and British publics in a fashion that would leave no room for cynical doubt.*

HEY, SUGINO, IT WAS SUPPOSED TO BE SAYONARA

One impetus for the kamikaze suicide planes used by the Japanese in the last year of World War II in a desperate attempt to sink American warships derived from an event in Japanese history that later proved to be misleading.

Japan's first use of suicide fighters in modern warfare had actually come in the Russo-Japanese War of 1904. At that time and for forty-two years since, the Japanese had immortalized Naval Warrant Officer Magoshiche Sugino as one of the first of Japan's suicide fighters. He was said to have given his life to sink a ship in order to bottle up the Russian fleet at Port Arthur. He was declared a great Japanese hero, with numerous statues later erected in his memory and songs written about him. His story and example were cited to Japanese children as a way of impressing upon them the heroism of sacrificing one's life for the emperor and the Japanese nation.

The truth, though, as the Japanese people learned after World War II in 1946, was that Sugino never died in his one-man assault on the Russian fleet. He survived and was picked up by a Chinese boat. Later, when he realized he was being praised as a hero for his suicide mission, he decided that the better part of valor was

---

*This passage occurs on p. 409 of *Crusade in Europe*. Interestingly, in another book on World War II, General Patton, known for his toughness, told of how he reacted upon seeing a concentration camp for the first time: He threw up.

66

not to return home and tell the truth about his "demise," but to stay hidden. He wound up in Manchuria, where he lived obscurely for the next forty years. Finally in November 1946, after World War II had ended, he was discovered and was returned home to Japan.

Thus, although Sugino never did die as a suicide fighter, his example, along with a Japanese tradition of self-sacrifice, became the basis for instilling in Japanese youth the honor of becoming a kamikaze in World War II.

The kamikaze, which means "divine wind," became a key part of Japanese military strategy from October 1944 until the war's end in August 1945. In the invasion of Okinawa, for instance, the Japanese threw more than 6,000 suicide planes against American forces. Although only several hundred were able to hit ships directly, the suicide planes caused thousands of deaths and much damage.

And the suicides were not limited to pilots of airplanes. A special type of kamikaze were gliders that, released from a bomber, were guided by a flyer into a warship. Also used to attack ships were suicide boats and rafts carrying swimmers with high explosives.

All of this activity was undertaken with Magoshichi Sugino as an early representative of selfless sacrifice in a heroic suicide mission on behalf of Japan. Except that all the time thousands of Japanese pilots, swimmers, soldiers, and sailors were participating in suicide missions, Sugino was living quietly in Manchuria.

WHERE DID THE SOVIETS PUT THE HIGHWAY OF LOVE?: THE TALE OF FIFTY YEARS OF MAP FRAUD

The Soviet Union, under Communist domination this century, has been a nation in which secrecy, mystery, and distortion have ruled. But little did most of its severest critics realize that for fifty years, under orders from Soviet secret police, Soviet mapmakers had deliberately falsified all of that nation's public maps.

The massive deceit surfaced in September 1988, when the Soviet Union's chief cartographer, Viktor R. Yashchenko, told the government newspaper *Izvestia* that authorities had now agreed to begin releasing accurate maps that had been classified as state secrets since Stalin's time. He said the public printing of correctly drawn maps was a result of Mikhail Gorbachev's policy of openness.

As a result, no longer would maps of Russia have misplaced rivers and roads, incorrectly indicated or absent features, tilted city districts, and distorted borders. For instance, in an example cited at the time of the admission about faked maps, it was shown how the town of Logashkino on the eastern Siberian seacoast appeared on the left side of a river in a 1939 Soviet atlas, disappeared altogether in a 1954 atlas, reappeared on the right side of a river in 1962, and then had its nearby river channel dropped in 1967. In another example, the official tourist map of Moscow was said to have only one accurate feature—the contour of the city.

The map falsifications started when the Soviet secret police took control of the mapmaking division in the 1930s. Spy mania and security concerns were high at the time and persisted with the coming of World War II and the Cold War. But long after these concerns had faded, the practice continued—even after the launching of satellites that enabled other countries to use space photography to map the Soviet Union accurately.

In fact the most reliable Moscow street map, used by diplomats and journalists, was put out by the U.S. Central Intelligence Agency. The detail on the map was drawn on a scale of one mile to one-half inch and included such significant landmarks as the headquarters of the KGB—a feature missing from Soviet maps.

It may be surprising to realize that maps can be manipulated for ideological causes, but this seems to have been one of the reasons behind the falsifications. The leadership of the Soviet Union in 1917 declared that cartography should be used for economic advancement, propaganda, and military needs. Lenin himself established what is today's Soviet mapping agency with a State Geodetic Service in 1919.

One of the original key motivations for the distortions may have also been military. Faking their maps, the Soviets hoped, would throw off enemy bombers and confuse military offenses. In this purpose, the Russians may have been more successful than they realized.

Ken McCormick and Darby Perry, in a letter to the editor published in *The New York Times* following the story on the faked

Soviet maps, wrote that in research they were doing for a book on World War II they came across statements by German military leaders indicating that the faked maps caused havoc to the Nazis in their invasion of the Soviet Union in 1941.

The writers cited Gen. Gunther Blumentritt, chief of staff of the German 4th Army, who declared that "the great motor highway" from the border to Moscow proved to be unfinished and his troops "were not prepared for what we found because our maps in no way corresponded to reality." He went on to list the problems encountered: "On these maps all supposed main roads were marked in red, and there seemed to be many, but they often proved to be merely sand tracks."

Field Marshal Karl von Rundstedt bemoaned that "the maps we were given were all wrong. The roads that were marked nice and red and thick on a map turned out to be tracks, and what were tracks on the map became first-class roads. Even railways that were to be used by us simply didn't exist."

So the Soviet map of lies may have helped stem the German invasion. But it took forty years after that war and in the face of space technology for the Russians to finally tell the truth—from the ground up.*

THE GULF OF TONKIN RESOLUTION MAY HAVE BEEN THE GULF BETWEEN TRUTH AND FICTION

The incident that marked the beginning of America's intensive involvement in the Vietnam War has always been enshrouded in controversy.

In the summer of 1964, a U.S. Navy destroyer, the *Maddox,* on routine patrol in the Gulf of Tonkin southeast of Hanoi, was said to have been attacked suddenly and without provocation by North Vietnamese PT boats. Although the *Maddox* was not damaged, other attacks were said to have been made on U.S. destroyers. President Lyndon Johnson immediately went before Congress

---

*Although a map of lies may have helped win a war, such maps in peacetime are costly. The *Military Engineer* magazine points out that "it is much more costly to deliberately and skillfully falsify maps than it is to produce reasonably accurate ones."

and urged that he be given congressional approval to defend United States interests in the area. He got it, in what has been called the Gulf of Tonkin Resolution (it passed 416–0 in the House and 88–2 in the Senate). Shortly thereafter, although he would promise in his campaign for the presidency that year against Senator Barry Goldwater not to send American boys into battle, Lyndon Johnson ordered the beginning of what became a massive buildup of men and materials in Vietnam.

Subsequently, after the patriotic fervor died down, the scenario that led to the Resolution—the firing on a United States ship—became suspect. Many now say that it was either an incident Johnson magnified to enlist congressional support for his plan to send United States troops to fight the Viet Cong or the episode was contrived and there had been no shelling or other act of aggression against the United States that day in the Gulf of Tonkin.

An opponent of the war and a critic of Lyndon Johnson was Senator J. William Fulbright (D.-Ark.), then head of the Senate Foreign Relations Committee. He always raised the possibility that Congress had been steamrollered into supporting the Gulf of Tonkin Resolution, thereby paving the way for the Vietnam War. In the motion picture documentary *Hearts and Minds,* a winner of an Academy Award for its look at the Vietnam War, Fulbright is interviewed about the Resolution and comes close to calling Johnson a liar:

"We always hesitate in public to use the dirty word *lie,* but a lie is a lie. It is a misrepresentation of fact. It is supposed to be a criminal act if it's done under oath.

"Mr. Johnson didn't say it under oath. He just said it. We don't usually have the president under oath."

But the deed was done. The Gulf of Tonkin Resolution opened the doors to what eventually became ten years of bitter fighting (one might almost say bitter fighting both abroad and at home) in which 55,000 Americans lost their lives in one of the most protracted wars the United States has ever waged.

And yet, ironically, it was not officially a war. Only Congress can declare war, and in the case of Vietnam, Congress never did. The closest it came was the Gulf of Tonkin Resolution, which—unknowingly for Congress at the time—may very well have been based upon a lie.

THREAT BARGAINING: TRUE OR FALSE

As an expert on foreign policy and negotiations between countries, Henry Kissinger, secretary of state under Richard Nixon, developed the strategy of threat bargaining, of using false and true threats to obtain policy objectives. One person who was not persuaded by threats—true or false—was the foreign minister of North Vietnam, Nguyen Co Thach. During the secret Paris talks between the United States and North Vietnam, Thach confided to Kissinger that he had read Kissinger's early writings about threat bargaining and, in his own words, cited Kissinger's philosophy that "it is a good thing to make a false threat the enemy believes is a true threat. It is a bad thing if we are threatening an enemy with a true threat and the enemy believes it is a false threat."

Thach then told Kissinger, "False or true, we Vietnamese don't mind. There must be a third category—for those who don't care whether the threat is true or false."

> "An ambassador is an honest man sent abroad to lie for his country."
> —Sir Henry Wotton (1568–1639)

"Should I chop or shouldn't I?" The famous tale of honesty was itself a lie.

CHAPTER III

"I cannot tell a lie. The other guy did it."

GREAT AMERICANS– AND THE NOT-SO-GREAT

. . . The Truth About the Honorable And the Dishonorable

How do you know when a lawyer is lying?
His lips move.
> —Scott Turow, practicing
> attorney and best-selling
> author, recounting a lawyer
> joke in the *New York Times*
> *Magazine*

As children, or even as adults, we all tend to want to think the best of our leaders and the other greats of our world. Although the tabloids may be filled with stories showing the feet of clay of our idols, we still consider them special and we still want to be able to worship our heroes.

One failing above all else threatens even this scenario. And that is the use of deceit. We tend to forgive all else—the drinking, the drug-taking, the fits of anger—but at least if our hero is honorable, we can believe he or she will eventually overcome.

For among our first teachings is the teaching of "Don't lie." That childhood innocence must remain intact with our heroes. Surely they do not or cannot lie. They have gained fame and the fervor of the crowd because they are better than others—not just in ability, but in their fitness to be famous and successful.

But into all lives, it seems, a little lying must fall. On closer inspection, many of our heroes can be seen bending the truth. And this is in addition to the notorious, who use deceit as a major tool with which they battle to achieve their goals.

Our own maturity comes when we recognize the way in which the world is played. Truth is not possible at all times, but neither should lies be permissible at all times. How our heroes deal with the twin-edged sword of truth and lies is an indication of how truly heroic they are.

Here is a gallery of how some of our famous—and infamous— have dealt with those of us who have revered—or reviled—them.

ACTUALLY GEORGE WASHINGTON'S MOTHER WAS THE LIAR IN THE FAMILY

No personage—other than possibly Pinocchio—is so associated with lying and telling the truth as is George Washington.

The Father of Our Country has long been associated with what must now be one of the most famous stories in literature—that of George Washington as a child chopping down a cherry tree, then admitting his guilt to his questioning father. The father, ecstatic at his boy's honesty, rewards George with a hug. History has rewarded George Washington with a special place in the pantheon of honest leaders (admittedly a very small pantheon).

The surprising thing about this story that has taught honesty to generations of schoolchildren is that the story itself is a lie and it was concocted by a preacher who lied about other things as well.

George Washington was basically honest and the apocryphal cherry tree story may have been a response to that innate honesty of Washington's, but the fact remains that the hatchet, cherry tree, hugging father, and "I cannot tell a lie" George were all fabrications of a shady character named Parson Mason Locke Weems.

Weems, born in Maryland in 1759, was a curious mixture of preacher, storyteller and con artist who sensed that he could make money writing inexpensive books about American heroes. He is reputed to have told a publisher, "You have a great deal of money lying in the bones of old George." And so Weems wrote a book containing numerous stories about George Washington. The title:

The Life of George Washington with Curious Anecdotes, Equally Honorable to Himself and Exemplary to His Young Countrymen. First published in 1800, the book was so successful it went through twenty-one editions during Weems's lifetime and provided the basis for other biographies.

The cherry tree story made famous by Weems was actually a later addition by him. It does not appear until the fifth edition, published in 1806. The story is introduced by Weems with the statement that it is "too true to be doubted" since it was told to him by "the same excellent lady" who recounted another incident that had also shown how George did not lie.

According to Weems, George was six years old when he was given a hatchet that, like other little boys, he liked to use to chop various things that he came upon. One day, while in the garden, he tried the hatchet "on the body of a beautiful young English cherry tree, which he barked so terribly, that I don't believe the tree ever got the better of it." The following morning George's father discovered the ruined tree, which also happened to be his father's "great favorite." Returning to the house, George's father could find no one who knew anything about how the tree had been badly barked (by the way, the tree was not chopped down in the Weems story). Whereupon, "George and his hatchet made their appearance."

Here, then, is the rest of the episode as told in the Weems narrative:

> "George," said his father, "do you know who killed this beautiful little cherry tree yonder in the garden?" This was a tough question: and George staggered under it for a moment; but quickly recovered himself: and looking at his father, with the sweet face of youth brightened with the inexpressible charm of all-conquering truth, he bravely cried out, "I can't tell a lie, Pa; you know I can't tell a lie. I did cut it with my hatchet."—
> "Run to my arms, you dearest boy," cried his father in transports, "run to my arms; glad am I, George, that you killed my tree: for you have paid me for it a thousand fold. Such an act of heroism in my son is more worth than a thousand trees, though blossomed with silver, and their fruits of purest gold."

George's instruction in truth and honesty seems to have been a major pursuit of his father during George's early years, if we are to believe Parson Weems, who in another part of the book cites the father's lesson for George: "Truth, George, is the loveliest quality of youth."

And so George Washington was inspired with an early love of truth. Except that not one word of the cherry tree or these interchanges between father and son are true. It was all fabrication by Weems, who thereby used the strange method of teaching the virtue of honesty by telling lies, of promoting truth by publishing a fiction.

Weems was not above lying about himself. On the title page of his book about Washington, Weems is listed as "formerly rector of Mount Vernon Parish." No such parish has ever existed.

As for the true Washington, George did have many admirable qualities, according to one biographer, but the virtue of truth telling, while present in large part, "occupied a place subordinate" to these other virtues. Ever the gentleman, Washington was not above couching his statements with a sensibility not to offend. And in his use of persuasion as a way to command, he tailored his message to his audience. "Thus, upon occasion," writes one biographer, "his letters to different people on the same subject deviate so far that his severest modern critic, Bernhard Knollenberg, has accused him of deceit."

In war he was especially willing and adept at coloring reports and using untruth as a military weapon. "An enemy is always supposed to be secret as to their real intentions and may generally be suspected of a view to deceive when they speak openly of them," Washington wrote during the Revolution. To keep up morale back home and among his troops after a defeat, he invariably accepted and spread exaggerated reports of enemy casualties. He tended to minimize bad news and maximize good. Wrote Washington in 1777, "It is our interest, however much our characters may suffer by it, to make small numbers appear large."

He Could Not Spell It or Tell It

Whether George Washington could tell a lie or not, we do know that he could not spell the word. In reviewing his writings, one can find that George, a poor speller, usually spelled *lie* as *lye*.

There was one Washington family member, however, who really did seem to have a problem with lying. This was George Washington's mother. An obviously troubled woman in her later years (some say she was senile), she publicly berated George when he was president, declaring that he was starving and neglecting her. None of this was true. But Washington's mother continued with her lies about her son, even going so far as to try to persuade the new government to pass a law that future presidents not be allowed to neglect their mothers.

So George had his problems with those who used tall tales and outright lies to build up and tear down the first president of this newest of countries. And then there were those who just liked to build stories around the Father of Our Country. Remember the one about Washington tossing a dollar across the Delaware River? Well, that was the made-up yarn of some drunken Continental soldiers. And then there was the story about George Washington that . . . well, when it comes to stories about the Father of Our Country, it may be time to cry uncle.

JEFFERSONIAN VIEWS ON NEWSPAPERS

Thomas Jefferson, who was deeply involved in the formation of the Constitution with its guarantees of freedom of the press, adopted a different attitude when he became the butt of newspaper attacks as president. He was castigated as a hypocrite and accused of fathering several children by a young slave named Sally Hemmings. The Federalist newspapers mounted such a vitriolic attack that he once declared newspapers should be divided into four sections with the following headings: "Truth," "Probability," "Possibility," and "Lies."

As for the latter two sections, Jefferson said that they "should be professedly for those readers who would rather have lies for their money than the blank papers they would occupy."

Historians, however, have generally come to view the stories about Jefferson's liaison with Sally Hemmings as true.

FRANKLIN THE FRUGAL?

Benjamin Franklin, one of the heroes of early America, has long been seen as a man of many virtues, especially that of thrift. After all, his writings are filled with wise sayings about the desirability of being thrifty. "A penny saved is a penny earned" was just one of Franklin's edicts.

But Franklin himself did not abide by his own maxims. While in England he shipped back to America a steady stream of extravagant presents—including fine china, silver-handled knives, carpets, and a harpsichord. While living in France as U.S. ambassador, he established a lavish wine cellar, in which at one point (September 1782) he had stocked 1,203 bottles. On the average, he spent more than $12,000 a year—a huge sum at the time—each of the eight years he was in France.

So heavily did Franklin spend that, according to Carl Van Doren's authoritative biography, the author of *Poor Richard's Almanac* admitted, in June 1782, that frugality was "a virtue I never could acquire in myself."

"Half a truth is often a great lie."
—Benjamin Franklin,
Poor Richard's Almanac

HOW HONEST WAS HONEST ABE?

Abraham Lincoln was known as Honest Abe, the president of such humble origins that he was born in a log cabin, walked miles to return a debt of pennies, and came to the presidency with clean hands and a pure heart.

How close to reality was this picture?

Close but not close enough.

Abe was indeed born in a log cabin and grew up poor, but what is overlooked is that he married wealth (Mary Todd came from a wealthy family, and friends and relatives felt sorry for her for marrying so beneath herself; she was, said one, "of the best stock and was raised like a lady''). And for thirty years, Abe was a Whig lawyer, connected to the power structure in his home state of Illinois.

As for his becoming president, Lincoln gained the Republican nomination in what political writer Garry Wills called ''probably the most corrupt convention in our history.''

Staying in his Springfield home while the convention of 1860 took place in Chicago, Lincoln ''let his agents do all the dirty work.'' To defeat William Seward, the favored candidate of the Republican delegates, Lincoln's lieutenants made certain that Seward's delegates were physically kept out of the meeting hall, saw to it that ballots were not printed during the time Seward held a clear lead, and offered posts in a Lincoln administration as bribes (and, according to Wills, these commitments were fulfilled).

Lincoln got the nomination actually because his opposition to slavery was vaguer than Seward's. He was touted as more electable because he had less of a record to defend. And during the course of the campaign, Lincoln built on that aspect of his background by actually refusing to give a single campaign speech—or even a statement in response to questions from editors. Lincoln stated that to do so and discuss the issues would be divisive. (A similar tactic was used 100 years later. In his 1968 campaign Richard Nixon talked of ending the Vietnam War but refused to say how.)

Ironically, then, we remember today that Lincoln debated Stephen Douglas for the Senate in 1858—a campaign Lincoln lost. But we do not seem to remember that Lincoln refused to debate in his campaign for president in 1860—a campaign Lincoln won.

And yet, once elected president, Lincoln dealt honestly with the American people, though he was often vilified for doing so, especially for championing the notion of equal rights. Among the many criticisms he received for pursuing such an honorable path were those from the *Chicago Times,* which was strongly anti-Lincoln. Commenting on the president's Gettysburg Address, the paper editorialized that his ''introduction of Dawdleism in a funeral sermon . . . was an offensive exhibition of boorishness and vulgarity.''

What the editors found particularly offensive was Lincoln's reference to ''the proposition that all men are created equal.'' The paper declared that the various provisions in the Constitution, for which the soldiers had given their lives at Gettysburg, did not provide for equality for all men. Asked the *Chicago Times,* how dared he, standing on the graves of officers and soldiers, "misstate the cause for which they died, and libel the statesmen who founded the government?"

And how had Lincoln libeled the dead soldiers buried at Gettysburg? Because, said the newspaper, "they were men possessing too much self-respect to declare that negroes were their equals, or were entitled to equal privileges."

Lincoln met such criticism head-on, and while he was vilified, he was also supported because throughout his presidency he adhered to the noble principles of truth and honesty.

In Letter Writing, Never the Twains Shall Meet

Mark Twain may have been a great writer of humor, but as a person he was plagued with depression and doubts, especially as he grew older. However, he sensed that to display this side to the public or to others would jeopardize his image, and so he kept this aspect of himself as shielded from view as possible.

One way in which he did this echoed Columbus's keeping of two sets of books on his voyage. Twain wrote two sets of his letters.

He regularly composed two letters when he was communicating with others on important topics. One letter contained his true views expressed in a blunt and honest manner. This letter, though, he put in his desk. The second letter, written with what was the popular sentiment of the time, is the one he sent.

Explained the author of such classics as *Tom Sawyer* and *Huckleberry Finn,* "I have a family to support, and I can't afford to tell the whole truth."

CAPONE WAS A REAL CARD

Al Capone (1899–1947) has the reputation of being the leading mob figure in American history. He was certainly the most successful. According to the *Guinness Book of World Records,* Capone holds the title for the "highest gross income ever achieved in a single year by a private citizen." His earnings? An estimated $105 million in 1927.

Michael R. Milken, the Drexel Burnham Lambert Inc. junk bond king who was indicted in 1989 for fraudulent stock market activity, was said by the IRS to have been paid $550 million in salary and bonuses in 1987. But as the *Wall Street Journal* pointed out, Al Capone's 1927 income of $105 million was worth $600 million in 1987.*

How did Capone achieve such wealth? Through some of the most brutal and far-ranging lying and cheating in the annals of crime. Among his illegal activities were dealing in liquor and running stills during Prohibition, gambling, conducting "protection" rackets, and operating dog tracks, dance halls, and prostitution rings.

Capone's biggest lie, therefore, may have been the one he reserved for his business card. On it he listed his occupation as "Secondhand Furniture Dealer."

SAY IT AIN'T SO, J. EDGAR

Even notables in crime fighting have been known to lie. Take the case of FBI Director J. Edgar Hoover. Early in his career as director, he fabricated the story about the capture of George "Machine Gun" Kelly, a kidnapper and gangster, so that he could coin the expression "G-men" for his bureau.

In a 1946 issue of the *Tennessee Law Review,* Hoover wrote that the expression "G-men" came from Machine Gun Kelly when, upon his capture in 1933 on a farm in Tennessee, he threw up his hands and shouted, "Don't shoot, G-men, don't shoot!"

The trouble with this story is that Machine Gun Kelly was captured by a group of officers led by Memphis policeman W. J. Raney in the gangster's bungalow. What Kelly really said, according to national press accounts of the arrest, was simply, "Okay, boys, I've been waiting for you all night."

There is another good reason why Kelly did not say anything

---

*See Steve Swartz, "Why Mike Milken Stands to Qualify for Guinness Book," *Wall Street Journal,* March 31, 1989, p. 1.

about "G-men" upon his capture. No FBI agent was anywhere around at the time.

And there were other ways J. Edgar fudged the truth, especially when it came to making himself and the FBI look instrumental in the capture of a highly visible criminal. The Al Capone case, in which the notorious leader of the Mob was sent to prison for income tax fraud, had been the work of Elmer Irey and the Internal Revenue Service, with the FBI contributing only an investigation that led to a contempt-of-court conviction. But Hoover did nothing to dissuade those like *The New York Times* who declared that the Capone case had shown "the bureau usually gets its man." Indeed, Hoover's stated position was that Bureau involvement in a case automatically sealed the criminal's fate so that "whether or not the Bureau actually solved the crime, it deserved the credit." A stretching of the truth, to say the least.

Hoover also took liberties with the books, movies, and other materials that came out about the FBI. The first popularization of the FBI came in the pages of the *American Magazine*. Some of the twenty-three FBI stories published by the magazine appeared with Hoover's byline, but they were all written by Courtney Ryley Cooper, a Kansas City free-lance reporter who provided the trademark FBI formula that made the department famous. Cooper, who later put many of the stories together in a highly successful book, *The Ten Thousand Public Enemies,* referred to Hoover as "the most feared man the underworld has ever known."

All in all, Cooper helped launch the extensive publicity about the FBI and about Hoover's special role in building the department and becoming, as Cooper put it, "the master detective."

But Cooper went even further than writing the three books openly ascribed to him. He wrote one of Hoover's books for Hoover's byline, and of four movies listing Hoover as author of record, Cooper wrote them all.

Hoover also built his reputation by making certain he was featured front and center at the successful conclusion of big cases and that any indication of luck, chance, or payoffs was downplayed and FBI-oriented detective work was emphasized.

A case in point, and the most important in terms of the history of the FBI and Hoover's own personal history, was the capture of John Dillinger, the notorious bank robber.

Dillinger had long eluded police and the FBI, when an FBI agent, Melvin Purvis, got a tip from Anna Sage, an East Chicago brothel keeper who was facing deportation. She knew the whereabouts of Dillinger and was willing to inform on him for the reward money of $5,000 and a promise of help for her with the Immigration Bureau.

A trap was set for the next day—Sunday, July 22, 1934—when Sage said she, Dillinger, and another woman would be going to the movies at the Biograph. Under Purvis's direction, the theater was staked out and when Dillinger emerged at 10:30 P.M., the agents made their move. Dillinger tried to flee but was gunned down by Purvis. In the initial aftermath, Purvis became a national hero, to the great consternation of Hoover, who had been in Washington, D.C., the whole time following the moviehouse stake-out over the telephone from the library at his home. Hoover, along with Rex Collier, another promoter of the FBI, worked overtime to refocus attention back on the Bureau. Hoover downplayed the tip from Anna Sage, repudiated the controversial bargain between her and Purvis, implied that several agents and not just Purvis were instrumental in the final shoot-out, and conveyed the information that FBI scientific investigatory work that had been under way for months had led to the successful stake-out of Dillinger.

"By dint of constant restatement, Hoover finally managed to turn his treatment of the Dillinger case into the definitive version, and the classic victory in the FBI's war against crime," writes Richard Gid Powers in *Secrecy and Power: The Life of J. Edgar Hoover* (The Free Press, 1987).

Indeed, so central was the successful law enforcement—and public relations—conclusion of the Dillinger case to Hoover's success that he turned the anteroom of his office into a Dillinger museum, with a white plaster facsimile of Dillinger's death mask and souvenirs of the memorable night of the shoot-out on display thereafter.

Hoover also seems to have learned two PR lessons from the Dillinger case. Since the press turns whoever seems to be in charge of a case into a hero, Hoover let it be known throughout the Bureau that he was in personal command of every important major case and that was how it was to be described to the press. And since reporters base their stories on the interpretation provided by the first high-ranking official they talked to or who talked to them, Hoover was always ready with a press release and statement whenever there was a major story.

This was nowhere more obvious than in the Charles Lindbergh

baby-kidnapping case. The break in the case came when a customer used a ten-dollar gold certificate that had been placed in the ransom money by Treasury agents to buy gas at a gas station and the attendant noted the license number of the car (which turned out to be owned by Bruno Richard Hauptmann, who was tried and eventually executed for the kidnapping-murder of the Lindbergh baby).

Hoover, with only minimal involvement in the case at that point, rushed to New York so that he could be in attendance at the announcement of Hauptmann's arrest. He also posed for pictures shaking hands with some of the members of the New York City Police Department and other agents serving on the New York Lindbergh squad. Later Hoover was able to involve himself in the interrogation of Hauptmann.

"The Bureau of Investigation, of all the law agencies involved in the case, had done perhaps the least, but in the long run, after a year of incessant publicity . . . the public decided that the Lindbergh case was one more triumph for the Justice Department," says Powers.

Hoover was also not above using the truth in a harsh way. According to former agents, Hoover did keep a file on celebrities and members of Congress, with information fed to him by agents in the field who came across sexual or other potentially damaging information. Jack Anderson, the nationally syndicated Washington columnist who has won the Pulitzer Prize for reporting, told Ovid Demaris, author of *The Director* (Harper's Magazine Press, 1975), how Hoover would intimidate others with his files:

"He [Hoover] was certainly capable of blackmail. In fact he did it all the time, but it was implied blackmail. He would let senators know that he had picked up some information on them and he'd give it to them as an act of great charity, thereby doing them a favor but at the same time letting them know that he had the information."

Hoover stayed in power more than fifty years, basing his career on the general impression that crime was escalating in America and the belief that the country desperately needed a strong federal presence in the fight against corruption and criminals. Ironically in 1968 the President's Commission on Law Enforcement and Administration of Justice issued a report entitled *The Challenge of Crime in a Free Society*. Among its findings was the fascinating fact that crime statistics, although fragmentary for the period, show that the crime level from 1918 until after World War II—a period during which Hoover had warned of increasing crime—actually declined. It was the enormous publicity given to a small number of celebrity criminals that had led the public to believe crime was growing dramatically. As with so much else in our lives, the illusion became the reality, the figment of the imagination became the fact, by which people were guided and decisions were made.

How Two FBI Agents Outwitted Hoover

J. Edgar Hoover was not bested by too many people, but two who pulled the wool over the eyes of America's number-one crime fighter were his own agents—one with a weight problem and another who was going bald.

All agents were expected to maintain stringent weight levels, and those who didn't knew Hoover would penalize them if he ever found out. One overweight agent, who would later become special agent in charge of the Miami field office, used a ploy to survive a scheduled interview with Hoover. The agent went out and bought a suit and shirt several sizes too big—falsely creating the impression he had lost weight—and wore this to the meeting, where he thanked Hoover for "saving my life" by instituting weight requirements.

Another agent who tricked Hoover did so because the director did not like to promote bald men (it seems he didn't like imperfections in others) and this agent had gone bald since his last meeting with Hoover. But now the agent was slated to serve in one of the Bureau's overseas offices and he was fearful of keeping an appointment with Hoover. So he wrote to Hoover saying he knew how busy the director was prior to his annual appearance before the House Appropriations Committee and that it would be selfish and unfair to take up the director's precious time. Flattered, Hoover accepted the agent's offer to forgo the meeting and thanked him for his sacrifice.

"THE OTHER GUY DID IT":
THE STRANGE CASE OF RICHARD M. NIXON

If George Washington is known as the president who could not tell a lie, then Richard Nixon will be known as the one who would not tell the truth.

Harry Truman once called Nixon "a shifty-eyed, goddamn liar." Truman also described Nixon as "talking out of both sides of his mouth at the same time and lying out of both sides."

One could say that Truman, a Democratic president, was just getting back at Republican Nixon's attacks on the Truman administration. But consider, then, the statement by the conservative former Republican senator Barry Goldwater in his autobiography *Goldwater* (Doubleday, 1988):

"He was the most dishonest individual I have ever met in my life. President Nixon lied to his wife, his family, his friends, long-time colleagues in the U.S. Congress, lifetime members of his own political party, the American people, and the world. . . . No lie is intelligent, but his were colossal stupidity because they involved the Presidency of the United States."

Indeed, Nixon's political career seems to be characterized by lying. He was known during his vice-presidential years as "Tricky Dick." And the Watergate scandal, in which Nixon engineered the cover-up, led to his being the only U.S. president to resign from office. He was forced to do so less than a year after he told a convention of newspaper editors that "I'm not a crook." *

Nixon's troubles as president began in June 1972, during the presidential campaign. Five men, later found to be working for the Republican Committee to Reelect the President (aptly referred to as CREEP), were arrested for burglarizing the Democratic party's national headquarters, located in the Watergate office com-

---

*The remark came on November 17, 1973, in a televised question-and-answer session at the Associated Press Managing Editors convention in Orlando, Florida. Nixon stated, "People have got to know whether or not their President is a crook. Well, I'm not a crook." The statement has become a classic example of why not to use a negative to communicate a positive, since at the time and even afterward everyone seemed to focus on the word *crook*. Within nine months, on August 4, 1974, Nixon, the noncrook, resigned.

plex in Washington, D.C. Although no hard evidence exists that Nixon ordered the break-in, it is now clear that he did authorize the cover-up. It eventually emerged that not only did Nixon's closest advisors—Haldeman, Ehrlichman, and Mitchell—plan the burglary, they also engaged in such other nefarious activities in behalf of Nixon as employing political "dirty tricks," applying illegal pressure on campaign contributors, and using governmental agencies to quiet or compromise political opponents.

But through it all—and central to the cover-up—ran a concerted program of lying. Here, for instance, was how the top Nixon White House personnel decided to respond to press inquiries about a potentially damaging development in the Watergate story involving Dwight Chapin, a Nixon aide who later went to jail. As revealed by John Dean in his testimony before the Senate Watergate Committee, at a meeting of top aides summoned by John Ehrlichman on October 15, 1972, during the height of the presidential campaign against George McGovern, Ronald Ziegler, the president's press secretary, was extensively coached on how to handle press inquiries about Chapin. Ehrlichman suggested he say, "We are going to see all kinds of presidential friends, presidential staff, presidential relatives, dogs, etc., pictures on the front page of local newspapers to counteract the fact that McGovern is two to one behind. I am not going to try to cope with these unfounded stories." Dwight Chapin suggested Ziegler say, "I am not going to dignify desperation politics." Ehrlichman then suggested Ziegler declare, "Dwight Chapin is terribly offended at the treatment he got. . . . He said he would never again speak to any member of the press and he would like your apologies."

Altogether, twenty people, many of them close aides to Nixon, were convicted of various offenses in connection with Watergate (a total of twenty-nine were indicted). And one more person might have been found guilty, but he was pardoned.

The Strange Need for the Watergate Tapes

Central to Nixon's being forced out of the presidency was the existence of the White House tapes. Tip O'Neill, in his book on his years as Speaker of the House, has written that if Nixon had destroyed the tapes, although damaging in itself, Congress would have had little evidence with which to impeach him and he could have weathered the final two years of his second administration. Why, then, did he keep the tapes? And why did he even put in a taping system, especially since so much of the scheming and other damaging conversations were being recorded?

The answer seems to be due to Nixon's fears of being lied about.

Richard Nixon was very concerned about his place in history. And while he greatly admired Henry Kissinger and made him secretary of state, Nixon also worried that Kissinger, with his many friends in the media and in academia, would either be the recipient of accolades for foreign-policy successes in the Nixon administration or would later interpret events so as to give himself—and not Richard Nixon—the success and glory. By taping conversations and meetings, Nixon would not only have a record from which to draw when he wrote his memoirs, but he would also have a source of proof to counter any Kissinger attempt to overshadow Nixon.

Actually Nixon himself may have gotten the idea for the secret recording of conversations from Kissinger, who also did not trust those in the Nixon administration and worried about their lying. In his book on his years as Nixon's chief of staff, Bob Haldeman says that Nixon began the taping system in February 1971, with only Haldeman knowing about it. The idea came, though, from Nixon's knowledge that Kissinger kept a log of all his talks with Nixon.

"Nixon realized rather early in their relationship that he badly needed a complete account of all that they discussed. . . . He knew that Henry was keeping a log of those talks, a luxury in which the President didn't have time to indulge," writes Haldeman. But Nixon also felt that he could not trust Kissinger to be fully truthful about Nixon's role or Kissinger's position on matters. "He knew that Henry's view on a particular subject was sometimes subject to change without notice," Haldeman says.

Interestingly both Nixon and Kissinger shifted back and forth in their levels of trust and mistrust about the other. Seymour Hersh, in *The Price of Power: Kissinger in the Nixon White House* (Summit, 1983), quotes a Kissinger aide, who monitored many of his boss's telephone conversations with the president, as describing Nixon as "swinging from trust to lack of trust" in his dealing with Kissinger—a description, writes Hersh, that "perfectly matches Kissinger's attitude toward Nixon." And then we get the picture of two of America's highest officials jockeying to safeguard themselves from lies and deceit from the other. Writes Hersh:

"If the President coped with their unstable relationship by secretly tape recording all conversations in his office and on his telephone, Kissinger coped by tape recording his telephone talks with the President—and with everybody else. . . . Both men soon accumulated far too much—in writing and on tape—on each other."*

Nixon's Strangely Remarkable Background

Ironically, for a man of such deviousness and paranoia Richard Nixon went into his presidency with some remarkable achievements. He had shown brilliance and political leadership as a college youth. He had wanted to go to Harvard and had even won a scholarship, but lack of finances forced him to go to nearby Whittier College. He graduated second in his class and was the undisputed campus leader—president of his freshman class, the student body, the history club, and a male social club (the Orthogonians). He also played on the school football team and was an outstanding debater. He so impressed Whittier president Walter Dexter that in a letter of recommendation to the dean of Duke University School of Law, Dexter wrote, "I believe that Nixon will become one of America's important, if not great leaders." Nixon, who won a scholarship to Duke, often had the highest class rank during law school and graduated third in his class.†

Nixon went on to win election to the House of Representatives for two terms and then election to the United States Senate from

---

*Nixon was so concerned about his reputation that at one point he tapped the phone of his brother Donald to make certain he was not doing anything that might embarrass the Nixon presidency.

†An incident in law school involving Nixon and several of his classmates was an eerie harbinger of the Watergate break-in. When students became uneasy about the late posting of grades one semester, Nixon climbed through the open transom window of the dean's office one night, unlocked the door for two of his "co-conspirators," and together they found the key to the file where the grades were located. After Nixon saw his grades (he had dropped below third place in the class), they replaced the files and left. Decades later, as recorded on the White House tapes, Nixon told John Dean, who was complaining about the difficulty in getting tax files on prominent Democrats: "There are always ways to do it. (Expletive deleted), sneak in in the middle of the night."

California, one of our five largest states. He was elected vice president at the age of thirty-nine, the second youngest vice president in U.S. history. When he lost the presidential election to John F. Kennedy, Nixon was not much older than Kennedy. Finally Nixon came back, not only from this defeat but from a defeat for governor of California two years later to emerge triumphant as president in 1968—surely one of the most impressive political comebacks in U.S. history. And he shares with Lyndon Johnson the rare achievement of winning office to the four major elective federal offices—congressman, senator, vice president (twice), and president (twice). But Nixon stands alone in one respect: No one else in the history of the country has been elected twice to the vice presidency and twice to the presidency.

Nixon exhibited, on at least one very important occasion, that he knew full well the importance of being honest in dealing with others. The White House tapes, which recorded so much else that was venal and devious, also records Richard Nixon giving one of the most incisive rationales for being truthful. On April 16, 1973, he instructed John Dean, the young White House counsel, on how to conduct himself during the Watergate investigation. The advice, well-given, was obviously not followed by its giver. Said Richard Nixon, "Tell the truth. That is the thing I have told everybody around here—tell the truth! . . . That Hiss would be free today if he hadn't lied. If he had said, 'Yes I knew Chambers and as a young man I was involved with some Communist activities but I broke it off a number of years ago.' And Chambers would have dropped it.* If you are going to lie, you go to jail for the lie rather than the crime. So believe me, don't ever lie."

When a First Lady Was Not the Last to Know

How truthful was the picture of himself Richard Nixon presented to the world?

---

*In 1948 Whittaker Chambers claimed Alger Hiss had been associated with him in a Communist spy ring in the 1930s. Hiss declared Chambers was lying and sued for libel, but Chambers produced microfilms of secret documents purporting to show Hiss was involved in Communist activities. Hiss was subsequently convicted of perjury and jailed. Nixon had pushed for Hiss's imprisonment.

Henry Kissinger served Nixon as national security advisor and then as secretary of state. At his initial formal White House reception, Kissinger met Mrs. Nixon for the first time and he took the opportunity to praise President Nixon in lavish terms. Mrs. Nixon soon leaned over and stopped Kissinger, saying, "Haven't you seen through him yet?"

—Seymour M. Hersh,
The Price of Power: Kissinger in the Nixon White House
(Summit, 1983) p. 109

In the art of business, West meets East—or is it East meets West?

CHAPTER IV

"It's free—with absolutely no obligation!"

CONSUMER SCAMS AND SCOUNDRELS

. . . Surviving the Half-Lie of Marketplace Hype

A liar believes no one else.

—Leo Rosten

"We're really living in dishonest times."

The speaker was a Queens, New York, dentist, quoted in a July 1988 *New York Times* article on the secret cost of car rental. The good doctor said he had made a hobby out of researching the best deals for his vacations. What he had encountered was a welter of devious and confusing practices by car rental companies—deceptive activities that, the reporter noted, had been largely addressed in the airline industry, but had as yet "gone unchecked in the rental-car business."

No wonder. In January 1988 Hertz, the world's largest auto rental company, had admitted overcharging insurance companies $3 million and customers $10 million for car repairs. The company had fraudulently collected the $13 million through what was termed an insurance-and-repair scam in which, according to reports, Hertz used double-billing, fictitious repair shops, forged signatures of appraisers, and false damage estimates to collect money from customers who had damaged but not insured rental cars. The phony billing practices involved Hertz employees using razor blades, glue, "white-out," and copiers to alter repair bills sent to customers.

THE BOOK OF LIES

But the car rental business is by no means alone in being plagued by dishonesty. As we will see in this chapter, the problem is rife across industries—and professions.

And even those who are supposedly there to help the consumer can be equally dishonest. One particularly nasty scam: credit repair clinics.

Ostensibly set up to help people challenge derogatory information on their credit rating, one such company—Credit-Rite Inc.—bilked nine thousand people around the country out of $2 million paid to have Credit-Rite restore their eligibility for credit. Authorities called it the most extreme case of credit-repair abuse ever uncovered. Two of the operators of the company eventually went to federal prison, where it is hoped their own credit rating is now in disrepair for many years.

Since business and commerce deal with money, the temptation to lie and cheat in the pursuit of acquiring money appears to be overwhelming to too many people in our increasingly mercantile world. The only solution for the consumer is the age-old one of "Buyer beware," which has now been coupled with "Buyer, be aware." Another appropriate adage seems to be "A fool and his money are soon parted." But let's not be too hard on the consumer. After all, he is us.

What follows is a sampling of the lies that can be found in today's marketplace. If you're smart, you'll read and reap from the experience. Otherwise, someday you might just weep.

> In a newspaper cartoon a man is shown leaving a roadside gift shop. He is saying to his woman friend, "I've never been in a gift shop with so many plaques dealing with honesty and forthrightness." Above him is the sign with the store's name—TOURIST TRAP GIFTS.

THE LATEST DIET GIMMICK: A PATCH THAT GOES SKIN DEEP

The hottest new weight-loss gimmick in recent years was said to be a "diet patch."

The idea and product were simple (which is what made it such a hot gimmick). For anywhere from one to forty dollars, a consumer could buy a skin patch that supposedly could suppress the appetite by sending a message through the skin to the brain where, lo and behold, the appetite control center is.

The appetite-controlling message was to come from a few drops of special liquid embedded in an adhesive bandage that the customer would stick on the wrist.

The makers touted this as the "latest in transdermal skin-patch technology." Several different companies were even manufacturing the product, and health food stores and individual distributors all sold it.

The problem was that although widely available, the product was illegal. Representatives of the federal Food and Drug Administration said that no such over-the-counter skin patch was ever shown to be safe and effective. The concept seemed to mimic legitimate prescription patches that deliver drugs through the skin, such as those for heart problems. But there are only eight such FDA-approved skin patches—none of which deals with weight loss, or the appetite control center.

The director of the resource center for the National Council Against Health Fraud was quoted in newspaper accounts with a suggestion for those who were contemplating buying the product. To lose weight, he said, people should stick the patches not over their wrists but over their mouths.

Falling into the Quacks

The word *quackery* was apparently derived from the word *quacksalver,* which meant to boast of a cure. Thus, quackery exists in the promise of a cure and not in the product (vitamin C, for instance, is good in combatting scurvy but not in curing cancer). Quackery also has no relation to the promoter of the cure, since it could be a licensed physician or a national advertiser making the claim. Quackery, then, is the label that can be applied to a claim of a cure when the hope of that cure turns out to be built on a lie.

QUACKERY NOW COSTS BILLIONS A YEAR

The growth in false and misleading health claims has become so alarming in recent years that in 1988 the Food and Drug Administration began an accelerated campaign against quackery, which, the FDA said, was costing Americans several billion dollars a year. A 1986 poll showed that 26 percent of adults polled used one or more questionable methods of health care. A third of the people, however, said the questionable method they were using was highly effective, with only one in ten saying it was totally ineffective. The perceived effectiveness of quackery was seen as paralleling the placebo effect, which is the tendency for a person's belief in his getting better to bring relief in itself. (It has long been known that two-thirds of patient complaints are at least partly if not wholly based on emotion and that one-third of the cure for many ailments comes from the patient's belief in the treatment or the one prescribing the treatment.)

Quacks no longer come on the back of a wagon selling snake oil. Quackery can come from people with impressive credentials and professional memberships; they can tout their claim of cures on talk shows and in best-selling books.

Do not think that just because the FDA exists and a claim if untrue would be stopped that the FDA can prevent or eliminate all medical frauds. A case of mail fraud, for instance, can take several years to prosecute. FDA resources are limited, so they and the Federal Trade Commission cannot deal with all scams but must address themselves to the more serious frauds.

IS THERE A DOCTOR IN THE HOUSE . . . OF CORRECTION?

A high-ranking member of Congress called it "the largest medical scandal in recent memory."

The late representative Claude Pepper (D.-Fla.), then chairman of the House Subcommittee on Health, following a six-month investigation into the licensing of physicians in 1984, reported a startling discovery—10,000 people in the United States were suspected of having fraudulent medical degrees.

Said Pepper, "We have found evidence that some people posing as doctors have not even graduated high school."

A major source of the bogus diplomas were diploma brokers, some with mail-order businesses. For example, postal inspectors found a school in the Dominican Republic to have issued suspected medical degrees to 165 individuals who went on to practice as doctors. About 40 of those in six states had so far been prosecuted.

As a result of the findings, legislation was promised to make it a federal crime to use fraudulent medical credentials, but four years later in 1988, when the *New York Times* followed up on the story, no legislation had as yet been submitted to Congress.

QUIET—HOSPITAL CHEATING ZONE

Here's a thought to ponder the next time you're about to go in for surgery. In October 1983 it was learned that thousands of graduates of foreign medical schools had cheated on that year's special examination used to determine acceptance for U.S. medical training.

As many as 4,000 students were said to have had access to the tests, which were stolen, and thereby cheated on the exam. As a result, 10,000 graduates were forced to retake the test.

Most of these 10,000 were Americans who, unable to get into U.S. medical schools, went abroad to study at foreign medical schools. To practice in America, they must pass stringent tests to determine if their education meets U.S. medical standards.

Before the breach in security was discovered, the test was originally sold for $50,000, then resold for prices ranging from $10,000 to $5,000 to $1,000. Near the time of the test, some people were renting it for an hourly charge of $25.

Authorities believed that 3,000 to 4,000 students eventually had access to the exam.

The organization that runs the test—the Educational Commission for Foreign Medical Students, in Philadelphia—had to reschedule the entire testing program at a cost of $1 million.

The only bright spot in all this is that the monies lost by the cheating medical students were not covered by Blue Cross.

MADE IN JAPAN?

A number of products are either manufactured, named, or promoted in ways that border on the deceitful—if they do not fully tip over into the land of outright fraud.

Consider for instance the case of the Matsui line of electronics products.

This company's TVs, videotape machines, radios, and other consumer items come with a "rising sun" symbol and a catchy motto: "Japanese Technology Made Perfect."

Sounds like a fine Japanese company, doesn't it?

There's just one problem. Although components in the products come from Taiwan, South Korea, Malaysia, Yugoslavia, and Britain, not one element comes from Japan. All the products in the Matsui line are really the private brand of Currys, a major British electronics retail company.

Currys was eventually charged with misleading advertising by a British government consumer protection agency, was fined $7,400, and was forced to drop the motto about "Japanese Technology Made Perfect." But Currys was allowed to keep the name Matsui.

The Matsui name, however, carried its own problems. Unbeknownst to the company's marketing people, who made up the name because it sounded "nice" and "a bit mystical and foreign-sounding," Matsui proved to be not only a real Japanese name; it was also the name of one of Japan's worst war criminals.

But company officials were undaunted when they heard about the name's association in Japan. They said they would keep using the name because it had been successful, enabling the company to sell millions of items. They also said they would continue marketing another Japanese-sounding line, Saisho. This, too, was selling well in England.

The British, however, were not the first to use such a marketing ploy. Actually the Japanese did it first. After World War II, Japanese goods had a shoddy reputation. Products labeled "Made in Japan" did not get the reception they get today. And a company with a name like Tokyo Tsushin Kogyo Kabushiki Kaisha would not have gone over very well in the United States. So the cofounder of that company, Akio Morita, and his staff developed a name that had a Western, modernistic ring but could also be pronounced easily in Japanese. The name they came up with was Sony.

WOULD YOU BUY ICE CREAM CALLED "HAÄGEN–NEW JERSEY"?

Two "super premium" ice creams—the rich, gourmet kind—stand out with names that imply a totally imported Scandinavian origin. One is Haägen-Dazs, which comes complete with a map on its back panel showing Norway and Denmark and two big stars indicating Oslo and Copenhagen. Another is Frusen Glädjé, which goes so far as to have not only a map of Sweden, Denmark, and part of Norway, but a portion of the copy on some packages in a Scandinavian language. Both products, however, are made in the U.S.A. Haägen-Dazs is manufactured in Teaneck, New Jersey. Frusen Glädjé has its headquarters in Philadelphia, on JFK Boulevard.

(This information can be found on the labels—in small print. But you have to look for it, and not many people do, which is the idea, *ja*?)

FROM ODOMETERS TO FINANCIAL PLANNERS: SOME FACTS AND FIGURES ABOUT HONESTY IN THE MARKETPLACE

• If you've bought a used car or truck, there is a one-in-five chance you're the victim of odometer fraud, *Changing Times* magazine reported in 1988. According to the National Highway Traffic Safety Administration, odometers get rolled back an average of 30,000 miles on 3 million vehicles a year. This enables sellers to cheat buyers out of an average of $1,000 per car. NHTSA estimates that the odometers on more than 50 percent of all leased cars are rolled back.

• If you eat out, watch out. According to a study by Cornell University's school of hotel and restaurant management, one of every eight restaurant checks is computed incorrectly. While some of those mistakes could be honest errors, many are not, and the advice is clear—check your restaurant check.

• Manufacturers today offer some 50 billion rebate coupons a year. Distributed through ads, in the products themselves and on store shelves, these rebates are used to sell everything from appliances to toys. But although 60 percent of shoppers say they prefer products with rebates, manufacturers freely offer them because they know fewer than 10 percent of rebate coupons are ever redeemed. Manufacturers also knowingly contribute to the small return rate by specifically making the process complicated and deliberately designing their offers so that consumers are discouraged from redeeming the rebates. In fact, redemption rates are so low that on a statistical average, only one in three buyers would bother to seek a rebate as high as $5 on a $25 item. A *Better Homes and Gardens* survey of its readers found that 64 percent of respondents said they were often or always discouraged from seeking a rebate because of the procedure imposed on obtaining it. Indeed, since companies know redemptions are predictably low, there are cases of companies offering the come-on of rebates that are actually more valuable than the product on which the rebate is offered. One such example: The manufacturer of a hair dryer priced at $4.99 offered a $5 rebate.

• Financial planners have proven to be financial disasters if you don't find an ethical one. In 1988 the North American Securities Administrators reported to the Subcommittee on Consumer Affairs of the United States Senate that from 1985 to 1987, 22,000 people had lost at least $400 million— and possibly as much as $1 billion—through financial-planning abuse and outright fraud. The NASA survey found cases of ex-preachers, savings-and-loan officers, income tax preparers, and others with "extremely limited" backgrounds in financial matters presenting themselves to potential investors as financial consultants with formulas, information, or investment opportunities that couldn't lose. One such example: A financial advisor told investors they could expect a 30 to 40 percent return on a mix of bank

CDs, precious metals, and international arbitrage. Four hundred investors wound up sending the advisor $7 million for deposit in an offshore bank in the Marshall Islands. The money, however, went to a gas station owner in the Marshall Islands, who simply mailed the checks from investors back to the financial planner, who invested in the only sure thing he knew about—himself.

CHUTZPAH DEPARTMENT—EXHIBIT 1

As tax scams go, it was small stuff. Of course, he himself was a tax preparer, which made it doubly odd, but there it was—a Baltimore City tax preparer was sentenced to a year in prison, with all but four months suspended, after he pleaded guilty to failing to file his state income tax return for 1986. He was also fined $1,000 and ordered to make a $3,000 good-faith payment for tax liabilities.

All of that was somewhat routine as tax cases go. What made this cheater different was that he had a bank account under the name "Take the Money and Run."

In other words, he was honest about his dishonesty.

WHEN DIRECT MAIL IS DIRECTLY DECEITFUL

Everything about the piece of mail said U.S. Government. The business-size envelope was that manila tan with window that seems to say Internal Revenue Service or Treasury Department. Across the middle of the envelope atop the cellophane-window portion were imprinted in black type the words "BUY U.S. SAVINGS BONDS." Through the window could be seen a drawing of the Statue of Liberty, a series of computer numbers, a green check-like background, and the name of the addressee with "Pay to the Order of" clearly seen. Added to all this, on the envelope was imprinted the following message:

POSTMASTER:
TO AFFECT EXPEDITIOUS DELIVERY, HANDLE IN ACCORDANCE WITH SECTIONS 134.12 TO 134.82 OF UNITED STATES POSTAL SERVICE REGULATIONS.

With all this going for it, the recipient could not wait to rip open the envelope and get his hands on what undoubtedly was a check from the government for either: (a) an IRS refund; (b) a Treasury check for who-knows-how-much; or (c) something good (after all, wasn't the envelope telling him to buy U.S. Savings Bonds, so surely the government was trying to get him to reinvest what monies they were sending him).

So what did he find when he opened the envelope? He found a "check" good for "six months of FREE gas or $250" for coming in to a Buick dealer in the area and buying or leasing a new or used car. Add our friend to the suckers-born-every-minute list. He had *opened* the lousy piece of mail, which is exactly what the advertiser wanted.

Advertisers go through all kinds of creative contortions to get people to open their envelopes so that they can make their pitch and, it is hoped, conclude a sale. But usually this is done with some kind of offer or enticement on the envelope—you know, words like *free* or *new* or *Special Announcement* or *Look Inside for a Special Offer*. In this case the advertiser had gone to special lengths to deceive by wrapping the mailing piece in the Statue of Liberty, a U.S. government–style envelope, and a reference to the patriotism of buying U.S. Savings Bonds. And what about that reference to the postmaster, as though one government agency was trying to tell another agency (the Post Office) how to handle this valuable piece of mail.

Intrigued—or, better yet, furious—our friend decided to check out those sections 134.12 to 134.82 that were printed on the envelope. Guess what he found?

He found that Section 134.12 refers to mail sent by members of the U.S. Armed Forces, that it refers to postage-due mail, and that it refers to letters sent free of postage. In other words, those sections have nothing to do with mail sent by a Buick dealer offering free gas to anybody who will run out and buy or lease a new or used car from said dealer.

And what about those other sections alluded to on the envelope? Our friend found that they do not exist. There are no sections of the United States Postal Service Regulations above 134.12.

Car buyer, beware.

THEY DON'T JUST COUNTERFEIT MONEY ANYMORE

Sellers and buyers in the marketplace face one common problem—the growing flood of counterfeit products. More and more, such famous brands as Levi jeans, Rolex watches, and Reebok shoes are being duplicated in shoddy counterfeit imitations and either sold as the real thing or marketed as cheaper ways you can get a famous-name brand on your body, wrist, or feet.

Of course, some consumers like the cheap imitation—so long as the fraud comes with the right price tag and the right look. But the practice is decidedly illegal, and in recent years manufacturers have banded together to get tougher litigation and enforcement of existing regulations.

Companies like Reebok have found their T-shirts, sweatshirts, and sneakers being copied illegally in growing numbers. The company now employs about 100 investigators who track the production of fraudulent Reebok products and close copies of Reebok designs. With sales mushrooming from $1 million in 1981 to $1.4 billion in seven years, Reebok, based in Massachusetts, finds it has to watch out for counterfeiting both in the United States and overseas.

In fact, Reebok, along with police, have mounted raids in flea markets in California, North Carolina, Texas, Tennessee, New Jersey, and New York. A federal anticounterfeiting law makes such seizures of goods legal so long as police take part.

The Reebok people destroy all such merchandise—often in the thousands and all invariably of poor quality.

Another manufacturer that pursues bogus knockoffs of its products is Levi Strauss, the jeans manufacturer. Their aggressive campaign has paid off in recent years, with the company reporting the counterfeiting and copying of Levi design features now lessening.

Cartier International Inc. of New York has been another aggressive fighter of counterfeiters, suing everyone who tries to copy their design trademarks. They even use court orders to seize counterfeits from street peddlers.

What has helped stem the tide has been the passage of strong laws in 1986 and 1987 by several European and East Asian countries who have also moved to stop the problem. One country, though, where problems persist is Thailand, which does not have strict controls against pirating of product designs and trademarks.

Hong Kong, for one, has an open market, touted to tourists, with stalls featuring imitation watches (Rolex, Gucci, Cartier, Dunhill, Hermès) ranging in price from $30 to $50. For five blocks along its Temple Street night market, which is on most tourist maps, young vendors stand behind small tables on which are laid out plastic cards showing pictures of the watches. When anyone asks to see a watch, the seller hurries away, then returns with the watch. All of this is illegal, but it is still done. One journalist who had bought a "Rolex" watch had it opened; he discovered inside a Seiko works.

Most of these fake watches are made in Taiwan, some in Hong Kong. But for those who think of buying such watches and then bringing them back to the United States, a catch-22 exists: U.S. Customs could either make you pay duty on the real price of the watch or confiscate it as a counterfeit.*

AT LEAST YOU COULD SAY
THEY'RE IMPORTED SHOES

To see how counterfeiters work, the Reebok people once traced a shipment of counterfeit shoes ordered by a California retailer. They discovered that instead of being shipped directly from the place of manufacture to retailers, as is normally the case, the shoes followed a journey of thousands of miles. First, the items were manufactured by a company in Taiwan, then transferred to another Taiwanese company, which then shipped them to Singapore, where they were then sent to Japan, whereupon they were later sent to Belguim—before finally arriving in California.

---

*One overlooked counterfeiting scheme that goes on in Hong Kong is that of pirated software for computers. A popular word-processing program that might cost $700 in the United States would cost as low as $20 in Hong Kong.

HERE'S WHEN LYING WAS IN REALLY POOR TASTE

Our nominee for the worst counterfeit of a famous label product is that of the rip-off of the Johnnie Walker Red Label Scotch by a whiskey company in Bulgaria.

The Bulgarian brew was called "Johnnie Hawker Red Label Old Scotch Whiskey." Distributed to the West by the official Bulgarian state forwarding agency, Despred, the Johnnie Hawker "scotch" was packaged in a square bottle just like its famous counterpart, looking but not tasting like the real thing. It came to public attention when a shipment of 28,000 bottles was seized in Italy before it could do any damage at its expected destination of South Africa.

When tested by Italian customs officials, the whiskey was found to have been produced with chemical alcohol and "whiskey essence." According to one of the customs officials who sampled it, Johnnie Hawker was said to taste "like toilet water."

MAYBE THAT'S WHY THE WORD CASH
IS IN CASHMERE

You've seen the ads for cashmere jackets at special low—or at least cut-rate—prices. Or you've encountered a street peddler selling cashmere scarves for just $15 or $20.

What you are witnessing, most likely, is an example of the latest luxury fraud—counterfeit cashmere.

Authorities are now finding that many garments labeled "70 percent cashmere/30 percent wool" contain only about 5 percent cashmere. The other 95 percent is made up usually of materials like recycled rags, human and rabbit hair, acrylic, asbestos, and newspaper.

In recent years the demand for cashmere has increased while the supply has dropped off. The consequences have been twofold: cashmere has gone up dramatically in price and rushing in to fill the void for affordable cashmere are shoddy operators with their shady labeling practices. The result: It is estimated that nearly 30 percent of the cashmere sold in the United States is labeled falsely.

The problem has led to the formation of the Camel Hair & Cashmere Institute of America, a watchdog agency founded in 1984 by seven major textile companies. They have discovered that even major department stores are at times duped—usually with goods produced with cloth from Prato, Italy. (England and Scotland have strong laws that prevent such tampering.)

The temptation to cheat on cashmere products is intensified because the best cashmere comes from a relatively small supply—the hair of Kashmir goats raised in China and Mongolia. Such authentic cashmere costs up to $200 a yard, with lower grades from Iran and Afghanistan at $100 a yard. Attempts to breed goats elsewhere, such as in Australia, New Zealand, and even in such midwestern states as Iowa and Montana, have not proven successful.

Among the subterfuges being tried are using the hair of the yak or removing the coarse fibers from camel hair to make it feel like cashmere. Says an official with the Institute, "The cheating is limited only by the imagination of the cheaters."

How can you tell what is true cashmere and what is fake?

The Institute has one guideline hard to beat. Look at the price. An overcoat of even the lowest-grade cashmere is said to cost at least $800. A cashmere sweater should go for a minimum of $200.

Maybe they should just rename the real material "lots-of-cashmere."

THIS LEATHER IS A DREAM, AFTER ALL

Another material that is not what it seems is that "rich Corinthian leather" that actor Ricardo Montalban made famous in his Chrysler car television ads (of course, he pronounced this leather for the upholstery as "Co-REEN-thee-an").

The *Wall Street Journal* wondered in an article in April 1988 what is Corinthian leather, anyhow? And where does it come from? (See "Department of Shattered Illusions," April 11, 1988, p. B1.)

The answer, according to the *Journal:* "It's a label dreamed up by Chrysler marketing mavens for leather tanned to company specifications. Its quality is a matter of opinion. And it doesn't come from Greece, site of the ancient city of Corinth, but from places in the U.S., including Newark, N.J."

Acknowledges Montalban, "It's just a name, really, that's all."

It seems that the name was developed in 1974 when Chrysler wanted a moniker for the leather seats in its Cordoba luxury coupe that would reinforce the theme of Mediterranean elegance. *Corinthian* was chosen because it has the dictionary definition of "gracefully elaborate," although it also means "dissolute and loving luxury, as the people of Corinth were said to be."

While Corinthian leather has been described by Ricardo Montalban as "the best," the director of auto testing for *Consumer Reports* magazine says the material "doesn't feel terrific."

Never mind. Montalban, who also went on to tout the leather in ads for the Chrysler New Yorker, is invariably asked, wherever he appears for Chrysler, to give his pronunciation to the now-famous but utterly made-up name, "Co-REEN-thee-an leather."

THERE'S A WORD IN THE DICTIONARY FOR IT: DECEIT

One of the most common misconceptions in book buying is that a dictionary with the name Webster's in its title is linked with the famed dictionary compiled by Noah Webster and published as America's first collection of definitions.

The truth is that any dictionary maker can put *Webster's* in the name of its dictionary, because book titles cannot be copyrighted. Many small printing companies, trying to make a quick dollar in the lucrative dictionary market, simply tack the Webster's name onto the title of their book and an inferior, slipshod, or incomplete book of definitions enters the marketplace, misleading book buyers and playing havoc with the reputations of reliable publishers of dictionaries.

Actually, while a number of very fine dictionaries without the name Webster's are on the market, the authentic Webster's is published by G. and C. Merriam Company of Springfield, Massachusetts. Interestingly, the original dictionary compiled by Noah Webster and issued in 1828 in two volumes did not have his name in the title. It was called *An American Dictionary of the English Language*.

BUYER, BEWARE

To survive in the marketplace, you need to know what devious practices you face as you go down the supermarket aisle. Here are some:

Weights and Measures—In the old days, you had to worry about the shopkeeper pushing his thumb down on what he was weighing. Today it's the manufacturer playing games with the packaging. The reason is that there are no standard weights or descriptive names. What one manufacturer calls "medium" may be a 5-ounce package while to another it's 4.5 ounces. This is particularly true for detergents, cereals, shampoos, pickles, or any other product sold in containers of varying sizes. So manufacturers can and do deceive with the size of their package—a bigger carton masking a smaller product on which a "medium" label is put on to obscure comparisons.

Also, bigger does not necessarily mean cheaper by the ounce. The Fair Packaging and Labeling Act of 1966 required that the use of terms denoting a price savings—such as "budget size," "value pack," or "money saving" container—can only be used if the item represents at least 5 percent savings per unit weight from its original price. But this regulation interestingly does not require any such standards on the use of such terms as "family," "bonus," "giant," or "king" size. In fact, numerous instances can be found where the smaller package is cheaper per ounce than the larger. So you have to compute to be sure.

Plus there is another practice to be wary of. It is no longer rare to find a toothpaste or laundry detergent box labeled as the "large" size when in reality it is the smallest of all the sizes offered.

False Savings—Watch out for the use of words implying big savings. Terms such as "discount foods," "lower prices," "warehouse prices," and "buy and save" can mean true savings—or they can mean nothing more than items available at the same prices they were before. In fact many stores put up big signs reading SALE, but that could mean that the item being touted is simply available for purchase—after all, isn't that what a store is for, to have items available for "sale"?

Drastic Price Reductions—This is yet another term that can represent a true savings or be just another shady marketing practice.

Is the price reduction a true reduction from real prices or were previous prices just inflated for a while so that the dramatic reduction claim, signifying essentially nothing, could be made? A major department store and a major national chain both offer 20 to 50 percent reductions periodically, but these sales are held on such a regular basis—usually every two to four weeks—that the sale price is basically the regular price. This is particularly true on jewelry and on store-name appliances, where cost comparisons with other stores are difficult.

Trading Stamps—Stamps that are given by stores for purchases and then later redeemed by consumers for items had their heyday in the 1950s and 1960s (by 1963 an estimated 80 percent of all food stores offered trading stamps). Although they fell on hard times in the 1970s during the energy crunch and inflation, they are now reported to be making a comeback. But do they represent savings for the consumer or just a hidden cost for stores that is then passed on to consumers in higher prices? In a marketing survey published in 1966 by the U.S. Department of Agriculture, it was found that a store needed a 12 to 15 percent jump in sales just to break even for offering the stamps and that 26 percent of supermarkets with stamps wound up raising their prices. And yet, trading-stamp companies convey the impression that stamps are a free service for the consumer—all the way from calling the booklet in which stamps are kept a "saver's book" and the special centers where the stamps are redeemed for merchandise as "gift" centers.

Coupons—The first coupon was a one-cent-off coupon issued by C. W. Post for Grape Nuts cereal in 1895. Since then, couponing has grown into a giant business. By the start of the decade of the 1980s, 90 billion coupons were being distributed annually. But coupons are not so much a savings method as they are a promotional tool for the manufacturers, since the cost of the coupons—their redemption value plus the cost of advertising and processing the coupons—are added to the cost of the product being promoted by the coupon offer. Indeed, the cost of couponing for the industry is calculated at $1 billion annually. Ultimately that cost is passed on to the consumer in higher prices (in fact, within the supermarket industry there have been attempts by some chains to forgo coupons for lower prices, but competition has prevented them from abandoning coupons).

But do you really save money using coupons? Not really, not if the offer of a coupon makes you overlook an equally good alternative product that costs less even without a coupon reduction—and especially not if the availability of a coupon makes you buy a product when, without such a coupon, you would not have bought the product at all (what most people do not realize is that except for in-store coupons, coupons are generally only for national name brands that have higher prices). In fact, if you are a frequent user of coupons, you probably have a higher shopping bill. Industry studies have found that coupon clippers tend to buy higher-priced items and to spend more on impulse—no matter what age, amount of schooling, size of household, or level of income. In a 1981 survey commissioned by two large coupon distributors—John Blair Marketing and Donnelley Marketing—it was found that the non- or occasional user of coupons spent an average of $16.86 per shopping trip, as compared with $31.04 for regular coupon clippers—a whopping 84 percent higher rate of spending and certainly far above any savings inherent in the use of coupons.*

Shopping, then, is a lot like getting married. You have to watch what you're doing before you go down the aisle.

WATCH OUT FOR OLD COINS AND NEW WINE

The industries in which one has to be wary of fraud and deceit are numerous, varied, and surprising. Consider:

• Approximately 15 to 20 million Americans collect coins, yet scams in the coin industry are as prevalent as ever, according to a Federal Trade Commission consumer alert issued in 1988. Warned the report, coin investing is often "a financial disaster."

The most common form of rare-coin fraud is "false grading," in which a dealer ascribes a higher value to a coin than it is worth. In the recent past, when some dealers have been prosecuted for this tactic, they have not been able to meet the guarantees and other obligations they made when they sold the overvalued coins, leaving gullible buyers in the lurch.

A frequent practice of unscrupulous sellers is to issue fraudu-

*These statistics and supermarket practices can be found discussed in *Cut Your Grocery Bills in Half!* (Acropolis Books, 1983) by Barbara Salsbury with Cheri Loveless.

lent certification to back up their claims of value. In this regard, they use an old certificate to mislead the buyer into assuming that a coin's grade is accurate.

One widespread abuse is to cite the Salomon Brothers index of prices for twenty rare coins—an index that has seen the compound annual rate of return on coins going up 16.3 percent over the previous ten years. The problem is that those twenty coins are not indicative of most coins—they are extremely rare and valuable—and the index does not reflect the investment performance of coins in general.

Indeed, according to the FTC, millions of dollars a year are lost because of fraudulent or deceptive practices by some nefarious elements of the coin industry. And this does not count the money lost the old-fashioned way—by collectors selling coins too soon or when the market is down.

• Fraud has occurred in the wine industry, injecting an old human practice into the production of new wine bottles.

In 1988 three top executives in West Germany's important wine industry were charged with fraud for illegally adding substances—mainly sugar and cheap foreign wines—to 12.7 million gallons of Rhine and Moselle white wines produced from 1978 through 1982. More than 50 million bottles of the fraudulent wine at a value of $60 million were sold—a violation of West Germany's wine-purity laws and a deception of consumers through the use of false labels. It was said that the case involved the biggest wine-related criminal charges ever raised in the history of the Federal Republic. Unfortunately, it was not an isolated case, as recurrent scandals have wracked the West German wine industry in the past decade, primarily involving the addition of illegal substances. From 1980 through 1988, eighty-three instances of wine fraud were brought before the courts of Mainz, the city in the heart of the West German wine region.

Cheers.

IS THAT WHAT AT&T MEANT WHEN IT SAID, "REACH OUT AND TOUCH SOMEONE"?

The telephone is a wondrous instrument. It can save lives. It can save time. It can bring people and families together.

But the telephone is also being used—with seemingly increasing frequency—as a way of prying us away from our money.

The Direct Marketing Association, Inc., has estimated that fraudulent telephone schemes cost consumers $1 billion a year.

While many honest companies use the telephone to sell goods and services, shady enterprises and outright thieves also call to collect from us. The three major categories often subject to abuse appear to be travel clubs, office supplies, and investments.

With travel clubs, you are called and told you are the lucky winner of a free vacation plus bonuses but that you have to secure the vacation by putting its value on your credit card. But when the information about the vacation comes, the promises are not fulfilled and the vacation winds up either costing you or—worse—there is no vacation for the money you've already put up.

In another scam, you are called with the offer of a very cheap trip to Hawaii, Florida, or other points warm. You send your money and either (a) you never hear from the company again or (b) you are strung along, with one cancellation after another, until the promoter vanishes.

Then there is the office-supply scam. If you are in business, you might get a phone call from a company claiming to be doing a survey or a serial-number check on a copier. Later you might get a call offering either boxes of toner or paper at a bargain rate—or, even more devious, the call may be confirming an order that had never been placed. The next thing you know you receive a shipment of merchandise marked up two to five times the regular price—complete with large shipping and handling charges. To top it all off, the merchandise is usually shoddy. Although you can send the materials back, the scam relies on bookkeeping departments paying for office supplies received before any internal checking is done.

But if you think only you can be ripped off by phone, consider the supposedly sophisticated investors who were ripped off to the tune of $150 million in a scheme uncovered in mid-1988. It has been called one of the largest financial swindles in European history.

The scam actually began with a newsletter sent out to unsuspecting investors touting investment advice on multinational, well-known stocks, as well as on penny stocks. Called International Dateline Report and described as "very well done" by those who received it, the publication was soon followed by a phone call from a very persuasive salesman urging the recipient to buy one of the recommended stocks. The typical victim responded positively, often investing thousands of dollars over the phone. In fact, Swiss and French investigators who uncovered the scheme said that 10,000 or more investors from South America to Saudia Arabia to Sweden were bilked out of sums ranging from $1,000 to hundreds of thousands of dollars.

What was the catch that lured so many victims?

First, the stocks being touted were usually in companies whose prices had been inflated artificially, usually with falsely optimistic press releases and overly optimistic reports of income. Several companies were said to be paper shells that existed only to fool investors.

Second, the swindlers, according to one of those who had been swindled, were "frighteningly convincing." A lawyer retained by 150 of the victims said that her clients "were really very intelligent people" who had been taken in by high-pressure salesmen adept at selling by phone. "When these brokers got on the phone, they really knew how to influence decisions," the lawyer told reporters. "They must have studied psychology."

Interpol was orchestrating the investigation and more than twenty arrests had already occurred in France, Switzerland, and Germany. But unclear to investigators as the case unraveled was—what happened to the estimated $150 million that had been essentially stolen by phone?

SELLER, BEWARE

Consumers are not the only ones who have to beware of deceit in the marketplace. Sometimes, the seller has to beware too. Here are some industries and the scams they have to face:

The Airline Industry—One of the few ways you can get back nonrefundable airfare is to be sick and have a doctor vouch for you. But many people try to get around this when they want to cancel a ticket but aren't sick.

According to a *Wall Street Journal* article on the problem,* doctors report that an increasing number of perfectly healthy people are asking for medical excuses to get out of nonrefundable

---

*"Why People Get Sick Over No-Refund Fares," *The Wall Street Journal,* April 20, 1988, p. 25.

tickets. Some doctors will question the patient to see if there is a valid health reason for the request, but others automatically write the notes. And one doctor reportedly never denies a request because "he just thinks the airlines' policies are too unfair."

A spokesman for the airlines said they do look at the medical excuses and will turn down those where the illness does not seem to warrant the refund. But, according to the spokesperson, "We essentially rely on the integrity of the medical profession."

The Health Insurance Industry—*U.S. News & World Report,* in its July 4, 1988, issue, called health insurance scams "the latest trauma in the nation's health care industry." Health insurance fraud is now costing the industry an estimated $10 billion a year, with false or inflated claims escalating and getting more sophisticated. The ones perpetrating the fraud are not so much the patients as the health care providers—the labs, the doctors, and the dentists.

Fraud is becoming more common because health care providers are finding themselves squeezed by the cost-containment measures imposed in recent years to keep the rising price of health care under control. But some doctors and dentists, faced by capped fees, are persuading patients to sign inflated claims to reduce co-payments. Also prevalent are "rolling labs" that give free checkups, then bill the insurer for tests not given to the patient.

As a result, health insurers are fighting back with closer scrutiny of claims, establishment of special investigative units, and a campaign to remind patients that fraudulent claims lead to higher premiums. Law enforcement officials on both the state and federal levels are also planning to use mail fraud and racketeering statutes to prosecute the flimflammers. The idea is to make health insurance defrauders ill about lying.

Couponing—While only five in a hundred coupons are ever redeemed, one out of those five is redeemed fraudulently. Coupons turned into a store for cents-off offers are sent to clearinghouses, where the coupons are sorted and sent on to manufacturers for reimbursement. Store owners are paid a handling fee, usually an average of seven cents, plus the value of the coupon. Such amounts of money can lead to abuses.

Store owners are known to hand in coupons that they never processed. Bogus stores are sometimes set up by people who then redeem coupons for payment. Sales clerks also get into the act, putting in their own unused coupons along with customer coupons so that they can get the cents-off supposedly paid to shoppers. And finally the public becomes part of the problem by slipping in expired coupons or coupons for sizes not covered or even for other products in their shopping purchases. The result: the fraudulent redemption of coupons now costs manufacturers a quarter of a billion dollars a year.

But you and I ultimately pay for the fraud; manufacturers build in such costs into the prices charged for couponed products.

Rebates—In 1987 a U.S. attorney in Michigan charged a fifteen-person ring of rebate defrauders with having illegally collected more than $80,000 during three years from 1984 through 1986.

Under the code name Rebategate, the postal inspector's office, tipped off by an observant carrier who noticed a slew of mail from fulfillment companies coming to one woman's apartment address, conducted an investigation in which eight people were found to have committed mail fraud and seven others to have aided and abetted the crime.

The defendants were charged with using false names and addresses, counterfeit refund forms, and cash-register tapes. They were also accused of sending in proofs of purchase from packages they had not bought.

Among the companies defrauded were Gillette, Seagram, Dow Chemical, and Procter & Gamble.

A woman in her forties from Jenison, Michigan, with no prior arrest record, became the first person in the ring—and the first in the nation—to be convicted for this kind of fraud. For accepting a refund for a pair of Gitano jeans she did not buy, she was sentenced to four years' probation, ordered to pay $805 in restitution, and fined $5,000.

Since authorities believe many consumers are defrauding refunders, other rebate cheaters around the nation are expected to be caught eventually and prosecuted in coming years.

"I never lie unless it is absolutely convenient."
—Benny Hill,
British TV Comedian

The true symbol of Wall Street?

CHAPTER V

"I've got a deal for you that's too good to be true."

THE CORPORATE STRUCTURE

. . . When Business Gives You the Business

"Help Fight Truth Decay."
—sign in office of polygrapher
for Baltimore City Police
Department

We Americans may like to think that our government, with all its regulatory agencies, protects against fraud and deceit in the marketplace. But consider these facts:

• The Consumer Product Safety Commission is not authorized to supervise, recall, or ban harmless products that do not work.

• The Food and Drug Administration is prevented from acting in various cases by a provision that allows certain unproven medical equipment and devices to be sold.

• The Federal Trade Commission can stop companies from making false or unsubstantiated claims in their advertising—but the Commission has to find the time, the staff, and the funds to force a company to cease and desist, and in recent years, especially with budget cutbacks coupled with an increase in such products, the FTC cannot be relied on to do the job envisioned for it or needed by the public.

So don't feel that just because a product or service is advertised, it somehow has passed legal and ethical muster to make such claims.

And for those companies wishing to flout the laws and slither through the loopholes, the payback—even with fines factored in—can be sizable. For instance, the Environmental Protection Agency has declared since 1984 that products claiming to repel roaches, insects, even bats by emitting high-frequency vibrations have no credible evidence to make such a claim. And yet companies have sold more than $25 million of these products. The EPA, after spending $250,000 on tests and finding that animals and insects either ignored the high-frequency sounds or quickly acclimated themselves to it, sued fifteen companies manufacturing the products. Most settled by paying fines of just $2,500 to $5,000—which means that if all fifteen paid $5,000 fines, it cost these companies a total of $75,000 to make a total of $25 million.

When it came to the marketplace, the rule of law used to be "Buyer, beware." Little has changed to alter this, not so much because business hasn't changed but because human nature hasn't changed.

Anytime money is involved, the tendency for deceit is there. Many people try to conduct their business affairs properly and ethically. Some, however, are not above looking for all the help they can get.

Wall Street, for one, has become synonymous with hard-driving personalities reined in only by the energetic tug of watching agencies and the threat of prison sentences and sizable fines. Even so, the last several years have been marked by some of the largest insider trading scandals in history.

Other industries—from construction to defense to aerospace—have been besmirched by kickback schemes, bribery, and falsehoods as more and more companies and company leaders have striven for the almighty dollar.

It is in this atmosphere that businesses operate—or are tempted to operate.

The Song of Songs—Business-Style

Among the top business schools in the nation is the University of Pennsylvania's Wharton School. The pressure of exams and keen competition among students is lessened somewhat by the student body's annual rite of midwinter follies.

The 1988 show had an interesting song about business ethics. Sung to the tune of the Michael Jackson hit song, "Beat It," the lyrics had a segment that went as follows:

> I cheated, cheated
> And I probably sound conceited
> You're probably angry
> I'm overjoyed
> I work on Wall Street
> You're unemployed.

MADISON AVENUE INTRODUCES THE FIBBING SALESMAN

The advertising and automobile industries have for years teamed up to pummel us with probably the most dishonest-leaning advertising and promotions around. They threw ads at us with talk of prices below dealer invoice (oh, they're selling all their cars at a loss?) . . . overstocked lots with cars that just have to go (you mean that dealers don't know how to stock inventory like every other business?) . . . and claims of being authorized factory discount dealers (all auto dealerships are authorized by the factory, otherwise they could not be a dealership).

All of these promotions—and more—are conducted regularly in my state of Maryland—at least they were until the attorney general of Maryland cracked down on car dealers for such practices.

But while Madison Avenue drove roughshod over logic when it came to advertising cars—and while the hint of the word *liar* would drive a car dealer into a frenzy of looking back over his shoulder—there finally emerged a car campaign that took the shoddy image of the car salesman and turned it into a tongue-in-cheek attention-grabbing ad campaign.

Introducing Joe Isuzu, the fibbing salesman for the Isuzu automobile.

This is the campaign, first launched in 1986, that garnered all kinds of attention and awards. Using an actor by the name of David Leisure, the commercials on television and in magazines show a grinning, oily car salesman making outrageous claims for his product (such as that they cost $9 and can climb Mount Everest)—all the while the words "He's lying" are superimposed on the screen when he comes to an audacious statement. In print, the copy on one representative ad says, "Big Joe is a big liar."

Of course, the commercials put in key features of the auto and play off the hyperbole of Joe Isuzu with understated truths. It is all a surprisingly effective way to cut through the clutter of over-blown, intelligence-assaulting car commercials.

Joe Isuzu has therefore accomplished what the best salesmen try to accomplish: get noticed, get a message across, and make a sale. Barbara Lippert, advertising critic for the trade magazine *Adweek,* called the campaign revolutionary for its willingness to lie outrageously about the product—and then to correct the lie with a message superimposed at the same time on the screen.

The idea for Joe Isuzu came from the ad agency of Della Femina, Travisano & Partners of New York. It is said that most of those who worked on the campaign were thirty years of age or younger, which shows that a different, more open, and ironically more honest approach to car advertising is possibly being promoted by a younger generation fed up with trickery masked as honesty. Now, thanks to Joe Isuzu, we are starting to see honesty peering through sassy, with-it, eye-winking deceit.

In short, lying is so much a part of our culture and the sale of products in our culture that open references to lying are, surprisingly enough, refreshingly honest.

The Joe Isuzu campaign, after all, earned its writers and art directors a first-prize Gold Lion at 1987's International Advertising Film Festival in Cannes, France.

And the campaign even entered the international political scene when, in February 1988, President Reagan likened Nicaraguan communist leader Daniel Ortega to that "lying spokesman, Joe Isuzu."

The rest, as they say, is history.

THINGS ARE NOT GOING BETTER WITH ADS

In a survey of nearly 2,000 consumers during 1988, the Roper Organization found that the public felt a need for more stringent government regulations in the areas of disposal of toxic industrial waste, exposure to hazardous materials, and—third—honesty and accuracy in advertising.

Also during 1988, the Consumer Network, a Philadelphia-based company specializing in consumer research, polled a sample of more than 1,500 consumers to determine how honest they believed advertising was in eight product categories. The findings: 75 percent said cosmetic advertising was dishonest or not very honest; 64 percent said insurance advertising was dishonest or not very honest; and only 31 percent said they believed food advertising honest or somewhat honest. In the area of hospitals, banks, and drugs, the respondents split about 50–50. Only in the areas of department store ads (70 percent) and discount store ads (62 percent) did a majority of those polled feel the ads were honest or somewhat honest.

These studies confirmed a business fact of life—advertising has long had a problem about its believability. A Roper official, quoted on their study in *Adweek* magazine,* said their findings show "there's a built-in skepticism about advertising claims."

And consumers are not the only ones questioning ads. The National Association of Attorneys General (NAAG), the Securities and Exchange Commission (SEC), the Center for Science in the Public Interest (CSPI), the Federal Trade Commission (FTC), the Food and Drug Administration (FDA), and various other governmental agencies have cracked down on various misleading or outright fraudulent ad claims in recent years.

NAAG has moved to regulate ads by the airline industry and in

---

*Janet Neiman, "Misleading Ads Casting Shadow Over Entire Industry," *Adweek,* September 26, 1988, pp. 32–34.

1988 began investigating rental-car advertising. The SEC has created new ad guidelines for mutual-fund advertisers. CSPI, a citizen group that covers food advertising, has been pushing to root out deceptive claims in the areas of nutrition and health, especially those that exaggerate the benefits of beef, butter, eggs, and milk.

Among the deceptive ad practices cited was the Montgomery Ward ad for a swivel rocker that the Kansas attorney general's office found was deceptive because the chair was advertised as being "on sale" 65 percent of the time. Later, Montgomery Ward was cited by the National Advertising Review Board, an industry self-regulating body, for using the phrase "lowest prices guaranteed" because the store did not say that "the lowest price" resulted only when the customer could show that a competing store sold the same item for less. *

Ironically the number of misleading ads, according to industry observers, has not increased in recent years. The assistant director for advertising practices at the FTC said that although there are different types of ad problems now, "in general, the level of problems is no greater than five years ago."

But even though deceptive advertising has not increased, *Adweek* reported that a consumer suspicion of ads is up. And this factor alone makes advertisers' jobs harder, creating added barriers that advertising has to overcome.

Thus the lies and distortions over the years in advertising—though now being corrected—have had their toll. Consumers are depending less on advertising for information about a product or service. As the president of the Consumer Network states about today's climate for advertising, "There is a definite sense of consumers pulling back from ads."

THE TEN DANGER SIGNALS IN BUYING

When the author of this book served as director of public information and education for the attorney general of Maryland, the

---

*Another common practice in retail advertising is to list the price of an item as being "20 percent off" without specifying what the regular price or the sale price of the item is.

agency developed a pamphlet for the Consumer Protection Division that contained information about the ten most common shady business practices we had encountered. We ultimately printed a half million of these leaflets, distributing them throughout Maryland. Years later these ten consumer rip-offs are, unfortunately, still very much in existence. To help you spot—and avoid—them and to save you money and heartache, here are "The Ten Danger Signals in Buying":

1. *"BAIT and SWITCH" ADVERTISING*—Maybe you've inquired about a product advertised at an unbelievably low price, only to be told by the salesman that the article advertised is no longer in stock or that "it wasn't that good anyway." No matter how you look at it, the merchandise isn't available. What does the salesman do now that you've been "baited" into the store? He tries to "switch" you to a more expensive, more profitable item. And yet, later you find that the product you were led to believe was "sold out" is still being advertised. This type of practice is illegal and should be reported to authorities.

2. *UNORDERED MERCHANDISE*—If you receive merchandise in the mail that you have not ordered, you are under no obligation to pay—so long as you do not make use of the article. Your best bet is to return the merchandise at once to the sender at his expense. Some dishonest companies are in the habit of sending out merchandise nobody has ordered . . . and follow it up with bills and collection notices. Especially watch out for this kind of practice around the holiday season.

3. *"BARGAINS"*—Articles offered at prices that are hard to believe are in the long run rarely the bargains you think they are. The quality of merchandise and the guarantee should be carefully checked out to make certain the advertised article is what it is claimed to be. Check the price with that offered by other companies, since it might not be any bargain at all.

4. *BLANK CHECKS AND BLANK CONTRACTS*—Never sign a blank contract or a contract with blank spaces

in it, and don't forget to read a contract, especially the fine print, before you do sign. Insist that all details be in writing and get a copy of the contract you are to sign. Never sign a statement that states that work is finished until it actually is. Also, never sign a blank check in which the amount has not been written in.

5. *MERCHANDISE LEFT ON APPROVAL BASIS*— Some door-to-door salesmen leave merchandise on an "approval basis." Too often these salesmen never come back and you wind up with the bill. Always check a salesman's credentials and don't let him talk you into anything you don't want.

6. *ORAL GUARANTEES*—You are legally bound by what the contract says, not what the salesman tells you. Therefore do not accept oral guarantees. Get it in writing. Make sure you understand what it says and that it protects you fully.

7. *REFERRAL SELLING*—If someone tells you to sign up as one of his customers and earn extra cash simply by "referring" other customers to him, beware. The contract you are signing is for merchandise you're buying, whether you think so or not. As far as the "extra cash" for referrals—forget it. The salesman has.

8. *GOLDEN OPPORTUNITIES*—Never allow yourself to be rushed into buying anything by talk of a "golden opportunity" or that it is your "last chance to get in on a good thing." You're probably the "last chance" that person has to make the sale. Take your time and, to satisfy yourself, shop around and compare prices before buying.

9. *THE WRONG DELIVERY*—Any article delivered to you that is not the same as the one you ordered should not be used. Call the sender or return the article immediately. If the item was bought on time, notify the finance company in writing of the mistake.

10. *ORAL ESTIMATES*—As with guarantees, oral estimates are no assurance that you will wind up with the bill you expected. If a repairman wants to take a household appliance, radio, or television set from your home for repairs, first get a written estimate of the probable repair cost. Also, get written assurances that no additional charges will be made without your consent.

Also, DON'T make financial commitments you cannot possibly meet. DO investigate before buying. Any questions? Contact your state's Consumer Protection Division. (Every state has one. Usually it can be found in the office of the attorney general. If not, call your local telephone directory assistance and ask for the Consumer Protection office in your state.)

THE GREEDINESS BOOK OF WORLD RECORDS
(With all due respects to Guinness)

The largest fraud settlement in history was $115 million in fines and penalties paid by the Sundstrand Corporation in 1988. At that time the Illinois aerospace company admitted to four criminal counts of charging the U.S. government for cost overruns on fixed-price contracts, paying gratuities to government employees, billing the government for various personal expenses of company officials, and violating tax laws.

The Justice Department, in making the announcement of the company's agreement to pay the fines and penalties, said Sundstrand also acknowledged a conspiracy to overcharge the government millions of dollars on military contracts.

Among other charges, Sundstrand at one point moved spare aircraft parts to a warehouse owned by a Wisconsin storage company and received a nominal payment for the parts. Sundstrand then turned around and, acting as if it had sold the parts, claimed on its tax return that it had a multimillion-dollar tax loss.

The fastest growing fraud threat is said to be gold-connected schemes. An estimated tens of thousands of Americans lost $250 million in 1988 alone—a year branded by authorities as "the fool's gold rush of 1988."

The typical swindle involved a boiler-room telephone operation in which a salesman offered to sell 100 tons of dirt said to contain enough to yield 20 ounces of gold for $5,000. This would represent $250 an ounce—less than the then-current $430 an ounce. The problem was the gold existed in only microscopic levels in the dirt. Many of the mine sites, upon investigation, were found to contain less gold than exists in seawater.

In another case 2,000 investors were defrauded out of $20 million when they were talked into investing in a New Mexico mine they were told would generate $100 million in gold sales annually.

Another scheme involved investors in Wyoming and Minnesota being persuaded to pay an average of $6,250 for what proved to be worthless dirt in an inactive Utah gold mine. The perpetrator of the scheme was later found to be an inmate of a Wyoming prison serving time for fraud. He had used prison telephones to make his pitch to his victims.

In case you might think those who fell for the scams were untutored, the head of the Council of Better Business Bureaus said the victims were from all stations of life, "from unsophisticated elderly persons to professionals who think they understand the risks of investing."

But what undoubtedly characterized them all was a higher level of greed—something the victims obviously shared with their victimizers.

THE REPEAT VICTIM: AN INVESTMENT SCAM PHENOMENON

One of the amazing aspects about the fraudulent business practices that swirl about us—especially the investment scams—is that many people fall prey to scam artists not once but several times.

There appear to be several reasons for this. One is that a person who proves easily duped once can be easily duped again. But other factors include the fact that some people place their trust in a specific salesperson and are reluctant to change. Or the person may continue to deal with the same salesperson or sales company as a way of denying to himself that he has been bilked in the past. Or, finally, the victim may feel driven to recover his or her losses and will plunge into another questionable investment.

So prevalent is this psychology that in a *Wall Street Journal* article on the syndrome it was found that "some firms compile and sell 'sucker lists' of people known to buy by telephone, sometimes with information on their income and investment tastes." *

One former salesman recounted how he would carry lists of customers from one boiler-room job to another and solicit clients he had already defrauded (although he would use a new name and accent—after all, people aren't total fools).

Consider Stanley J. He lost $86,000 investing in a precious-metals company touted by a now-defunct Florida boiler room selling fraudulent contracts in precious metals. Then, when another company called, saying they could get silver so cheap and sell it for so much that he would get all his money back, he jumped at the chance. So Stanley, a seventy-three-year-old retired farmer, made seven payments totaling $27,000 over three months. He never saw any of his investment again—and later it was found that the second company that defrauded him was itself a boiler-room operation that preyed on the former customers of the first company.

But that's not all. Stanley has invested several more times with people soliciting him over the telephone. The latest: he was called and informed that he had won five American Eagle gold coins—it seems a computer had selected him, but to get his prize, he had to send in $349 (Stanley isn't quite sure why). In any event, Stanley sent in his money. He was still waiting for his coins several months later when his story appeared in the *Journal*.

The Business Strategist

Two rival merchants met in a railway station in Russia.
"Where are you going?" asked one.
"To Pinsk."
"Ahah!" said the other, "you tell me you are going to Pinsk because you think I'll think you are going to Minsk. But I happen to know you are going to Pinsk. So what's the idea of lying?"

—*A Treasury of Jewish Folklore*

---

*Martha Brannigan, "Victims of Investment Scams Seem Condemned to Repeat Past Errors," *Wall Street Journal*, March 24, 1988, p. 33.

ALMOST AS EASY AS TAKING CANDY:
THE BABY APPLE JUICE SCAM

The nation's second largest baby food firm, its former president, and a former vice president were all found guilty in what an assistant U.S. attorney called "one of the largest consumer frauds ever to be prosecuted by the Department of Justice."

The crime: selling phony apple juice for babies.

The Beech-Nut Nutrition Corporation pleaded guilty on November 15, 1986, of marketing during the early 1980s a product touted as "100 percent pure" apple juice that turned out to consist of sugar water, beet sugar, cane sugar syrup, corn syrup, and apple flavoring. There was little or no apple juice.

The company was fined $2 million plus $140,000 in investigative costs. The $2 million fine was the largest ever imposed in the fifty-year history of the Food, Drug and Cosmetic Act.

Two years later a federal judge, saying the case was "extraordinary" and noting how millions of adulterated bottles had been sold and consumed, found the two Beech-Nut executives guilty of a total of 799 counts of conspiracy, mail fraud, and violations of the Food, Drug and Cosmetic Act. The executives were eventually sentenced to six months of full-time community service, placed on five years probation, and fined $100,000.

In his defense the former president of Beech-Nut said he did not know about the distribution of the fraudulent product until several years after it was being sold, and then he allowed the distribution to continue based on the advice of four lawyers—an obvious dual mistake (to continue distribution and to rely on the advice of four lawyers).

The mislabeled and fraudulently promoted apple juice was sold for several years before being pulled in 1983. Shipments went to twenty states, Puerto Rico, the Virgin Islands, and five foreign countries. Since then the company says it has invested over $10 million to ensure the purity of its product. Among steps it has taken include upgrading authenticity testing, hiring experts to review quality procedures, and setting up a hot line for employees who want to report any concerns about product quality.

The employee hot line is a little like the closing of the barn door after the horse has gone. The juicy juice scandal actually first came to light when a Beech-Nut employee—the then director of research and development—became suspicious that the company was selling a bogus apple juice. When he informed company officials but they did nothing, he quit and later wrote an anonymous letter about his suspicions to the FDA. The letter spurred the federal investigation that began in 1982.

The former Beech-Nut employee had signed his letter, "Johnny Appleseed."

SOME STATISTICS ABOUT CRIMINAL LIARS (CRIME MAY NOT PAY, BUT IT COSTS)

Banks lose much more through the twin deceptions of fraud and embezzlement than they do through robberies. Consider: from 1950 to 1971 fraud or embezzlement caused 100 banks to fail. And in one six-month period in recent years, commercial banks lost almost five times as much money from fraud and embezzlement as they did from armed robberies.

* * *

In the 1970s about 500 U.S. companies spent $1 billion to bribe foreign officials (source: *Louis Rukeyser's Business Almanac*).

* * *

Credit card fraud is a massive headache. By the mid-1980s, this crime was costing banks and consumers $700 million a year. With the development of new technology such as holograms on the cards, losses by banks and consumers were reduced. But by 1987 stolen credit cards were still costing $164 million annually.

* * *

Among America's 500 largest corporations, 115 were convicted during a ten-year period in the 1970s of at least one major crime or paid civil penalties for serious misbehavior (source: *U.S. News & World Report* survey in 1987).

* * *

The U.S. Justice Department estimates that $5 billion to $15 billion of illegal drug money is laundered each year through the American and international financial system—thereby enabling organized crime and criminals to use their money. Not figured into this amount and generating billions of dollars more in laundered money are those involved in insider investment trading, embezzlers, swindlers, and dealers in counterfeit bonds and securities. As much as $9 billion in taxes are lost to the U.S. Treasury in this way, according to the IRS.

* * *

Shoplifting and employee theft are major problems for retailers. In a euphemism of the trade the problem is called ''shrinkage,'' but the shrinkage is expanding. In 1980 shoplifting alone was costing $20 million a day or $7.3 billion annually. Employee theft costs American business at least another $5 billion, with estimates ranging as high as $40 billion (the U.S. Commerce Department).

* * *

It is estimated that the cost of white-collar crime ranges from $40 billion to more than $100 billion annually. In contrast, according to a 1986 study by the President's Commission on Organized Crime, the Mob steals $50 billion a year.

* * *

Inside trading scams on Wall Street grew so large in the 1980s that one such culprit, Ivan Boesky, earned $50 million to $100 million in illegal profits from 1982 to 1986. But once he was caught, indicted, and convicted, Boesky was fined $100 million and sentenced to three years in jail. One other punishment: He was forced to set aside $5 million for legal costs (the total legal costs for cases connected with Boesky were said to be more than $20 million).

THE LATEST THING IN LIES: HIGH-TECH FAKE

Here are just some of the ways high-tech fakery is now being used, especially in a business setting:

Yuppies who can't afford to have it all—such as a car phone— can now have the supposedly next best thing: a product called the Cellular Phoney.

Yes, it's a fake car phone that is a highly realistic copy of the status device. First produced in 1988, the Cellular Phoney comes with a realistic handset and a fake, stick-on antenna. Priced at

$15.95, the novelties were being made by a small company in Los Altos, California, called—appropriately enough—Faux Systems. At first report, more than 40,000 had been sold, largely in the Los Angeles area, where freeway fashion is an important consideration.

The owner of a Dallas store where hundreds of these had been sold told a reporter, "It's so incredibly real-looking that you have to begin to wonder how many people driving around out there with an antenna on the back of their car actually have a phony."

Indeed, another product on the market forgets the fake phone and just sells the fake antenna.

And then there is the audiotape you can buy that will provide you with the sounds of a fake office in the background. The idea was the brainchild of a Kingston, New York, woman working at home who worried that the only background sounds her clients who called her heard was that of her four small children, television, and other domestic noises. So she recorded the sounds of a typewriter, adding machine, file cabinet, and other office appliances, and played the tape of sound effects whenever a client called.

The fake office worked so well for her that she got the idea to market the tape of small-office sound effects to office-supply outlets. The price: $14.95.

The product is seemingly so real that sometimes when the fake telephone rings in the background, people on the line ask if the phone needs to be picked up. How does the inventor of the tape handle this?

"I say, 'No it's being taken care of.' "

WHAT'S-IN-A-NAME DEPARTMENT

The successful business is usually the one that packages and promotes itself in the most imaginative way. Sometimes, however, this leads to exaggeration, better known as stretching the truth, even better known as lying. Consider the case of one of the most successful sports enterprises in history.

The Harlem Globetrotters, founded by Abe Saperstein in 1927, did not originate in Harlem or in New York City. Saperstein started the team in Chicago, where he lived, but wanting a name that would connote a black team, he chose Harlem, which then as now was heavily populated by blacks.

As for Globetrotters, here, too, Saperstein fibbed. He wanted a name that connoted something that the team wasn't—a team in wide, international demand.

Actually it took more than twenty years after their founding for the "Globetrotters" to play their first game outside the United States.

---

*An Ode to the **

Yes, the asterisk.

A cute little fellow. Almost looks like a star, twinkling so innocently on the page or in the ad.

But oh so deceptive, so diversionary, so dangerous.

For the * is a signal that something more—or less—lurks elsewhere on the printed material.

Where could that be? Is it here, off to the side? Or right under the headline? Or is it far below? Yes, there it is at the bottom. But it's oh so tiny—and the words that come after the tiny * are also very tiny down there. Why is that? Don't they want us to be able to read it?

Do you think there is a reason why tiny *s and real tiny type always seem to go together?

And do you think that the use of *s is specially taught in advertising school (so many *s are used in ads you would think copywriters need special training in it, just as lawyers get training in defending murderers and doctors take seminars in combatting malpractice suits).

But nowhere does the * seem to multiply the way it does in car ads and on car dealer lots. Why, there seems to be a colony of *s marching all over the car industry. Maybe we should just write the name of car companies like this:

G*E*N*E*R*A*L* M*O*T*O*R*S*

Yes, with all those *s in our ads, do you think they're trying to tell us something? Or maybe they're trying *not* to tell us something? In any case we would like to believe

---

that the * is not the punctuation of the liar. So here's a little poem in salute to all the *s in the world—both born and unborn:

> Twinkle, twinkle little asterisk,
> Makes no difference if things are slow or brisk.
> When you appear in any kind of ad,
> We'll try to think of you as good, not bad.

"My fellow Americans, I'm not a crook, I did not know about the Iran-Contra affair, and I will make this a kinder, gentler nation."

CHAPTER VI

"I'm not a crook."

ᎢPOLITICS AS ᎢUSUAL

. . . A Look at the Deception Process

Politics have no relation to morals.
                    —Niccolò Machiavelli

Politics has always been fraught with a dual image. On the one hand, we want to believe the best about those who represent us. Among the most highly regarded individuals in our history have been our presidents. And this high regard has usually extended to their wives, who are seen as the most highly respected women in the nation.

But we are also wary of and denigrate our political leaders and representatives. We tend to make fun of their ethics and snicker about payoffs and pressures for their votes.

And periodically we seem to be proven right to be so caustic. Whether it was the Teapot Dome Scandal in the 1920s, Watergate in the 1970s, the Iran-Contra affair in the 1980s, we have seen various presidential administrations wracked by lies and cover-ups. We have now had a president resign in disgrace (Nixon) and a vice-president resign to avoid a jail sentence (Agnew)—a far cry from the cherry tree image of George Washington and the honesty of an Abe Lincoln.

Indeed the loss of confidence in the honesty of our presidents has been severe. In a national poll in 1975, 69 percent of those interviewed supported the statement that "over the last ten years, this country's leaders have consistently lied to the people."

Possibly because of this growing mistrust of our leaders, the turnout at presidential elections has been dropping. By 1988 the campaign for president won by George Bush experienced the lowest voter turnout in sixty-four years.

Of course, we the electorate are not much better about lying to our elected officials. Following the 1988 presidential campaign, *TV Guide* magazine conducted a survey to find out the public's attitudes and feelings about the election. When people were asked if they had voted, the magazine reported that "an astonishing 85 percent said yes," when in truth only 50 percent of America's eligible voters had bothered to go to the polls.

"VOTE EARLY AND OFTEN": VOTING PATTERNS IN THESE UNITED STATES

One of the tenets of the American system is that we have free and fair elections. This, after all, is the root of democracy. Only totalitarian regimes or dictatorships have rigged elections, stuffed ballot boxes, and intimidated voters.

If you believe that, consider these snapshots of elections past in the United States:

• Edgar Allan Poe is said to have died on a Baltimore street after being given far too much to drink by political bosses and then taken in a drunken state from polling booth to polling booth in the city to vote the ballots of dead people still on the rolls.

• Under Lincoln, voting in the slave-owning border states was closely supervised. Because of fear about where their sympathies lay, the voters in these states in at least one election were made to hold up a colored ballot showing their party preference and proceed to the ballot box between lines formed by Union soldiers. Few were willing to hold up a ballot with the colors not endorsing the party of Lincoln.

• In the Nixon-Kennedy race of 1960, only 112,707 votes separated the two candidates out of 68 million cast. Kennedy won in the popular vote and in the Electoral College (303–219), but Nixon would have won the electoral vote if just Texas (he lost there by 46,000 out of 2 million cast) and Illinois (9,000 out of 4.5 million) had gone for him. (The outcome in electoral votes would then have been Nixon 270, Kennedy 252.) In fact Nixon points out in his book *Six Crises* that in three precincts in Texas and three in Illinois in which Kennedy won big a further examination shows that many more votes were actually cast than there were registered voters. Interestingly Nixon never contested the voting in this or any other part of the country, saying he did not want to cause delay, confusion, or bitterness at home or affect the image of the United States abroad. Since Nixon would later fight tooth and nail for the nomination in 1967 and even more so for renomination in 1971 (remember Watergate?), he may have had other reasons not to call for a recount—such as Republican irregularities elsewhere.

• One United States president remains dogged by stories of ballot-box stuffing and tampering that helped his career get off the ground. That president was Lyndon Johnson. In 1948, after being elected to the House of Representatives several times but losing one bid for the Senate in 1941, Johnson finally won his coveted Senate seat from Texas. But he did so after winning the Democratic primary by one of the closest margins in history—87 votes out of nearly 1 million cast. Ugly rumors and charges of election-day shenanigans swirled around Johnson (he won one precinct by 202–1), but his eyelash victory stood. So did a nickname that trailed after him for years: "Landslide Lyndon."

(Lyndon, himself, may have been the victim of vote fraud in an earlier campaign. In his losing race for the Senate in 1941, he at first seemed to win by 5,000 votes—until returns started coming in from his opponent's bailiwick. Although the vote totals looked strange in terms of numbers and distribution, the ballots were accepted, and LBJ went down to a narrow defeat. It was the last time he ever lost a race in Texas.)

• One future president did not let vote irregularities go unnoticed and his decision to challenge election results helped launch his climb to the presidency. That office seeker was Jimmy Carter.

When Carter ran for the Georgia State Senate in 1962, he found himself losing the election by 139 votes out of 6,000. But when he studied the results, he noticed what he thought was suspicious activity at one of the precincts he lost. He had the names of voters in that precinct printed in the local newspaper, then found many of them coming forward to say they had never voted in the election. Carter then challenged the results and had the ballot box opened in court, where it was discovered that ballots were missing. As a result, the precinct-vote totals were disallowed and Carter was declared the winner by 85 votes.

Watch Your Step . . . and Where You Sit

The drawing by *Kansas City Star* editorial cartoonist Bill Schorr, published during the final year of the Reagan administration, showed a maître d' at the door of the White House dining room greeting two guests. He asks the two dining patrons where they want to sit by gesturing to the seating arrangement in the restaurant and saying, ". . . Indicted or nonindicted . . .?"

THE SELECTION OF "THE FRAUD PRESIDENT": THE MOST DISPUTED NATIONAL ELECTION IN U.S. HISTORY

The most disputed—and possibly most corrupt—presidential election in United States history occurred in 1876, with the selection of Rutherford B. Hayes (1822–1893) as America's nineteenth president. The controversy over the outcome was so intense that it lingered throughout Hayes's four years in the White House.

Ironically the presidential campaign of 1876 was between two men known for their honesty and integrity. Hayes, nominated at the Republican convention on the seventh ballot, had gained national recognition as an upright political figure who was the first person elected governor of Ohio for three terms. The Democratic candidate was Samuel J. Tilden, who had become governor of

New York in 1875 and who was famous as the leader of the attack on the New York City political boss Tweed and his "Tweed Ring," which had swindled millions of dollars in municipal funds.

The campaign between the two was hotly contested, with the Democrat favored because of the eight years of corruption in Republican Grant's administration. But just before election day, responding to complaints about KKK intimidation of black voters, Grant sent federal troops into several southern states, thereby raising charges among Democrats that the Republicans were trying to influence the outcome by enlisting the black vote.

In the ensuing election, Tilden won the popular vote—4,284,020 to 4,036,572—and garnered 184 undisputed electoral votes. But the results in Florida, Louisiana, South Carolina, and Oregon were thrown into dispute, with both Democrats and Republicans charging vote fraud and submitting different sets of returns. In all, 20 electoral votes were in question. Tilden needed just one of the disputed 20 to put him over the top with 185 electoral votes.

Republican and Democratic party leaders traveled to the states to investigate. Each side found irregularities, forgery, bribery, ballot fraud, even shootings and murder. Also uncovered was the fact that many blacks, who would have voted for the Republicans as the party of Abraham Lincoln, had been kept from voting by KKK-type tactics.

When the Electoral College finally met in December, all of the 20 disputed electoral votes were awarded to Hayes and he was named winner—185 electoral votes to Tilden's 184.

The Democrats were incensed. In January 1877, after prodding by Democrats challenging the actions of the Electoral College, Congress established a special fifteen-member Electoral Commission (comprised of eight Republicans and seven Democrats) to review the voting. Deciding along party lines, the Commission also awarded the election to Hayes.

What also boosted Hayes into the presidency and finally seemed to quiet many of the Democrats was an agreement, termed the Compromise of 1877, in which the Republicans agreed, in Hayes's name, to withdraw federal occupation troops from the South and provide federal funds for rebuilding states still affected by the Civil War if southern Democrats would endorse the election of Hayes. Since the agreement would solidify the Democratic hold on southern states, the political deal was struck. Hayes was finally named president just fifty-six hours before the scheduled inauguration day of March 4, 1877.

The press, the public, and rival Democrats, however, never let Hayes forget his slim, suspect victory. During his four years as president, his more vociferous opponents referred to him as "His Fraudulency," "The Fraud President," and "Rutherfraud."

Machiavelli—A Name You Can Mistrust

It is necessary that the prince should know how to color his nature well, and how to be a great hypocrite and dissembler. For men are so simple, and yield so much in immediate necessity, that the deceiver will never lack dupes.
—The Prince (Chapter 18)

These observations about political thought and action—and others of an equally cynical, cunning nature—were written by Niccolò Machiavelli (1469–1527), whose name has become synonymous with treachery, deception, and unscrupulousness in political strategy.

An Italian statesman, Machiavelli served for fourteen years as the first secretary of the council of the Republic of Florence before being dismissed by the return to power of the Medici family. After being imprisoned and tortured by them, he was released and spent the last fourteen years of his life in retirement, writing poetry, comedy, and books about history and politics.

Today he is remembered primarily for his political thinking, which—especially in *The Prince* (written in 1513 and published in 1532)—focused on how one gains and keeps power. He advocated the concept that the end justifies the means, that a leader is smarter to rule by fear than by love, and that a ruler can use any method to strike down his enemies and make his followers obey.

But Machiavelli's own employment of his tactics did not always work. It is said that he wrote his treatise on politics to gain favor with the Medici family (he dedicated *The Prince* to Lorenzo dé Medici), but they rejected his advances, and he lived out his life away from politics and power.

He has had an effect on others, however. Down through the years many political figures have been intrigued with some or all of his thinking. Among those said to have been heavily influenced by Machiavelli this century were Joseph Stalin, Adolf Hitler, and Benito Mussolini.

Nice going, Nick.

THE FEDERAL GOVERNMENT'S FIRST MILLIONAIRE

In politics you are often only as good as the people you appoint to office. In that regard, President Andrew Jackson had a problem by the name of Samuel Swartout, who holds a notorious distinction.

Swartout, of New York, was named by President Jackson as collector of the Port of New York—despite the opposition of his secretary of state, Martin Van Buren, who warned Jackson against the appointment.

Swartout soon repaid Jackson's confidence in him by carrying out a confidence game of his own. From 1829, when he was appointed, until 1838, when he escaped to England, Swartout embezzled $1,225,705.69—a huge sum for then. He thereby holds a record. Swartout is said to be the first person to embezzle more than a million dollars from the federal government—or at least he's the first person we *know* embezzled more than a million dollars from the U.S. Treasury.

HONEST ABE DEALS WITH A BAD APPLE HIS WAY

Another president who had to deal with an appointment that went sour was Abraham Lincoln. In the rush to mount a war effort against the South, Lincoln's administration had to do things in short order, a factor that often leads to waste and corruption. The worst such situation was found in Lincoln's War Department, which was headed by Simon Cameron.

Under Cameron, it was later discovered, mismanagement was

rife, competitive bidding often went by the board, and favored middlemen—many of whom were dishonest—provided the bulk of war supplies at exorbitant prices. The inflated prices would have been bad enough, but the items purchased were usually of inferior quality—such as disintegrating blankets, spoiled meat, horses near death from disease, and uniforms that fell apart in the rain.

Eventually complaints about the conduct of the War Department grew so loud that the House of Representatives investigated Cameron's conduct as secretary. The result was an indictment of more than 1,000 pages. Although Cameron's mismanagement was singled out, no evidence was found that Cameron had taken graft or kickbacks. Rather his management style, or lack of it, had enabled the waste and graft to surface around him.

Lincoln, having to get rid of his secretary of war, decided to kick him not upward but sideward . . . to send him if not to Siberia then close by. He made Cameron the American ambassador to Russia and packed him off to St. Petersburg. However, writing to Cameron in a private letter, Honest Abe gave a demonstration in the use of the little white lie. He praised Cameron for his "ability, patriotism, and fidelity to public trust."

RESPONSES OF THE PRESIDENTS TO CHARGES OF MISCONDUCT: A LOOK AT AN UNUSUAL RESEARCH PROJECT

One of the more unusual documents in the history of political ethics in America was prepared during the height of the Watergate-related impeachment inquiry against then president Richard Nixon. It was a work devoted entirely to a historical review of charges—from high crimes to misdemeanors—that for various reasons had been leveled against the presidents of the United States from George Washington to Lyndon Johnson, Nixon's predecessor.

The study was commissioned by John Doar, special counsel of the Impeachment Inquiry Staff of the House Committee on the Judiciary then investigating charges against President Nixon. In mid-May 1974 he asked the distinguished American historian C. Vann Woodward, Sterling Professor of History at Yale University, to direct a study of any charges of misconduct in administrations from George Washington to Lyndon Johnson and how these presidents responded to such charges. The members of the Impeachment Inquiry Staff found that their investigations took them back in time through American history and that "historians could provide a study which would prove useful in debates in the House of Representatives should resolutions of impeachment be recommended and, if such resolutions were adopted, also in the trial proceedings in the Senate."

Doar also wanted Dr. Woodward and his staff of historians to examine the ways in which presidents responded to charges of misconduct—whether the chief executives were helpful or antagonistic to Congress in their investigations, how presidents reacted if and when individuals in their administrations were found guilty, and whether actions were taken to protect or "cover up" illegalities in their administrations.

In all this it could be seen that Doar and his staff wanted to determine how Nixon's actions may have differed from those of other presidents and why he should be subjected to removal while no others were. The study, Doar emphasized, was to be factual and nonjudgmental. The work had to be completed by July 1.

Dr. Woodward, writing later about the assignment, said that despite the extremely short time line and the fact that the period of year was especially busy in the academic world, fourteen historians willingly plunged into the project.

The result was eventually published in book form in 1974 by Delacorte Press in a 400-page edition entitled *Responses of the Presidents to Charges of Misconduct*. Dr. Woodward, in an introduction, calls it a book "without precedent."

Among some of the findings of this unusual historical review:

- Ulysses S. Grant "had to respond to more charges of misconduct that took the form of financial corruption than any other president. No department escaped congressional investigation."

  Accused of misconduct at one time or another during his term in office were Grant's cabinet members, secretaries, members of his family, and the president himself. The entry on Grant runs thirty pages and covers such issues as the manipulation of the gold market that led to the Gold Panic of 1869 . . . such scandals as the Safe Burglary Conspiracy . . . the implication of Grant's vice president in a stock scheme involving shares in the company building the Union Pacific Railroad . . . how his secretary of the navy began office with a net worth of $20,000, but after his department began dealing with a small grain and feed firm on a large scale, soon showed bank deposits totaling $320,000 . . . and the whiskey frauds, in which it was found that over a four-year period 12 million to 15 million gallons of whiskey had escaped tax annually—a fact that was linked to whiskey distillers and Internal Revenue Commission agents conspiring to make false reports of production to avoid tax, a practice that had started in the Lincoln administration but that some evidence showed had been carried out by Grant's closest associate, his secretary of the treasury, Orville E. Babcock, "and perhaps the Grant family itself."

• No president, except for William Henry Harrison, who died after only one month as president, was free of some charges of misconduct or corruption. But "allegations are not proof," and some administrations, such as those of Washington, Jefferson, and Truman, were more vigorous and virtuous than others, but also had their critics—more so than others, such as Harding, who later proved to have one of the most suspect administrations.

• Grover Cleveland, the only person to be elected to two separate terms as president, entered the White House with a widespread reputation for honesty—both on a personal and on a political level—and after each term he left with his reputation intact. No historian, says the study, ever seriously questioned Cleveland's integrity or the honesty of his administration.

• Franklin D. Roosevelt, the president with the longest term, also had one of the cleanest administrations in United States history. During the twelve years of his tenure—a time marked by close scrutiny by Roosevelt's critics and opposition—not one member of FDR's White House staff or any major administrator in the New Deal was convicted, indicted, or even forced to resign because of a scandal.

• While Roosevelt's administration was free of corruption, just ten years before FDR, America endured an administration said to be judged by historians "as the most corrupt in the twentieth century." Warren G. Harding, president from 1921 to 1923, saw three of his appointees, including a member of his cabinet, imprisoned. Harding's attorney general almost went to jail, too, but avoided that fate after being tried twice by juries that could not reach a verdict. He eventually committed suicide after rumors surfaced that he was involved in questionable deals. The chief counsel of the Veterans' Bureau (now the Veterans Administration) also killed himself. But Harding himself was never personally implicated or found to have benefited from any of the scandals that swirled around him.

Teapot Dome and Harding—The Scandal and the Slob

It was in Harding's administration that the most notorious political scandal prior to Watergate took place—Teapot Dome. (The picturesque name came from the teapot configuration of the land sitting over the dome of oil reserves in Wyoming.) An investigation by Congress followed by court testimony eventually revealed that Harding's secretary of the interior, Albert Fall, had persuaded the secretary of the navy to transfer government oil reserves in Teapot Dome, Wyoming, and Elk Hills, California, to Fall's jurisdiction. Fall, without competitive bidding, then leased the rights to these reserves to private oil producers for large sums of money that Fall pocketed—$300,000 alone for the Teapot Dome oil leases. The illegal arrangement was not fully uncovered until the last year of Harding's life (he died in office in 1923), but only when Harding's vice president, Calvin Coolidge, took over was Fall prosecuted and found guilty. He was eventually jailed for accepting a bribe. (Strangely enough, the two oil men who gave him the bribes were never convicted of bribery.)

When Harding died, the dimensions of the Teapot Dome and other scandals were not fully known to the public. They may also not have been known to Harding, since Harding, a poor administrator and politically naive, was seemingly unaware of wrongdoing around him. Harding, himself, was viewed with great affection by the American public at the time. Millions of people turned out to pay their respects as the funeral train carrying Harding's body crossed the country. *The New York Times* called the outpouring of emotion "the most remarkable demonstration in American history of affection, respect and reverence for the dead."

Surfacing after his death were also scandals about Harding's private life, including alleged adulterous liaisons with several women and a baby he was accused of fathering out of wedlock. None of this was said to have affected or compromised his role as president. The most telling assessment of Harding may have come from Alice Roosevelt Longworth, the acerbic daughter of Teddy Roosevelt and a longtime observer of Washington. "Harding was not a bad man," she once said. "He was just a slob."

In a special introduction to the published book (this introduction was not part of the original study), Dr. Woodward assesses what this overview of all the presidents shows about their ethical behavior, as contrasted to actions alleged to have been taken by Richard Nixon. He notes that in previous administrations "typically the president was the victim of some manner of betrayal." The presidents themselves, he points out, were never the beneficiary of misconduct. Neither did they direct misconduct or cause it through plan or any conspiratorial arrangement. Usually the president had no knowledge or only partial knowledge of what others in his administration were doing, his offense thereby being at the most a lapse in correcting the situation or firing the culprit.

In short, as noted by Dr. Woodward:

• No president before Nixon was proved to be the chief coordinator of the crimes charged against his own administration.

- No president was ever shown to be the chief beneficiary of misconduct in his administration "or of measures
taken to destroy or cover up evidence of it."

- No president demonstrated that any malfeasance in
office had an "ideological purpose" or "constitutionally
subversive ends."

- No president was ever accused of "extensively subverting and secretly using established government agencies
to defame or discredit political opponents and critics, to
obstruct justice, to conceal misconduct and protect criminals, or to deprive citizens of their rights and liberties."

- No president was ever charged with "creating secret
investigative units to engage in covert and unlawful activities against private citizens and their rights."

The five and a half years of the Nixon administration, then,
proved unlike any previous administration in the nature of its actions. Concludes Dr. Woodward, "A search of the long history of
misconduct charged against the presidents down to 1969 . . . fail[s]
to disclose many of the abuses of that office, many combinations
and concentrations of abuses, and many new uses and purposes
of such abuses, that have subsequently become increasingly familiar to American citizens."

In other words, although this nonjudgmental work does not say
it, the picture that emerges is that the Nixon actions in the Watergate scandal were not "politics as usual." His behavior was
without precedent and may well have justified the first impeachment of a president of the United States.

THE WATERGATE SCORECARD

By the time Richard Nixon resigned the presidency in 1974 in the
wake of his involvement in the Watergate cover-up, many prominent White House or Republican-party personnel were either forced
to resign or were sent to prison. In all, a total of twenty-nine

prominent people were indicted, pleaded guilty, or were convicted of Watergate-related crimes.

Among those found guilty were:

- Nixon's White House chief of staff

- Nixon's main domestic advisor

- Two attorneys general

- Three White House counselors

- Nixon's own attorney

- The chairman of Nixon's campaign finance organization

- Nixon's deputy campaign manager

- Nixon's appointments secretary

Nixon also was found to have:

- Ordered the telephone tapping of seventeen government employees, none of which was done with a proper court order

- Made improper use of the Federal Bureau of Investigation

- Made improper use of the Central Intelligence Agency

- Forced the Internal Revenue Service to audit or harass opponents and others in disfavor with the administration

- Compiled an "enemies list" of those who were to be watched or hounded

- Authorized a "plumbers unit" to stop the leaking of classified information, with the result that the unit engaged in at least one illegal burglary of the offices of the psychiatrist of Dr. Daniel Ellsberg, one of many suspected leakers.

The result of all this? One former president.

The Votes Are Coming In, Still Coming In . . .

. . . and then there is the cartoon showing a TV news correspondent, microphone in hand, reporting from a Mexican street, a ballot box and voters lined up behind him. Staring at the viewer, the correspondent announces: "With 265 per cent of the vote in . . . it looks like we have a winner in the Mexican election . . . back to you, Dan. . . ."

YOU COULD SAY HE HAD A WAY WITH WORDS

President Eisenhower gained a reputation as a mangler of language and syntax bordering almost on the inept during his eight years in the presidency. The reputation came primarily from his performances at press conferences, where he seemingly butchered the English language as he responded to reporters' questions with answers often difficult to decipher.

But the evidence has emerged that Eisenhower may have mangled his words on purpose as a way of deceiving reporters and avoiding answering questions he did not want to answer.

He was, after all, an accomplished writer. Not only did he write the successful *Crusade in Europe* about World War II and his command of Allied armies, but as an earlier aide to General Douglas MacArthur in the Philippines he wrote the speeches that gained for MacArthur the reputation as a silver-tongued speaker. Later, as president, Eisenhower worked with his speech writers on his addresses.

But at his presidential press conferences, Eisenhower often turned incomprehensible. One of his profilers said of him, "He was a masterly performer. He went to these conferences knowing exactly what he planned to say and what he intended to avoid saying by employing vague and evasive language."

A case in point was the May 1954 incident when world tensions rose over the Republic of China's threats to take control of some of the islands in the Formosa Strait. Just prior to one of his regularly scheduled press conferences, his press secretary, James

149

Hagerty, warned him that the State Department felt the crisis was so delicate that "no matter what question you get on it, you shouldn't say anything at all."

Ike responded, "Don't worry, Jim. If that question comes up, I'll just confuse them."

And he did—in a 150-word display of mangled syntax.

JFK'S SENATE CAREER WAS HELPED BY A FIB

When John F. Kennedy, then a member of the U.S. House of Representatives, made his first try for the U.S. Senate in a campaign against Henry Cabot Lodge, he encountered a problem with Jewish voters in Massachusetts. Lodge had brought into the state to campaign for him the Jewish Republican senator from New York, Jacob Javits. Addressing a large Jewish audience in Boston, Javits repeatedly pointed out that Jack Kennedy was "the son of his father." The Jews knew what he was referring to: Joseph Kennedy was considered an anti-Semite who, as U.S. ambassador to England, had voiced support for Adolf Hitler before the war. Javits also attacked Jack Kennedy for being anti-Israel and for offering an amendment that would have cut aid to Israel (actually what he had voted against at the time was aid to the entire Middle East, not just Israel).

The speech, well received by Jewish voters in the state, caused consternation for the Kennedys. Joe Kennedy then called on his friend John McCormack, the longtime Massachusetts political figure and powerhouse in the Congress, for help. McCormack was considered such a friend of the Jews that he was sometimes referred to as "Rabbi John."

A few days after Javits's speech, the Kennedy campaign held their own rally before a Jewish audience in the same theater where Javits had spoken. McCormack, whom JFK had not spoken to in years and whom he had no particularly high regard for, appeared at the rally and gave a dramatic speech in behalf of Jack Kennedy. He particularly singled out for comment Javits's attack on Kennedy for his vote on the aid package.

"Let me tell you what *really* happened on aid to Israel," McCormack declared. "We had heard that the Republicans were going to defeat that bill and take out the money that was supposed to go to Israel. I walked up and down the aisle, looking for somebody who would put forward an amendment to soften the blow. And finally I found Jack Kennedy, and he agreed to offer an amendment that included only a token cut to Israel. *He* was the one who stood up there with guts and with courage. *He* was the one who saved the aid package to Israel.''

The crowd's reaction was enthusiastic, and the threat to Jewish support of Kennedy was diffused.

The story is recounted by Tip O'Neill, Speaker of the U.S. House of Representatives, in his memoir, *Man of the House* (Random House, 1987). He also recounts Jack Kennedy's reaction of disbelief and delight about what McCormack did. For McCormack had lied about JFK's actions. There had been no such interchange between McCormack and Kennedy and no JFK attempt to soften any blow to Israel.

Kennedy, who had later told the story to O'Neill, recalled the incident. ''The audience went wild,'' O'Neill quotes Kennedy. ''But the whole story was a figment of John McCormack's imagination. He made it up to save my ass, knowing damn well that I didn't deserve his help.''

Kennedy, however, profited handsomely from the help. He went on to defeat Lodge and win a seat in the U.S. Senate. From there JFK was able to make his successful move into the presidency. And all the while, he had the overwhelming support of Jewish voters.

''When we got into office, the thing that surprised me the most was that things were as bad as we'd been saying they were.''

—John F. Kennedy

THE REAGAN NOMINATION SPEECH: THE GIPPER BECOMES THE GRIPPER

One of the high points of Ronald Reagan's political career was his acceptance speech of the Republican nomination as president at the 1980 Republican convention. And the high point of that speech came at the end.

Nearing the conclusion of his prepared remarks, Reagan suddenly paused and, peering around the audience and then looking into the TV cameras, he declared, "I have just thought of something that is not part of my speech, and I am worried about whether I should do it."

After another pause, Reagan went into a tribute to the United States as a place of refuge for people "who yearn to breathe freely."

After which he stated, "I'll confess that I'm a little afraid to suggest what I am going to suggest. I'm more afraid not to."

What he then suggested was that everyone join him in a moment of silent prayer in behalf of the "crusade" he would now be waging.

It was a gripping, dramatic gesture, all the more so because it was seemingly extemporaneous and spur-of-the-moment. Reagan the former actor had become a hit as Reagan the political leader.

Later, however, it became known that Reagan's ending had been carefully orchestrated. Rather than being off-the-cuff, the climactic close of his nomination speech had been crafted carefully before presentation. The prepared remarks handed out to the press before Reagan's appearance did not contain the closing sentiments heard by the public, but all along they were on the three-by-five cards used by Reagan during his speech.

"Since politicians don't believe what they say, they are surprised when the people believe what they say."
—Charles de Gaulle

A LIAR? WHO DID HE CALL A LIAR?

New York's Mayor Ed Koch and the Rev. Jesse Jackson became embroiled over a number of issues during the 1988 Democratic presidential primary campaign, but none proved as explosive as the time Koch attacked Jackson "for lying" twenty years previously.

Koch, opposed to Jackson in the race and supporting Tennessee senator Albert Gore, accused Jackson of trying to magnify his role at the time the Rev. Dr. Martin Luther King, Jr., was assassinated in 1968.

It was a charge that had been made many times before by others. For shortly after the assassination, Jackson had said he was the last to cradle Dr. King's head as he lay dying. Jackson even appeared the following day wearing a shirt stained with what he said was Dr. King's blood. Some of Dr. King's followers have long disputed Jackson's claims, saying he exaggerated his role, and Jackson no longer says he cradled Dr. King's head; instead he talks of "reaching out" for him.

Koch used these discrepancies during an interview on an ABC-TV news program to remark that Jackson had used Dr. King's assassination "in a way that was false and to feather his own nest." He pushed his point by asking, "Do you want a president who under stress is not capable of telling the truth?"

Always ingenious in his way with words, Koch later explained to a reporter following up on the story that he was not calling Jackson a liar. Said Koch, "I don't call him a liar. I just say under stress that he will do what's convenient, and if lying is convenient, that's what he will do."

YOU CAN QUOTE ME ON THIS

The political process requires our elected officials to make their views and positions known in speeches, statements, and reports. The words that comprise these statements are often crafted by others—usually by aides, press secretaries, or speech writers. Many times the final remarks have few if any words from the official himself.

To those on the outside this may seem surprising, but to those on the inside this is how it has been done for generations. While nothing stops politicians, from the president to a city councilman, from writing their own statements—and many do—the sheer number of activities often demands that an aide draft the sentence or the speech that gives the elected official his official voice. What is hoped for and expected is that the aide captures the essence of the political figure's vision and beliefs in the final statement—and the official at least has the opportunity to approve or make changes in what will go out over his name.

This whole process came into glaring public view when Larry Speakes, a former press secretary to President Reagan, revealed in his book *Speaking Out: Inside the Reagan White House* (Charles Scribner's Sons, Macmillan Publishing Company, 1988) that he had on two occasions fabricated quotes for President Reagan and had offered them to the press as authentic presidential sentiments—without ever clearing them with Reagan. A furor erupted when it became public that Speakes had lied to the press about the validity of the quotes and when Reagan himself said that this was the first he even knew about the quotes being issued.* Speakes was forced to resign from his job as vice president and spokesman for Merrill Lynch and to apologize for the deceit of putting words in the president's mouth.

But Speakes's guilt lay not in making up the quotes but in not clearing them—and then boasting in a book about his deception of the press. It was as though someone had violated the rules of polite society by doing in public what everyone was doing in private. Speakes had lifted the curtain enshrouding the little deceits involved in the political process, and for this his punishment was to be smacked on the wrists, labeled a liar, and sent out of the room.

All the notoriety given to Speakes's actions also led to some Washington humor. Soon after the flap, a press secretary to the Senate Finance Committee chairman, Lloyd Bentsen, telephoned a newsman with a statement on a bill before the committee.

"I want to give you a made-up quote," he said to the reporter. "It was made up by Senator Bentsen."

---

*One of the made-up quotes was issued during the Geneva summit of 1985. Noticing that Gorbachev was stealing the scene, Speakes manufactured the following line for Reagan and gave it to the press: "There is much that divides us, but I believe the world breathes easier because we are talking here together." (*Newsweek* magazine termed the quote "pompous," although "pathetic" might be better.) Another time Speakes spoke for the president occurred when, after the Soviets shot down a Korean airliner in 1983, he took remarks actually made by Secretary of State George Shultz and issued them as Reagan's.

THE HEART OF THE HART AFFAIR
WAS THAT THE *HERALD* HERALDED WRONG

We all know how Gary Hart, the then leading candidate for the 1988 Democratic nomination for president, was forced out of the race by disclosures he had hosted a beautiful young model named Donna Rice in his Washington townhouse for part of a weekend. But what is not generally known is that Hart may have been deceived by the press into resigning.

The story was first published by the *Miami Herald* in a May 3, 1987, front-page story, which began, "Gary Hart, the Democratic presidential candidate who had dismissed allegations of womanizing, spent Friday night and most of Saturday in his Capitol Hill townhouse with a young woman who flew from Miami and met him."

The paper noted Hart's response—which was that "ten or fifteen minutes" after they had arrived on Friday night at eleven, Donna Rice had left the townhouse by a back entrance. But, in a key passage, the newspaper stated in so many words that Hart was lying: "Hart's explanation was not consistent with what was witnessed by a team of *Miami Herald* reporters who conducted surveillance of the townhouse from the time the woman arrived in Washington from Miami until the time of the interview."

The problem with the paper's statement is that it is now clear the *Miami Herald* did not have all the facts at the time that would warrant the paper making such an assumption. For later it became known that the *Miami Herald* did not have the Hart townhouse under full and continuous surveillance, as it said. In an analysis of the reporting of the Gary Hart sex scandal, journalist John B. Judis, writing in the *Columbia Journalism Review* soon after the episode, states that "the *Herald* did not have a 'team' watching the townhouse during the time Hart claimed that Rice had left, but only a single reporter, Jim McGee. And McGee could not have seen anyone leave from the back—the usual exit from this townhouse."*

---

*See "The Hart Affair," *Columbia Journalism Review,* July/August 1987, p. 21–25.

Judis also points out the paper had "failed to mention that Hart's friend William Broadhurst had told the paper's reporters that he and Hart had driven Rice and another woman around suburban Washington on Saturday afternoon—a period during which only *Herald* photographer Brian Smith had a clear view of people entering and leaving Hart's house."

Indeed the manager of a delicatessen in Alexandria, Virginia, had told the *Los Angeles Times* that Hart, accompanied by another man and two women, had been in his store on Saturday afternoon—"at a time when the *Herald* had claimed that Hart and Rice had been together in Hart's townhouse."

The *Herald* actually changed its account several times during the following week of how it covered the Hart story. The paper's political editor had told the *Washington Post* on the day the story first broke that "a minimum of two people" had watched through Friday night "and five of us at various times on Saturday." By a week later, on May 10, the *Herald* acknowledged that reporter McGee was by himself during the critical time period on Friday and that the paper had no one keeping an eye on the townhouse between 3 A.M. and 5 A.M. Saturday.

But by then the damage to the Hart campaign had been done. Two days before the *Miami Herald* finally acknowledged its own lack of reporting the full truth, Gary Hart withdrew from the race.

While Gary Hart may have self-destructed eventually anyway, the newspapers did not know as much as they strongly suggested. But then again, that sleight of hand—and phrase—is often how the press does operate, leading interviewees to believe the reporter knows more than he does and thereby getting the interviewee to offer information or confirmation about matters of which the reporter is, in actuality, in the dark.

In any other field that's called lying. In journalism it's called investigative reporting.

ANNOUNCING THE "BUSH/QUAYLE SHAMOMETER"

As the 1988 presidential campaign entered its final weeks, the Michael Dukakis people, frustrated with the claims and criticisms being hurled at their candidate by the Republicans, created a device to help reporters gauge the degree of untruthful statements being made on the campaign trail by the other side.

The device, to be worn on a string around the neck, was a simple movable pointer on pasteboard that went from a low rating of 0 to 120, the highest form of lying. The reporter was instructed to turn the pointer on what was named the "Bush/Quayle Shamometer" to the proper level when Republicans made a statement.

The Shamometer ratings were as follows:

0—"Not Entirely False"

20—"Not in the Loop"

40—"Don't Remember"

60—"He's Fibbing"

80—"Real Whopper"

100—"Joe Isuzu"

120—"I'm an Environmentalist"

THE TRUTH SQUAD SHALL MAKE YOU FREE
(FREE TO DISTORT, THAT IS)

The Bush campaign dusted off an old political tactic during the 1988 election, gave the maneuver a new twist, and used it supposedly to separate lies from truth.

The tactic was the formation of a "Truth Squad." During the summer of the election, the Bush people, feeling that the Democratic candidate Michael Dukakis was making unchallenged claims, sent Republican senator John S. McCain III of Arizona to precede Dukakis in his travels and present questions about Dukakis's record. Then, either McCain or another Republican stalwart would stay to answer any of the Democrat's charges or claims.

The operation of a Truth Squad appears to date from the 1952 election between General Dwight David Eisenhower and Governor Adlai Stevenson. William Safire, in his column on language, finds the earliest citation to come from the *Tuscaloosa News* of November 3, 1952. The Alabama paper reported that day, "The Republican 'Truth Squad,' after trailing President Truman across the country on his campaign trips, passed down its final verdict today that the President was 'guilty of over 100 lies, half-truths and distortions.' "

A "truth squad" may have a nice ring to it and may even bring benefits to a candidate who can apply pressure to his opponent with such a probing, questioning attack. But in the heat of a campaign, it is doubtful a partisan group of politicos—even one with the self-given label of "truth"—could really correct the incorrect and shed unbiased light for all. Adlai Stevenson may have summed up such a tactic best when, in his 1956 campaign, with a Republican Truth Squad dogging his moves, he stated, "A truth squad bears the same relationship to 'truth' as a fire department does to 'fire.' "

THE RESULTS ARE IN: YOU CAN'T FOOL 90 PERCENT OF THE PEOPLE

How did the American electorate view the honesty of the presidential candidates in the election of '88—an election fraught with charges and countercharges of lying? *Parents* magazine surveyed 1,000 American adults and, in its November 1988 issue, reported that

    • 79 percent said they believed both candidates were insincere and "just saying what they think the voters want to hear."

    • and *only 10 percent said they believed the presidential hopefuls were honest* (italics mine, conclusion yours).

Actually, while this reinforces the feeling that dishonesty may be increasing rather than decreasing on the political scene in this country, those 90 percent who were not hoodwinked should renew our faith in the perceptiveness of the public.

Of course, this finding must be tempered by the fact that the survey also revealed that 49 percent of those polled found prime-time television more interesting than the election.

IS IT TRUE ABOUT THE "SLEAZE FACTOR"?

During the 1980s the phrase "sleaze factor" arose to characterize the growing corruption being uncovered in Washington. But were there really more nefarious doings in D.C. than ever or was it just more of the same—or even less of the same?

The U.S. Justice Department seems to have provided the answer. In their "Report to Congress on the Activities and Operations of the Public Integrity Sector for 1986," the Justice Department issued statistics for the number of federal officials indicted, convicted, and awaiting trial in 1985 versus 1975.

Herewith the sleaze factor proved:

	1975	1985
Indicted	53	563
Convicted	43	470
Awaiting Trial	5	90

The Politician—Pro in a Con Game

"Politics, in a sense, has always been a con game . . . and as the American voter insists upon an illusion, the politician must embellish the illusion, particularly if he wants to be president. . . .

"On TV it matters less that a candidate does not have ideas. He need be neither statesman nor crusader—only show up on time."

—Joe McGinnis
The Selling of the President

WANT TO SEE CAPITAL LOW LIFE?
TAKE THE SCANDAL BUS TOUR

By late in the 1980s Washington, D.C., had become such a site for political scandal that some enterprising young Washingtonites began offering a seventy-five-minute tour of the low spots of capital political life.

Labeled the Scandal Bus Tour and priced at $20 per seat, the narrated excursion brought a visitor up close and personal with such lurid sightseeing spots as the building complex where the Watergate scandal began . . . the Tidal Basin, where exotic dancer Fanne Foxe, accompanied by her companion, the then powerful Wilbur Mills, chairman of the House Ways and Means Committee, took a late-night dunk . . . the Georgetown townhouse where presidential candidate Gary Hart was said to have stayed with model Donna Rice . . . the buildings where Abscam and Koreagate took place . . . the Executive Office Building, where Ollie North shredded documents and Vice President Spiro Agnew took his kickbacks . . . the Pentagon, where, as the tour guide noted, toilet seats are purchased at "a bargain of $6 billion a dozen."

An actors' group, which billed itself as the Gross National Product, was behind the tour. (Its theater show at the time was called *Bushcapades: An Administration on Thin Ice.*) The idea for the Scandal Tour came when one of the members noted that his out-of-town friends were becoming bored with the usual Washington tourist attractions. Instead they said they wanted to see Watergate and Gary Hart's townhouse.

From this was born a tour like no other in the country—although plans were afoot to launch a similar tour in London because, said the leader of the group, "their scandals are so much better than ours. They have espionage, sex, and money all mixed together. Most of ours are only one or another."

But as for the American version, the members of the Gross National Product expressed confidence that the Scandal Tour would always remain fresh and invigorated with new material.

"I don't think we'll ever run out of scandals or alleged scandals," said one. "The day we run out of scandals is the day that Washington quits printing money."

"I never did give anybody hell. I just told the truth and they thought it was hell."

—Harry S Truman (1884–1972)

"What do you mean, the devil made you do it?"

CHAPTER VII

"I have a headache tonight."

LIES BETWEEN THE SEXES

. . . How the Sexes Really Do Their Battle

An old divorce lawyer once told me, "They [husbands and wives] all lie. The secret of success is to get your client to tell better lies."
—Mike Royko,
syndicated columnist

The relationship between the sexes has often been referred to as "the battle between the sexes." Maybe that is why this area of human life has been so wrapped up in mystery and deceit; after all, as we have seen earlier, wars and battles have always been fought with deceit as a weapon, so why should the sexes act any differently?

Of course, the first deceit in the relationship between the sexes may well be the willingness to deceive oneself. As the Ukrainian proverb says, "Love tells us many things that are not so."

That may not be so bad. If it were not for "beauty being in the eye of the beholder," few if any would find a mate, especially for a lifetime. We either have to learn to look away when it comes to personality or physical traits or we allow love to do the softening, the enhancing, the "lying" for us.

And then, too, we need those little acts of deceit and deception to woo and wed another. In his *Art of Love,* the witty Roman poet Ovid offered the advice that a young man interested in a girl should seek out opportunities to touch her. And if no such opportunities existed, the male should make do with a subterfuge. Wrote Ovid, "If a speck of dust should fall on her gown, flick it off with your finger; and if no speck of dust falls—then flick it off anyway!"

Of course, some people tend to abuse the "dance of deceit" involved in the dating and mating process. Consider the case of Giovanni Vigliotto. At his trial for bigamy in San Francisco in 1982 one of his wives testified she was attracted to Giovanni because he had the "honest trait" of looking directly into her eyes. He must have hoodwinked a lot of women with his eyes. It was estimated he may have married as many as 100 women.

WHEN EVE LOST A RIB

French actress Anna Held, wife of Flo Ziegfeld, was known for her figure—especially for her eighteen-inch waist. At her sudden death in 1918 doctors said she had died of myeloma, inflammation of the spinal cord. Only after reporters investigated the death was it found that she had died from excessive crash diets and internal injuries caused by overly tight lacing of her corsets. It was also discovered that the famed tiny waist had been kept that way because Held, when entering her forties, had had her lower ribs surgically removed.

THE QUALIFICATIONS OF A MARRIAGE BROKER

According to an old Jewish saying, "A person who can't lie can't be a marriage broker."

LYING IN THE MARRIAGE BED—AND OUT OF IT

Lying between the sexes does not stop with marriage. It often escalates. Experts on the sexual conduct of adults estimate that 60 percent of married men and a third of married women today engage in adultery sometime in their married lives.

HOW HONEST ABE USED A LITTLE WHITE LIE TO DEAL WITH MARY TODD

Abraham Lincoln and Mary Todd, as do many couples, had almost diametrically opposite traits. She was stingy to others, even though she came from a wealthy family; he was more charitable, even though he had grown up in poor circumstances.

But Abe had learned a technique for getting along with Mary, especially when it came to donating to a charity.

As recounted by Carl Sandburg in *Abraham Lincoln: The Prairie Years,* Abe, then a lawyer, was once approached by the local volunteer fire department to contribute to the purchase of a new hose cart. In response, Lincoln told the fund-raising committee how he was going to get Mrs. Lincoln to go along with his giving a donation:

"Boys, when I go home to supper—Mrs. Lincoln is always in a fine, good humor then—I'll say to her, over the toast, 'My dear, there is a subscription paper being handed round to raise money to buy a new hose cart. The committee called on me this afternoon, and I told them to wait until I consulted my home partner. Don't you think I had better subscribe fifty dollars?' Then she will look up quickly and exclaim, 'Will you never learn, never learn? You are always too liberal, too generous. Fifty dollars! No, indeed; we can't afford it. Twenty-five's quite reasonable enough.' "

Lincoln then chuckled: "Bless her dear soul, she'll never find out how I got the better of her; and if she does, she'll forgive me. Come around tomorrow, boys, and get your twenty-five dollars."

> "Honesty has ruined more marriages than infidelity."
> —Charles McCabe
> (1915–1983)

WHEN THE ALMIGHTY TOLD HALF THE TRUTH

There are times when telling the truth in a marriage or a relationship only results in hurting someone's feelings. Thus there are times when, in a sense, only a fib will do. One such case occurs early in the Bible, and the one who demonstrates this is the Almighty Himself.

This episode occurs in Genesis 18: 12–14. Angels have come to Abraham and Sarah to tell them they will have the child they have long awaited. When one of the angels informs Abraham privately, Sarah overhears. Since she and Abraham are now advanced in years (the Bible says, "It had ceased to be with Sarah after the manner of women"), her reaction is to laugh, saying, "After I am waxed old shall I have pleasure, my lord being old also?"

In the very next verse, verse 13, the Almighty says to Abraham, "Wherefore did Sarah laugh, saying: Shall I of a surety bear a child, who am old?" But note that God does not quote Sarah's reference to Abraham ("my lord being old also").

In other words, the Almighty does not tell Abraham all of what Sarah had said, since she had cast aspersions on Abraham as well as herself. But the Lord here safeguards Abraham's feelings by only telling him the disparaging remarks that Sarah said about herself.

As one of the biblical commentaries points out, this passage is a demonstration that to keep peace between husband and wife, it is permissible to refrain from stating the whole truth or to shade the truth when that truth will only hurt the feelings of one of the spouses or provoke a quarrel in the marriage.

Abraham and Sarah went on to have a child, as prophesied. They called him Isaac, an appropriate name considering Sarah's initial reaction to the news she would conceive a child. "Isaac" is Hebrew for "laughter."

THE VEILING OF THE BRIDE: A CEREMONY TO GUARD AGAINST TRICKERY

One of the most fascinating of wedding rituals occurs in the Jewish ceremony with the *badeken,* the veiling of the bride by the groom just before the wedding procession begins.

In this activity the groom is escorted by his singing and dancing friends to the bride, who sits without her veil over her face. He places the wedding veil over her face, after which the ceremony that will marry the two begins.

This act is undertaken to assure the groom that his bride is the woman he has selected, unlike the biblical Jacob, who was tricked into marrying Leah.

This episode occurs in Genesis 29: 16–30. Jacob falls in love with Rachel, the younger daughter of his uncle Laban. When Jacob offers Laban his labor for seven years as compensation for marrying Rachel, Laban responds, "It is better that I give her to thee than that I should give her to another man; abide with me."

Jacob serves the seven years for Rachel, "and they seemed unto him but a few days, for the love he had to her." But when the time comes for the wedding, Laban hoodwinks Jacob into marrying the older daughter, Leah. Laban brings her to the ceremony heavily veiled and at night. When Jacob discovers the treachery the next day, that Laban has switched daughters on him, Laban's excuse is lame if not an outright lie. To Jacob's question— "Wherefore then hast thou beguiled me?" (verse 25)—Laban answers, "It is not so done in our place, to give the younger before the firstborn" (verse 26), something Laban had conveniently forgotten to say when he made his deal with Jacob seven years before. Now, however, Laban says he will give Rachel to Jacob to marry the following week if he agrees to work for another seven years.

Jacob agrees—thereby acquiescing to one of the most outrageous liars in biblical literature.

Since then every Jewish wedding ceremony is marked by the colorful veiling of the bride so that the groom knows exactly who he is getting as a bride—even if he doesn't quite yet know what he is getting into as a groom.

THE BARD ON LYING BETWEEN LOVERS

Shakespeare, who always seemed to have something to say about everything, devoted one of his sonnets (138) to the lying that goes on between lovers. But here the lying cited is the kind that is done to suppress the truth that can only hurt the loved one. (Note in the next to last line how Shakespeare uses the word *lie* in both its moral and carnal sense.)

When my love swears that she is made of truth,
I do believe her, though I know she lies,
That she might think me some untutored youth,
Unlearned in the world's false subtleties.
Thus vainly thinking that she thinks me young,
Although she knows my days are past the best,
Simply I credit her false-speaking tongue;
On both sides thus is simple truth suppress'd.
But wherefore say not I that I am old?
O, love's best habit is in seeming trust,
And age in love loves not t'have years told.
  Therefore I lie with her, and she with me,
  And in our faults by lies we flattered be.

TRUTH AND XXXXXXs

When a lady or gentleman signs a love note with *XXXX*s to signify kisses, she or he may not realize that the origin of such a symbol is not romantic but legal—to ensure honesty.

The use of the *X* appears to have its beginnings in Christian symbolism. The sign of one of the apostles, Saint Andrew, was an *X,* and using the *X* for one's signature was a statement that the signer was pledging in the name of Saint Andrew to carry out the promise and that the document being signed was true.

During the Middle Ages, people would kiss their signatures as a way of swearing to the veracity of what they were signing. This was referred to as "the kiss of truth," and the act itself became known as "sealed with a kiss."

The connotation of the *X* as a symbol of truth eventually disappeared with the passage of time, but its representation for the kiss—this time the kiss of affection—remained.

Interestingly, in male-female relationships, expressions of affection must often be accompanied with signs of trust and honesty, else the entire relationship will not endure beyond the physical attraction. In that sense the *X* certainly marks a crucial spot in the relations between the sexes.

"I'LL ALWAYS LOVE YOU" DEPARTMENT

Voltaire, the great French philosopher of the eighteenth century, was not considered a man of high personal ethics. In fact, in his candidacy for membership in the French Academy in 1745, according to Will Durant in his monumental *Story of Philosophy* (Simon and Schuster, 1926) Voltaire "lied inexhaustibly" (he lost, but the year later finally succeeded).

In dealing with the opposite sex, Voltaire was not much better. As "a madcap boy" in his late teens living away from home, he fell in love with a girl he called "Pimpette" and wrote her passionate love letters. Each one he ended with the sentiment "I shall certainly love you forever."

When the affair between the two was discovered, Voltaire was sent back home. The love he had expressed so hotly now cooled so quickly. "He remembered Pimpette for several weeks," writes Durant.

Later in his life Voltaire found his love for another woman, Mme. du Chatelet, also cooling after fifteen years (they had even ceased to argue, a devastating sign). But then he soon discovered that she had fallen in love with a handsome young man, Marquis de Saint-Lambert. At first, Voltaire raged against the deception, then came to accept the triumph of youth over age.

"Such are women," he said. "I displaced Richelieu, Saint-Lambert turns me out! This is the order of things; one nail drives out another; so goes the world."

The changing emotions between men and women must have fascinated Voltaire, for he wrote a tale called "Zadig" about a Babylonian philosopher "as wise as it is possible for men to be; . . . he knew as much of metaphysics as hath ever been known in any age—that is, little or nothing at all."

To make certain of his wife's fidelity, Zadig makes arrangements to fake his death and have a friend, an hour after the death, make an overture to the wife. Zadig fakes death and is laid out in a coffin, whereupon the friend first consoles the wife, then proposes marriage. At first the wife resists and protests she would never consent. But then, "protesting she would ne'er consent, consented." Zadig rises from the dead and flees into the woods.*

---

*Zadig later teaches a king how to determine who is the most honest among applicants to be a minister in the royal court. He tells the king to choose the lightest dancer among the applicants after they go alone and unwatched through a vestibule that leads to the royal dance hall. The vestibule is filled with loose valuables that are easily stolen, and the idea is to see who would try to take the valuables by hiding them under their clothes. When the applicants emerge into the hall, they are asked to dance. Writes Voltaire, "Never had dancers per-

"IT'S A SIN TO TELL A LIE"
(THE GOOD BOOK COMES TO TIN PAN ALLEY)

The songs of endearment between the sexes are peppered with allusions to the fear of being lied to. These songs seem to ask, How really true is my love's love for me—and how true is my love for her (or him)? These refrains, voiced over and over again in one form or another, show the insecurity of loving and being loved. This insecurity is nowhere better shown in a relationship than in the presence or absence of face-saving white lies.

This is captured in the famous song "It's a Sin to Tell a Lie," which was first introduced in 1936 by Kate Smith. In the song, the singer tells the loved one to be sure he isn't lying when professing his love. If he does, the party who receives such false sentiments will suffer a broken heart and die. Thus, "it's a sin to tell a lie."

The huge success of this song (it was revived in 1955 by Something Smith and the Redheads and became a best-selling record) led to a parody in which a sobered-up singer tells how he got drunk and professed his love to a rather unappealing girl. Now, he moans, if she leads him to the altar he'll be sunk, because he can't tell the preacher that he was drunk. Because of this experience he is a changed man.

HE COULD HAVE BLAMED IT ON HIS MICKEY MOUSE WATCH

Walt Disney loved his wife, but he also loved his work. After he married, he would take his wife, Lillian, out to dinner, then tell her he wanted to drop by his studio to do some work, saying it would only take a couple of minutes. While Lillian napped on the couch, Walt would begin working—and keep on working, forgetting about the time. Typically he would finally remember the time at one o'clock in the morning. He would then wake Lillian and take her home, telling her it was only ten-thirty.

formed more unwillingly or with less grace. Their heads were down, their backs bent, their hands pressed to their sides."

ACTUALLY HE WAS MORE A PRINCESS CHARMER THAN A PRINCE CHARMING

Sometimes the deception conducted between the sexes is done not for love but for money. Consider the case of Lee J. Sawaya.

Sawaya must rank as one of the most unlikely of Casanovas. He was short, pudgy, balding, middle-aged, and had droopy "puppy" eyes.

But he also had such a way with women that police alleged he charmed scores of women out of millions of dollars with phony investment deals.

According to newspaper reports at the time he was captured in the late 1980s, detectives were unraveling the case coast-to-coast. San Francisco police alone were talking to twenty women who had identified Sawaya as "a man with the hypnotic power of Svengali, capable of persuading businesswomen to hand over thousands of dollars."

All in all, more than a dozen police agencies wanted to talk to him, including police in Arizona, Oklahoma, Pennsylvania, Florida, Louisiana, and New York.

In addition, Los Angeles authorities had already charged him with grand theft, a warrant was outstanding in Virginia, and in New Jersey he was wanted on federal charges of income tax evasion and wire fraud under the name of Anthony Lamonica for allegedly defrauding as many as 1,000 investors of $2.3 million between 1983 and 1987.

Sawaya might never have been captured if it had not been for someone showing Sawaya's wedding picture to a woman who realized Sawaya was the same man who had earlier charmed, then cheated her.

How did he hoax so many women? Police authorities said that more than one woman had reported that Sawaya was an exceptional lover.

He must have been. When he was arrested at a San Francisco restaurant, he was dining with his wife of three days. He had proposed to her the day he met her.

THE CLASSIC DIVORCE SPAT

In the annals of spats between divorced couples, the following must rank as the classic in the attempt of one spouse to get back at another. This time the effort was made through an abuse of truth and outright lying that borders on the hysterical—which is what divorced couples usually are at some point.

In a story reported by the *St. Paul Pioneer Press Dispatch* in 1988, ex-husband Gerald was living at the couple's old address in a suburb of St. Paul, Minnesota, while his former wife, Sharon, had moved to another state. One day Gerald received a letter for Sharon. Instead of sending it along to her, he opened it and found a questionnaire from her old high school class of 1958. The purpose of the questionnaire was to gather information for a newsletter that would be sent to all of the classmates telling them what each was doing thirty years later.

But Gerald, with a gleam in his eye, a sneer on his lip, and a pen in his hand, filled out the questionnaire for his ex-wife and sent it back. Someone on the other end, without much common sense or editorial acumen, went ahead and published all of "Sharon's" responses as is. And what responses they were! Consider:

Sharon's "Occupation"—"Retired on third husband's divorce settlement."

Sharon's "Achievement Most Proud Of"—"My three divorces and how each time I married into more money to the point where I am now living on the $400,000 settlement and interest from my third divorce."

Sharon's "Outrageous, Unusual, or Interesting Experience"— "Going out to Virginia . . . on my job and having an affair with two different guys while my third husband was back in Minnesota working two jobs."

Sharon's "Hobbies"—"Night clubbing, partying, and looking for new and wealthier husbands."

Sharon's "Secret Ambition or Fantasy"—"Seeing if I can't get married as many times as Liz Taylor and gain my riches through divorces, not work."

After all of her classmates read these statements in the newsletter, Sharon had the most interesting reaction—she sued Gerald for $50,000 for embarrassment and mental anguish.

As of this writing, the case has yet to come to trial, but it is obvious that editorial license and the marriage license do not go hand in hand.

THE MYSTERY OF THE BABE'S BABE

In the battle between the sexes, one area fraught with possible duplicity is that of the parental origin of the child born of marriage or a love affair. One person with a past he tried to cover up was the great baseball slugger, Babe Ruth.

Babe Ruth's first child was a daughter named Dorothy. Everyone assumed she was the child of the Babe and his first wife, Helen Woodford, who died in a fire when Dorothy was eight.

It now seems that Helen was not the mother, even though Babe Ruth let it be believed that she was. When Dorothy, then said to be sixteen months old, was for the first time shown in public on September 23, 1922, people were surprised. No one had been aware that Helen, who had had several miscarriages, had been pregnant during the previous two and a half years. Also, in giving out birth dates and other details, the Babe and Helen provided conflicting information.

Suspicions grew that Helen was not the true mother, but according to Dorothy, not even the Babe's second wife, Claire, who was Dorothy's stepmother, knew the truth.

Dorothy herself did not learn who her natural mother was until 1980, when Juanita Jennings of California, two weeks before her death, revealed she had given birth to Dorothy. Juanita had had an affair with Ruth in 1920. She later married a friend of the Babe's, Charlie Ellias.

All of this is told in *My Dad, the Babe* (Quinlan Press, 1988) written by Dorothy Ruth Pirone with Chris Martens, a senior producer for Major League Baseball. At the time of publication Dorothy had five surviving children and nine grandchildren, giving the Babe fifteen living descendants. Not one is a baseball player.

THERE ARE NOT ONLY LIES BETWEEN THE SEXES, THERE ARE ALSO LIES OF THE SEXES

Billy Tipton was a noted jazz musician who had a wife and three lovely adopted sons. But he also had a secret, which was not disclosed publicly until he died in January 1988 at the age of seventy-four.

It was then found out that Billy Tipton was not a he, but a she.

None of the adopted sons, now all adults, knew, nor did any of Tipton's friends or fellow musicians. Only the funeral director, preparing the body for burial, realized the truth and broke the story to one of the adopted sons since he did not want the son to learn about it later from the death certificate.

"I'm just lost," the son told the *Spokane Spokesman-Review,* a newspaper in Spokane, Washington, where Tipton had died. "But I think that he should have left something behind for us, something that would have explained the truth."

The woman whom Tipton had married in 1960 (they separated in 1979, after nearly twenty years together) said that "no one knew," but she declined to discuss their life together and said that Billy Tipton had died with the secret, which should be respected.

It appears that Billy Tipton, born December 29, 1914, in Oklahoma City and brought up in Kansas City, Missouri, decided to appear as a man to increase her chances of being a successful jazz musician. She was a saxophone and piano player and, dressed as a man, performed with the Jack Teagarden, Russ Carlyle, and Scott Cameron bands. In the 1950s she formed the Billy Tipton Trio and performed in nightclubs throughout the West.

One of the players with the trio for ten years, a drummer, said he never suspected Billy was a female, although he now remembered how some individuals would joke that Billy's baby face and high singing voice made him appear feminine.

Billy Tipton's oldest adopted son reminisced that the musician was recently ill with ulcer problems but would not go for medical help. "Now I know why I couldn't get him to a doctor," the son said. "He had so much to protect and I think he was just tired of keeping the secret."

Another of the adopted sons, the one who said he was "just lost" when he heard the news about the sex of his father, had a final thought. He told the newspaper, "He'll always be Dad."

THE BIG QUESTION IN A MARRIAGE TODAY—WHO CHEATS AND HOW CAN YOU TELL?

The surprising news from the front lines in the war between the sexes is that the picture today is changing in the area of infidelity.

During recent decades researchers have generally agreed that 50 to 65 percent of men and 25 to 50 percent of women cheat at least once during their marriage. But now some studies are showing that more married women are having affairs than ever before.

Annette Lawson, a sociologist and author of *Adultery: An Analysis of Love and Betrayal* (Basic Books, 1988), reports that based on a one-year study, she found that 66 percent of women and 68 percent of men had had at least one affair during their first marriages and that 39 percent of these women and 42 percent of these men had an affair during a current marriage.

Lawson also found that women are starting to cheat earlier in a marriage. Women married after 1970 actually waited less time on the average than men to have an affair—four and one-half years for the women versus five years for the men. Those married before 1960 acted more in form—the men waited eleven years, the women fifteen.

Says Lawson, "Women are beginning to look more like men in both attitude and behavior."

The other surprising development is that women and men seem to be cheating for reasons that reflect a role reversal among the sexes.

In an interview with *USA Today* on the topic, a representative of the Marriage Council of Philadelphia reported, "We see women in affairs thought possible only for males in the past—the brief sexual encounter with little attachment."

Women, especially working women, are being found able to "compartmentalize relationships with men," saying that this person is my husband, this my boss, this my lover. The result: more women are turning men into sex objects.*

---

*Michelle Healy, "More Women Have Cheating Hearts," *USA Today*, December 6, 1988, p. D6.

Among the reasons cited for the changing behavior in women are the increasing numbers of working women, more women going back to school (cited is the growth in adult education classes), and the changing roles for women in society—all affording more opportunity and time to meet members of the opposite sex.

These reasons, however, do not explain why there has been a surprising shift in male motives for affairs. Researchers are finding that today's married men are not cheating just for sex—they often want romance.

So, how can you tell if your spouse is cheating?

USA Today ran these warning signals:

- Your mate's hours change
- Your mate begins dressing differently
- Sex is different between the two of you
- You find unexplained bills or other mysterious items
- Your mate takes phone calls in another room
- Other people voice suspicions
- There are slips of the tongue
- You feel anxious

While one or several of these situations do not indicate someone is cheating, the more you find evidence of these changes or situations, the more likely it is your spouse is having an affair.

As for those most likely to have an affair, the profile looks like this:

- A family history of infidelity, separation, or divorce
- Physical or sexual abuse as a child
- Finding fault with a spouse's longtime traits
- Sexual problems with a spouse
- Compatibility problems with a spouse
- Three major changes in a person's life during the past year (such as a parent's death, job stress, auto accident, etc.)

- Obsession with aging or appearance

- Suffering from psychological problems or drug abuse

- Fantasizing more about another person

- Boredom with life and craving excitement

- Becoming more open to the topics of divorce and infidelity

More than five of these ingredients in a person is a warning that such a person is vulnerable to having an affair.

"Eighty percent of married men cheat in America. The rest cheat in Europe."

—Jackie Mason

If Groucho Marx had played in *Gone With the Wind,* as its author had suggested, the dialogue might have been too honest. "Frankly, my dear, you're too damn heavy." "I may be, Rhett, but I'm not a butler." "Then carry yourself, Scarlett. This ain't duck soup."

CHAPTER VIII

"Frankly, my dear, I don't give a damn."

HOLLYWOOD SCENES AND SINS

. . . Lying in the Land of Illusions

*The secret of staying young is to live honestly,
eat slowly, and lie about your age.*
                                        —Lucille Ball

What can one say about an industry that calls its product "motion pictures," but the pictures are all stills? Twenty-four still pictures to the second, to be exact.

It is only an optical illusion—literally faking the eye—that enables these static pictures to appear to move and come alive. That which was once a parlor trick—in which photos of a horse or person were flipped fast enough to make them seem to show motion—is now a multibillion-dollar-a-year industry called Hollywood.

And the deceptions of Hollywood do not stop with the projection of still images that only seem to move. The deception extends to the creation of the images we see on the screen. Makeup, lighting, staging, dubbing, and editing are used to alter the physical presence of the actors and actresses we see.

In addition, noses are bobbed. Wigs and toupees are fitted. High heels and elevator shoes are worn. Hair is dyed or darkened. Busts, shoulders, and fannies are padded.

The result is a fantasy world encompassed on a screen fifteen feet high with a force sufficient to turn artificiality into its own reality. Even brief showings in the movies can lead to widespread fads among the populace. Clark Gable takes off his shirt and reveals he is not wearing an undershirt—and undershirt sales soon plunge. Joan Crawford plucks out her eyebrows, paints on false ones, and the women of America start doing the same. Rudolph Valentino, shy and unsure of his own virility, plays romantic leads, and a nation so believes that this basically retiring person is the epitome of the dashing lover that 30,000 women turn out for his funeral.

Thus the power of Hollywood—to alter old images, to create new images. And both are done by fooling the eye and lying to the mind.

IN HOLLYWOOD, NAME-DROPPING HAS TWO MEANINGS

The most graphic symbol that Hollywood is a tinseltown with a fake facade can be found in the contrived names given to or freely adopted by many of its leading actors and actresses. No other walk of life or pursuit of a livelihood sees people so widely changing their names as they do in Hollywood. In such other public arenas as the professions, athletics, politics, or the arts, rare are the individuals who alter their names and go about in public wrapped in a sham moniker (even in literature the noms de plume are few and far between).

Of course, a large part of this name-dropping has to do with creating—or at least not destroying—the romantic and exotic aura of Hollywood. Consider, for instance, the sex goddesses who have graced the silver screen. Would we have been so enamored of Greta Garbo, Rita Hayworth, Susan Hayward, Marilyn Monroe, and Brigitte Bardot if they had gone around clothed in their real names: Greta Gustafson, Margarita Cansino, Edythe Marrener, Norma Jean Baker, and Camille Javal?

But here, too, Hollywood has often gone too far. Among the first screen sex goddesses and the first to be called "vamp" was Theda Bara. An extra in 1915, she was catapulted to stardom in the early silent movies by a publicity campaign that said she was the daughter of an Eastern potentate and that Theda Bara was an anagram of "Arab death." The truth about her background and her name was far more prosaic. Theda Bara was really from Cincinnati, she was not Arab but Jewish, and her real name was Theodosia Goodman.

Hollywood's treatment of its leading men has been no less devious. Here is a sampling of movie marquee make-believe:

Screen Name	*Real Name*
John Wayne	Marion Morrison
Rock Hudson	Ray Scherer
Cary Grant	Archibald Leach
Rex Harrison	Reginald Carey
John Garfield	Julius Garfinkle
Edward G. Robinson	Emanuel Goldberg
Paul Muni	Muni Weisenfreund
Omar Sharif	Michel Shalhouz
Kirk Douglas	Isidore Demsky
Melvyn Douglas	Melvyn Hesselberg
Karl Malden	Mladen Sekulovich

Some of Hollywood's famous changed not their last names but their first. Gary Cooper was originally Frank Cooper. And as for that duo of Bob Hope and Bing Crosby, their last names are really Hope and Crosby, but their true first names are Leslie and Harry.

Then there are the cases of siblings taking different directions. Olivia de Havilland kept her name, but her sister Joan changed hers to Joan Fontaine.

Sometimes one can well understand the name-dropping. Stefanie Powers may have been professionally hampered no matter what she did if she had kept calling herself Stefania Federkiewicz. Ellen Burstyn was born Edna Rae Gilooly. Albert Brooks definitely would have had a problem if he had kept his real name of Albert Einstein. And Laurence Harvey, who played suave Englishmen, would not have gone far in such roles with his given name—Larushka Mischa Skikne.

But Hollywood is so infused with name changing (not to mention name-calling) that even those who write about it have altered their names. The two biggest chroniclers of the gossip of Hollywood—columnists Louella Parsons and Hedda Hopper—each could not resist the lure of lying about their bylines. Louella Parsons's real name was Louella Oettinger. Hedda Hopper's was Elda Furry.

> Some Hollywood names do not seem true, but are. Among those using their real names were Clark Gable, Tyrone Power, Henry Fonda, Clara Bow, Ava Gardner, Alan Ladd, Errol Flynn, and James Dean. Special mention must go to Gina Lollobrigida, the Italian sex symbol who resisted movie mogul demands that she change her name or else she would never be a star. She showed Hollywood that when it came to names, Shakespeare may have been right all along: "A rose by any other name would smell as sweet."

THE IMAGE ON THE SILVER SCREEN IS OFTEN TARNISHED

Hollywood became the land of make-believe in large part by making over the actors and actresses who are projected larger than life on the screen. This meant molding, remolding, or creating the physical aspects or personalities of people who would be movie gods and goddesses. To make a star, Hollywood moguls figured they had to help boost a performer into the firmament.

One way this was done, as we have seen, is by altering names. But there was often more that had to be done, as truth was fudged and optical illusions embraced.

Here are some examples of how the screen image differed from reality:

- Katharine Hepburn—Because of her long neck, cameramen had to shadow her from her chin down.

- Claudette Colbert—She always insisted on being photographed from just one side. Special sets had to be built for her so that she could enter from the direction that best showed off the side she wanted.

• Marlene Dietrich—When she first came to Hollywood from Germany, she was plump and did not project a sophisticated image. This sleeker look came only after Travis Banton, a fashion designer with the Paramount studio, worked closely with her.

• Errol Flynn—The handsome, sword-playing, woman-chasing figure on screen was bisexual off screen, even engaging in a sexual relationship with Tyrone Power.

• Carole Lombard—On screen she projected an angelic, self-assured image; she was, however, so shy with others that she had to have someone walk with her when she went through the studio commissary.

• Jean Arthur—Self-assured on screen, she got so nervous before scenes that she sometimes vomited.

• Alan Ladd—He played the aggressive leading-man roles, but he was short and whenever he appeared in a love scene with a tall actress, either a platform was built for him to stand on or a trench was dug for her to stand in.

• Tyrone Power—The handsome leading man was actively bisexual off-screen.

• Rock Hudson—The movie and TV star was famed for his Doris Day movies and leading-man roles, but he was homosexual in his private life. He once married, but the wedding was a hurried-up situation to counter a pending magazine article about his homosexuality. After several months the marriage disbanded and Hudson eventually got a divorce, never marrying again. He died of AIDS.

• Cary Grant—He was the debonair star in Hitchcock films and played opposite Audrey Hepburn, but he, too, was bisexual, having a continuing sexual relationship with Randolph Scott, who himself played macho cowboy heroes.

• James Dean—The young actor who developed a large cult following after starring in *Rebel Without a Cause* in

1955 was a lonely, insecure person. "He was not the self-assured person everybody believed he was," Ann Doran, who played his mother in *Rebel,* has said. "He had great doubts about himself and where he was going. He was *that* lost."

• Marilyn Monroe—A natural brunette, she peroxided her hair to make it blond and, to improve her looks, bobbed her nose and chin.

IT'S THE OLD QUESTION: WHAT'S REAL AND WHAT'S ACTING?

James Cagney, who played tough guys in numerous films, was quiet and reserved in real life. Once a Warner Brothers studio employee, after meeting Cagney and noting how he was so unassuming in real life, asked, "Now, when are you acting—on screen, or off?"

JUST THE FACTS, FANS

The studios have never been known to restrain themselves in stretching the truth to promote a film. One instance of going overboard in this regard happened with the movie *We Live Again,* issued in 1934 by the Goldwyn studio and featuring Goldwyn's latest discovery, a European actress named Anna Sten.

The advertising department created a poster that touted "THE DIRECTORIAL GENIUS OF MAMOULIAN," "THE BEAUTY OF STEN," and "THE PRODUCING GENIUS OF GOLDWYN." All of this was said to have combined to create "THE WORLD'S GREATEST ENTERTAINMENT."

When shown the poster, Goldwyn responded, "That's the kind of ad I like. Facts. No exaggeration."

WHO SAID TALK IS CHEAP?

It was 1928 and Gary Cooper and his costar Nancy Carroll were about to finish a silent movie, *The Shopworn Angel,* when their studio realized how well sound was being received by the public with *The Jazz Singer,* issued late in 1927. So, with virtually the entire sixty-minute film finished, Cooper and Carroll were given dialogue for the final scene—a wedding.

The dialogue: Cooper said, "I do," and Carroll said, "I do."

On the basis of this, the movie was released and promoted as a talkie.

When It Came To Telling The Truth, Isadora Duncan Didn't Dance Around

Isadora Duncan, the dancer and actress, once began what she intended to be her autobiography. She never got beyond the first chapter in a dictation made to a secretary in 1924. The first paragraph ended as follows:

> I want to tell the truth about my loves and my art because the whole world is absolutely brought up on lies. We begin with lies and end on nothing but lies. We begin with lies and half our lives at least we live with lies.

CHARLIE CHAPLIN ENCOUNTERED SLAPSTICK IN REAL LIFE, TOO

Charlie Chaplin, who had an eye for women, was once thwarted in his pursuit of a beauty by a cruel hoax. While in Germany on a visit arranged by the Blumenthal brothers, he was introduced to the exotic new film star Pola Negri, then in her early twenties. Chaplin was immediately taken with her. At a reception to which they were all invited, Chaplin whispered to one of the Blumenthals, "How do you say in German, 'You are the most beautiful woman I have ever seen'?"

For some unexplained reason—since the brothers had been helpful to Chaplin—Blumenthal responded, "*Du bist ekelhaft.*" But this really meant, "You are disgusting."

In a scene that could come right out of a Chaplin movie, the great screen star then turned to Miss Negri, bowed, and said, "Madam Negri, *Du bist ekelhaft.*"

The beauty's reaction was immediate. She slapped Chaplin's face and immediately left.

Interestingly, several years later back in America, the two became engaged, but only for a brief time before they split up . . . again.

IN—AND OUT—LIKE FLYNN

Actors and actresses often engage in devious publicity stunts to promote themselves or their movies. But one highly revealing case of an actor creating a publicity hoax involved Errol Flynn.

Flynn, who played in numerous swashbuckling films, has been ranked by one journalist—George Seldes, author of *Witness to a Century* (Ballantine Books, 1987)—as "the number-one son-of-a-bitch" he encountered in nearly eighty years of journalism. Indeed, according to Seldes, some 200 government documents now available under the U.S. Freedom of Information Act reveal that Flynn was a Nazi spy both before and during World War II and that he took pictures of U.S. naval installations and sent them to Japan.*

Seldes himself witnessed Flynn in action. The two found themselves together on a bench at the main Paris police station waiting for travel permits to enter Spain during the Spanish Civil War in the 1930s. Flynn told Seldes he was going to Madrid as a representative of numerous Hollywood people and that he was bringing a million dollars to help supply a hospital for the Republican soldiers and medicine and food for the International Brigade.

Once in Spain, Flynn asked if he could be taken near the front lines, but when the shooting began to hit the building from where he was observing the fighting, the actor, who had fought pirates on screen, decided he wanted to see another aspect of Spain. "Do any of you know of a good, clean whorehouse?" he asked. He was directed to the old red-light district.

---

*These and other facts about Flynn can be found in *Errol Flynn: The Untold Story* (Doubleday, 1980) by Charles Higham.

The following day Flynn went to the office where telegrams could be sent out of the country and gave the censors what appeared to be an innocuous statement he wanted to send to Paris. The telegram passed through the censors, but what they did not know was that the message carried a prearranged code releasing a hoax that had been planned in Hollywood.

The hoax soon became apparent. The following day the New York *Daily News* published a front-page story with the headline, ERROL FLYNN KILLED ON SPANISH FRONT. The article went on to report that Flynn had been killed "by machine gun bullets on the Guadalajara front."

This was soon followed by a statement from Warner Brothers in Paris that Flynn had not been killed but had been wounded on the Spanish front. The *Daily News,* in its next day's editions, clarified its earlier story, saying now that Flynn had been "wounded on the head."

The actor soon emerged in Barcelona, Spain, and to questioning reporters showed a bandaged left arm. He then left Spain.

Observing that the bandage covered what was probably "a self-inflicted scratch," Seldes writes that Flynn's visit led to none of his stated objectives: "There were no ambulances, no hospital, no medical supplies, no food for the Spanish Republic, and not one cent of money. The war correspondents said bitterly it was the cruelest hoax of the time. Flynn was one of the most despicable human beings that ever lived, and had used a terrible war just to advertise one of his cheap movies."

Oddly newspapers at the time did not print the truth about Flynn's self-serving escapade but continued to treat him as a hero. Only years later did the story of his departure from the war front for a night in a whorehouse appear in a book. Flynn thereupon announced a libel suit for $2 million, but, when Seldes and other war correspondents offered to testify they had witnessed Flynn's actions, the actor dropped his suit.

Interestingly, when Flynn died in 1959 at the age of fifty, *Life* magazine said of him that "the truth was not in him when a lie made a better story." The headline of *Life*'s obituary referred to him as "the Fabulous Flynn."

HOLLYWOOD MAKEOVERS

If the facts or features about a person aren't good enough, Hollywood doesn't seem to mind tampering with the truth. Here are some famed make-over attempts with hair, nose, age, even tears.

HAIR
Now It Can Be Told: Elvis Dyed His White Hair

Women are not the only ones who use wigs and bleach or blacken their hair in Hollywood. Besides being big users of toupees (Humphrey Bogart and Burt Reynolds, for example), males, too, engage in various hairy lies. One who did was Elvis Presley. His hair was normally sandy brown, but he dyed it jet black for years—as did his wife, Priscilla, who dyed hers to match his.

Elvis's hair beneath the dyeing eventually turned white, as had his father's at an early age. Several months before Elvis died, Larry Geller, Elvis's personal hairdresser, suggested that Elvis let his hair grow and revert to its natural color of white, which would make his hair healthier and would dramatically highlight his show suits. Elvis responded that letting the public see him with long white hair at that time would be too drastic, but that he would "give it some thought."

Before he could give it further consideration, Elvis died at forty-two.

NOSE
How Danny Kaye Almost Lost His Nose

One of the things Hollywood likes to tinker with are the noses of its leading men and women. Again, the idea is the ideal—to have everything about the heroes and heroines of the silver screen just right for adulation and emulation. And what usually needed adjustment more than the nose?

So rhinoplasties are widely practiced in the movie industry to carry out the make-over and to provide a better setting for make-believe. But not everyone targeted agreed to a nose job. Consider the case of comedian and entertainer Danny Kaye.

When Kaye (born David Daniel Kaminski) came to Hollywood for his first movie role in *Up in Arms* (1944), Samuel Goldwyn (born Goldfish and Jewish) thought Kaye looked too Jewish and told him to get his nose bobbed. When Kaye refused, another movie mogul, Louis B. Mayer (also Jewish) came up with a novel if ludicrous idea—he offered to pay to have Kaye's brother's nose changed so that Danny could see how it looked. Kaye declined again.

Goldwyn, beside himself, suddenly came up with a solution one night during the filming. He ordered that Kaye's wavy reddish-brown hair be dyed blond. Kaye finally agreed to this, and that is how he appears—with a mane of wavy blond hair—in *Up in Arms*. Once issued, the film propelled Danny Kaye into an international star—and his blond hair thereafter became his trademark.

A footnote to this story is that once Kaye proved popular, Goldwyn spent lavishly on Danny Kaye movies. In fact it was in connection with Kaye's films that Goldwyn is reported to have uttered one of his famed Goldwynisms: "Our comedies are not to be laughed at."

AGE
When a Star Is Born

Besides the name, the nose, and the image, Hollywood often concerns itself with making certain an actor or actress has the right age—even if it means a little lying about when a star was born.

Here is how *Time* magazine, in 1949 at the height of Hollywood's power, showed how the movie industry arrived at just the right age for an actress:

> To find the age of an actress, a Hollywood press agent takes the year of her birth, subtracts it from itself, then burns the paper the figures were written on. The publicist next adds last week's fan mail to the box-office receipts from the star's last picture, subtracts her salary, divides the remainder by the number of press agents assigned to her, subtracts the number of her

marriages, adds three months for every child she has had, and knocks off ten years for gallantry. If the age is still higher than the one the boss ordered, he works in slight mathematical errors until the result comes out right.

TEARS
You'll Cry Today and Tomorrow

Make-believe tears that look real are a necessary staple of the movie-making industry. One way in which tears were made in early Hollywood (besides the language in divorce settlements) was by blowing menthol through a handkerchief into the actor or actress's eyes. But this was not always possible, and the preferred method was to make the performer somehow able to summon up real tears from real tear ducts.

Take child stars, for instance. Jackie Cooper, one of the most famous of the child stars of the 1930s, had trouble crying on demand. In *Skippy* (1931) this was especially trying because the script called for three crying scenes.

The first time, the director aroused tears by sending on the set another boy dressed in Cooper's costume; the thought of someone else taking his part set Cooper crying. Another time the tears rolled when, after the director had exhausted his yelling at the child to cry, his mother took him in her arms and explained the reason the part called for crying; Cooper began weeping without further encouragement.

Yet another time came when the director had the dog in the movie taken off the set and warned Cooper the dog would be shot if Cooper didn't cry. When Cooper still could not make the tears roll, a gun went off in the distance and Cooper was told the dog had been shot because it had been distracting Cooper and preventing him from crying.

Now Cooper began to sob and kept on sobbing throughout the scene. The dog was then brought back and reunited with Cooper, who was then given an ice-cream cone for his realistic performance.

Another time—in a famous scene in Cecil B. deMille's *The Ten Commandments* (1956)—an announcement of a death among the cast was used to elicit an appropriate response for a scene. In trying to film the Israelites receiving the Ten Commandments, de-Mille felt the throng of extras were not providing the proper serious emotion. So he called everyone together and announced that one of the cast had just died that morning, leaving eight children. He asked the stunned crowd to stand for two minutes of silence. As everyone stood quietly, De Mille had the cameras begin running and sweeping the sorrowful and downcast looks. After two minutes de Mille had his somber crowd scene on film and dismissed the assemblage. But there had been no death among the cast. A Cecil B. de Mille lie had enabled the successful filming of the giving of the Ten Commandments.

ONLY IN HOLLYWOOD

William Wyler, the director, had a habit of shooting and reshooting scenes without explaining to actors what he was after so that they could respond to his desires. In the first sequence of the film *The Letter* (1940), he went through thirty-three takes before he declared himself satisfied. Hal Wallis, the producer, grew exasperated with Wyler and decided to do something to stop his overshooting. After the thirty-three takes, Wallis invited Wyler into the projection room to see how the selected take looked. The sequence, which involved Bette Davis in a night scene, looked captivating. When the projector was turned off, Wyler, smug at the results, turned to Wallis and said, "Now you see why it was worth thirty-three takes." To which Wallis responded, "We printed the first take."

* * *

Chariots of Fire was a highly acclaimed movie that won the Academy Award for Best Picture in 1981. Among its accomplishments was the sense of authenticity it captured in its telling of the true story of three friends competing in the 1924 Olympics. The film, however, credited sprinter Harold Abrahams with the accomplishment of a feat never before done—racing around the Great Court at Cambridge's Trinity College at noontime before the clock could toll the hour, literally beating the clock. But it was actually another of the three men—Lord Burghley—who accomplished the feat—and he did not do it until 1927. The peer, seventy-six years old when the film came out, was deeply offended by the liberties that had been taken with a film said to be so authentic. He protested by refusing to see the movie.

Watch Out: Autobiographical Movie Ahead

Stand by Me, a movie based on a Stephen King book, is supposedly derived from a King friend's boyhood experience involving four youths' discovery of a boy's body beside the train tracks. But the real story involved the boys' finding not the dead body of a boy but of a dog. Later, in discussing how he had reshaped the story for his purposes, King pointed out why one cannot trust an autobiographical movie or book. Citing something author John Irving had once told him, King said, "Never believe a writer when he seems to be offering you autobiography, because we all lie. We all edit it and we say, well, this is what happened but that doesn't make a good story so I'll change it. So it's mostly a lie."

NOW IT CAN BE TOLD: WALT DISNEY NEVER LAID A HAND ON CINDERELLA

The name Walt Disney is synonymous with animated cartooning. But Disney was not that good a cartoonist. In fact after *Snow White and the Seven Dwards* in 1937, he concentrated on coming up with the ideas for the movies that bore his name but did no drawing for these films. He hired a stable of animators to do that for him.

So while the Disney mind can be seen in such classics as *Fantasia* and *Cinderella* and the Disney name is associated with them all, the Disney hand is nowhere to be found in any movie after *Snow White.*

FRANKLY, MY DEAR, THERE'S A LOT OF DUPLICITY IN HOW VIVIEN LEIGH BECAME SCARLETT

The contrived publicity stunt—one can almost call it the duplicity stunt—is a staple of Hollywood. It may have been employed at its most effective in the ballyhooing of one of the greatest films ever to be made—*Gone With the Wind*. Released in 1939 and the winner of eight Academy Awards including Best Picture, it stands today as the most-watched movie in history.

Gone With the Wind, based upon the best-selling book, was given added publicity throughout the making of the movie by an astute campaign orchestrated by David O. Selznick, the producer, who had bought the rights for the then high sum of $50,000. While Clark Gable was the obvious choice to play Rhett Butler, the actress to play the green-eyed, headstrong beauty Scarlett O'Hara was less obvious. As a result, Selznick announced he would mount a national search for the right actress.

In response, many actresses came forward seeking the role. Among them were Bette Davis, Joan Crawford, Tallulah Bankhead, and Katharine Hepburn (she told Selznick, "The part was practically written for me," but Selznick told her, "I can't imagine Rhett Butler chasing you for ten years").

Since the preparations for filming the movie were to take two years, the talent search was stretched out almost until the filming began, with another $50,000 invested in scouring the country to see if a girl existed somewhere in America who was just right for the Scarlett part. The director, George Cukor, sent to the South to scout locations, was also said to be looking in on high school plays. Women wishing to be tested were allowed to do so, most in simple reading tests, some brought before a camera for a screen test.

As time for production neared, Scarlett fever was at a high pitch, but still no Scarlett. And then it supposedly happened. David Selznick, the public learned, had found his Scarlett. On December 10, 1938, at one of the scenes already being filmed—the burning of the Atlanta ammunition dump during the Civil War (but was really the old sets for *King Kong* and *Garden of Allah*)—a young

British actress named Vivien Leigh was being escorted on the set by Selznick's brother, Myron, a top Hollywood agent. He introduced her to his brother as "your Scarlett O'Hara!" As the story was later told to the press, with "the flames glowing on her face," David Selznick saw that the green-eyed beauty was the Scarlett for whom he had been searching. She was tested three times and passed grandly.

America had found its Scarlett O'Hara in an English actress who, it turned out, had the same Irish and French background as the Scarlett O'Hara of *Gone With the Wind*.

Ah, but the truth of how Vivien Leigh came to be chosen to play Scarlett is different than the legend, which appears to have been elaborately constructed.

Vivien Leigh was hardly the little-known actress who needed discovery. She had appeared in several films and had been in numerous stage plays in England. Her beauty and acting ability had attracted the attention of others, among them David Selznick, who had screened her movies and had a private print of one, and Laurence Olivier, with whom she fell in love. Olivier's agent at the time of their affair was Myron Selznick, David's brother.

Standing in her way of getting the part of Scarlett—a part that Olivier said she "had almost demonic determination to play"—were two factors. One was that she was not a native-born American. Would the nation accept a foreign-born actress playing such a famous role in such an American story?

Second, her love affair with Olivier had scandalized England. They were both married to others at the time they began seeing each other.

The solution: While no actual records exist to substantiate the following without dispute, film historians generally agree that a scenario was devised in which Vivien Leigh would be discovered at the last minute after an extensive search for the right Scarlett had not been successful. In this way the foreign-born aspect would be diffused, especially since Scarlett, the character, and Vivien, the actress, shared the same Irish-French background. And with Olivier and Leigh agreeing not to move for a divorce at the time, the scandal would be abated in the flurry of good news that the Scarlett part had finally been filled.

Indeed the various elements of the discovery scenario do not hold up. Myron had actually arrived on the set somewhat drunk and late, so the introduction between David Selznick and Vivien Leigh occurred after the fire had been put out, the set leveled, and the filming over. The testing of Vivien Leigh also appears unnecessarily overdone.

What makes the legend certainly suspect is that David Selznick, an inveterate memo writer and diary keeper, is somehow suddenly speechless—or certainly wordless—about the casting of Vivien Leigh. Rudy Behlmer, author of *Memo from David O. Selznick,* points out that "correspondence regarding Selznick's initial meeting with Vivien Leigh, her testing for the role of Scarlett, the reactions to the tests, the unofficial selection of her for the role . . . is all conspicuous by its absence in the Selznick files."

But the ploy worked. The movie, as had the book, was greeted with great enthusiasm. It was an immediate success and its popularity has not waned in more than fifty years.

One can only sigh with relief that no equal national search—with an equal hidden agenda and selection—was made in the case of Rhett Butler. Everyone then and since seems to agree that Clark Gable made the best Rhett Butler. Everyone except possibly Margaret Mitchell, the author of *Gone With the Wind.* When the search was on for a Scarlett O'Hara, she refused to choose an actress, but she had her own ideas about someone to play Rhett Butler. Her choice, offered with a trace of humor (and probably with her fingers crossed behind her back), was, she said, for her favorite performer—Groucho Marx.

WAS TARZAN A LIAR?

Johnny Weissmuller is probably the most famous Tarzan of the many actors who have played the King of the Jungle in the movies. What made him so famous—and what led to his being chosen to play Tarzan— was that off screen he was a champion Olympic swimmer who had won a total of five gold medals representing the United States in the 1924 and 1928 Olympics.

But evidence has since surfaced that Johnny Weissmuller was

not born in the United States as he claimed and was therefore not a U.S. citizen eligible to compete in the Olympics as a member of the U.S. team. At the time he won the medals, he was actually a citizen of Romania.

During his lifetime, however, Weissmuller repeatedly stated that he was born in Windber, Pennsylvania, after his parents, Peter and Elizabeth Weissmuller, had traveled from Romania and settled in the United States. But the actual scenario appears to be that he was born on June 2, 1904, in Freidorf, a small town in the Banat region of what is now Romania (but was then part of Hungary before boundary changes were made in 1918). Seven months later Johnny was brought by his parents to the United States, and the family lived for a brief period in Windber, during which time Johnny's brother, Peter, Jr., was born.

Questions about Weissmuller's nationality first arose in April 1924 as he trained for the Olympics. A member of Congress, Illinois representative Henry Riggs Rathbone, publicly expressed his doubts, and *The New York Times* reported the story, but Weissmuller's father declared that his son was born in Chicago. That pacified the media and the public. But no record exists that Johnny was born in Chicago.

In fact, when Johnny Weissmuller later that year wanted to get a passport to travel to the Olympic games in Paris, he had to show proof of citizenship. He thereupon produced documents not from Chicago but from Windber, Pennsylvania. He presented the baptismal records of St. John Cantius Catholic Church showing an entry for Petrus John Weissmuller, but the entry is undoubtedly for his younger brother, Peter. The name John can be seen written in between the first and last names in different ink and in a different style of writing. However, Weissmuller claimed his name was really Peter John (and his brother, in support, said his name was really John Peter, even though he had people call him Pete).

The document assured officials, though, and Weissmuller got his passport and competed in Paris, where he wowed the world, winning three gold medals in the 1924 games.

From there he went on to fame and fortune, becoming a double gold medalist at the next Olympics. In all, he set more than fifty American and world swimming records in the 1920s, then went on in the 1930s to star as Tarzan in the movies.

Interestingly no one in the United States now questioned his American birth. And in 1950 his "birthplace" town of Windber gave him a welcome-home celebration. Schools were closed and a parade was held down Main Street. The pastor of the church where Johnny had said he was born gave him a copy of his birth and baptismal certificates.

But there were those who knew Weissmuller's secret and did not tell—such as some of the other immigrants from the Banat region who had settled in Chicago near where Johnny grew up, as well as those back in Freidorf who remembered the family. Both groups took pride in Johnny's accomplishments and understood why he had had to show a birth on U.S. soil.

In recent years, however, the truth about Tarzan Weissmuller has begun to emerge into public view. Romania has pointed to him periodically as a native son, with Romanian newspapers showing his birth records from Freidorf. He has been included in an anthology of notables born in Banat, and a cousin, Jakob, who lived in Freidorf, was quoted in a 1979 article in a Banat newspaper as saying, "Tarzan comes from Freidorf."

Johnny kept the secret about his birth from his wives (all five of them) and even from his only son, Johnny, Jr., who was stunned when after the death of his father a reporter told him about the Freidorf birthplace. Johnny, Jr., said he had never even heard of Freidorf.

In an interview cited in *Sports Illustrated* soon after Weissmuller's death in 1984,* Johnny, Jr., wondered what effect the truth about his father's secret could have on his father's Olympic honors. "Will they take away his medals?" he asks. "They did that to Jim Thorpe for a buck and a half."

As of this writing, no action has been taken. The infraction seems slight. After all, Weissmuller lived his entire life in the United States—except for his first seven months. And he won the medals fairly, even if he might have been on the wrong team to do so. But Jim Thorpe, a native American, was stripped of his Olympic medals when it was found he had taken money for playing base-

---

*Much of the information presented here comes from a *Sports Illustrated* article, "Johnny Weissmuller Made Olympian Efforts to Conceal His Birthplace," by Arlene Mueller.

ball and was therefore not an amateur athlete eligible for Olympic competition.

Weissmuller's son may have had the right perspective on what his father had done. Said Johnny, Jr.: "He sure could keep a secret. I guess he was a better actor than any of the critics knew."

That Tarzan Yell Was Actually a Fake

The Tarzan victory call—an unusual earsplitting sound that characterized Tarzan movies—was actually not made by any of the Tarzans, although the movie studio and each of the Tarzans let the public think that it was. Actually at first the yell was three voices put together—a baritone, a bass, and a hog caller. Later the father of Tarzan Buster Crabbe did all the yells. The famed Tarzan yell is simply another Hollywood deception.

TO BE SPIEGELED IS AS BAD AS IT SOUNDS

In the annals of great Hollywood filmmakers, one name is always present—Sam Spiegel. And that's because in the annals of great Hollywood films four of them were produced by him: *The African Queen* (1951), *On the Waterfront* (1954), *The Bridge on the River Kwai* (1957), and *Lawrence of Arabia* (1962).

It is all the more surprising, then, that in Hollywood Spiegel gained a reputation for deviousness.

Consider:

• In his press handouts, Spiegel said he was born in Austria, but he was really born in Poland.

• In Hollywood in 1939, he avoided the Immigration Service by taking the name S. P. Eagle (a name by which he billed himself until 1954).

• During his rise in Hollywood, he invented a nonexistent background to generate much trade-paper publicity; he knew the bogus background would be difficult to check because of the war.

• And then, to assemble the casts he wanted for his movies, he used trickery—or, as John Houseman termed it, "Parlaying a pack of lies into a motion picture."

• His technique of casting, for example, was to tell Charles Boyer that Charles Laughton had agreed to appear in a film, then get Laughton and his wife, Elsa Lanchester, to appear by telling them he had gotten Boyer, Edward G. Robinson, and Ginger Rogers.

But Spiegel's tactics eventually caught up with him. Based on his life-style, a new Hollywoodism emerged to denote being lied to. The expression became "to be spiegeled."

HOW OL' BLUE EYES REALLY GOT STARTED (AND DON'T FAINT WHEN YOU READ THIS)

Many performers get their beginnings or boosts to their careers from artful manipulation of reality. Consider the case of Frank Sinatra, one of the most successful entertainers of all time (he even won an Academy Award—for best supporting actor for his role in *From Here to Eternity*).

A vivid image from Sinatra's early career is that of bobby-soxers swooning and fainting during his singing at New York's Paramount Theater in 1942. And yet, prior to this event, Sinatra's singing career was going nowhere. Why the dramatic change?

The change came about when a Sinatra show business friend suggested he shift publicity agents and hire George Evans, a forty-year-old press agent who then handled such leading entertainers as Duke Ellington, Glenn Miller, Dean Martin, and Jerry Lewis. Evans went to see Sinatra perform at the Paramount, where he was appearing as a supporting act to the Tommy Dorsey band. Walking down the aisle to get a better look at Sinatra, Evans saw a girl stand up and throw a rose at the stage, while the girl next to her gave a slight moan. Thus was born the germ of an idea.

To engender not only publicity but a mass following for Frank, Evans decided to try to fill a theater with girls moaning over the younger singer. According to Kitty Kelley in *His Way: The Unauthorized Biography of Frank Sinatra* (Bantam Books, 1986), Evans hired twelve long-haired young girls in bobby sox for $5 each and trained them to jump, scream, yell, moan, and faint when Frank sang. In the basement of the Paramount, he drilled them in hollering when Frank delivered parts of his songs. "They shouldn't only yell and squeal, they should fall apart," he is quoted. The girls were taught to scream "Oh, Daddy," when Sinatra, in singing "Embraceable You," came to the words, "Come to Papa, come to Papa, do." And as two of the girls fainted, the others were instructed to moan together as loudly as possible.

To add to the effect, on the day of the performance when all this was to happen, Evans packed the theater by giving away tickets to hundreds of youngsters. He even rented an ambulance, put it in front of the theater, gave ushers bottles of ammonia with which to revive any swooning patrons, and alerted newspaper photographers.

The result: The next day's newspapers carried photos of young girls being carried out of the theater after fainting from Sinatra's singing. In a clear example of mass psychosis, although Evans had hired twelve girls, thirty fainted.

The effect of the publicity was immediate and widespread. Within days people were waiting in lines to buy tickets to Frank's performances at the Paramount, and newspapers were running stories about the young crooner who was making girls swoon and women scream. By the next month, after further buildup in the press with the start of Sinatra clubs around the country (Evans told reporters that more than one thousand Sinatra clubs had been formed within weeks), Frank came back to the Paramount and was besieged by thousands of screaming girls who broke through the doors. As one eyewitness recalled, "It was absolute pandemonium. This time they threw more than roses. They threw their panties and their brassieres. They went nuts, absolutely nuts."

And so was born Frank Sinatra's spectacular entertainment career that has lasted more than fifty years.

As for publicist George Evans, several years later Sinatra fired him in a dispute over expenses.

"If you can't give me your word of honor, will you give me your promise?"

—Samuel Goldwyn

Journalist H. L. Mencken got himself into hot water with a hoax he could not stop.

CHAPTER IX

"And here is Big Foot's actual shoe."

HOAXERS AND
THEIR HOAXES

. . . Telling Some Tall Tales

A liar's punishment is that he is not believed
even when he tells the truth.

—The Talmud

One vast refuge of the liar is the hoax.

A hoax can either be lighthearted—a practical joke, for instance—or devastating—as in the forging of historical documents or evidence.

Indeed, according to historian Allan Nevins, forgery is one of the oldest and commonest of human offenses. "One of the first warnings the teacher of Renaissance history must give students of Luther, Erasmus and numerous other figures is to beware of the stream of manufactured documents attributed to them. The forgery of letters purporting to be by Marie Antoinette has long been a thriving industry, and still continues," he writes in *The Gateway to History,* (D. C. Heath & Co., 1938, 1962).

There are so many faked letters of Franklin, Washington, Jefferson, Lincoln, Poe, and others that the New York Public Library maintains a large collection of false autographic material.

Over the span of centuries there have been many hoaxes that may have started out as practical jokes but that have lingered and grown until they played havoc with reality and truth. Such could well be the case with the Loch Ness Monster, Big Foot, and the Abominable Snowman. In each case sightings have been made and tabloid stories have been published, but somehow there never seems to be the clear photo or the unmistakable piece of evidence or the appearance of the "thing" in public. Note how those spotted aliens from outer space and UFO's seem to love backcountry roads or remote areas. Aliens certainly seem unlike humans—they do not care for the bright lights of Broadway.

But in recent times hoaxes have continued, if not escalated. We had the episode where the supposed diaries of Adolf Hitler—sixty volumes in all—surfaced and reputable publishers in Europe and in the United States paid over $2 million for the rights to publish the diaries before it was learned that the works were forgeries—and crude forgeries at that. And then there was the case of the *Autobiography of Howard Hughes,* the reclusive billionaire whom no member of the public had seen for decades because he liked to hole up in the top floors of Las Vegas hotels and watch movies. But he seemed to find time to meet with Clifford Irving, a writer, and work with him on his autobiography. Or so said Irving, who convinced a major American book publisher and a major magazine to pay huge sums to him for the rights to publish the Hughes manuscript.

All went well—Irving even held up under questioning and lie detector tests that corroborated his story—until Hughes, over a telephone hookup at a press conference, denounced the Irving text as a hoax. Irving was eventually found guilty of lying and jailed for several years for the fake autobiography.

These are just recent examples that show audacious hoaxers and their hoaxes are still very much with us. A lie is no less a lie for being dramatic or fascinating. After all, most liars are deceptively charming and fascinating—that's what makes their deceptions and lies so effective.

The real question we must ask ourselves is—what hoaxes are still out there being believed because we have yet to find out that we've been hoaxed?

THE GREAT IMPOSTOR

One newspaper called him "Genius Without Portfolio."

Another paper headlined a story about his latest exploit: GENTLE MASQUERADER AT IT AGAIN.

Robert Crichton wrote a book about him entitled *The Great Impostor*.

Ferdinand Waldo Demara, Jr., born December 12, 1921, wanted to lead a life of service to others, thereby gaining a measure of adulation for himself. He had a remarkable memory. He had an uncanny ability to pick up information and skills quickly and easily. He was supremely self-confident.

He also did not know when to accept society's limitations. For during the course of his adult life, Demara posed as:

- A surgeon lieutenant in the Royal Canadian Navy, performing major operations while at sea aboard a destroyer

- A doctor of psychology and dean of the School of Philosophy at Gannon College in Pennsylvania

- An assistant warden in a Texas prison, where he helped reform a cell block with some of the nation's most hardened criminals

- A law student, zoology graduate, cancer researcher, and teacher at a Maine junior college

- A teacher in a village in Maine

- A Trappist monk

In the course of being found out, he was charged with desertion from the military, fraud, forgery, car theft, embezzlement, resisting arrest, vagrancy, and public drunkenness. The charges against him at one time could have brought him forty-seven years in jail. And yet, because of help from his family, friends and even the authorities, Demara was released after serving just several weeks.

In addition, after being informed of Demara's deceit, many of those he deceived indicated they would be willing to have him back. The men of the *Cayuga,* the Canadian destroyer he served on as surgeon, sent him a large Christmas card with a picture of the ship and poem by Berton Braley entitled "Loyalty," which among its passages says, "He may be six kinds of a liar . . . but I love him, /Because—well, because he's my friend."

Among the psychological theories that Crichton cites in his book to explain Demara's actions, he notes that Demara's father lost all his money and with it the family lost their home and social status when Demara was very young. "Many feel that he had been going through life in another guise trying to find it [social status] again."

Demara himself, in response to Crichton's queries about why he had assumed so many guises, summed up his reasoning: "It's a rascality, pure rascality!"

Crichton concluded that Demara was the champion rascal of his age, "one of the last sad playboys of the Western world."

Ferdinand Waldo Demara's desire to become a hero did lead to one achievement, certainly a highlight in the life of any American. His many lives and careers caught the fancy of Hollywood. In 1960 a movie was made of his life. *The Great Impostor* played in movie houses nationwide, with Tony Curtis starring as Demara.

Demara had become a motion picture star, without trying.

Should We Thank Our Liars?

"If there were no falsehood in the world, there would be no doubt; if there were no doubt, there would be no inquiry; if no inquiry, no wisdom, no knowledge, no genius."

—Walter Savage Landor,
philosopher

FATHER, FORGIVE HIM . . .

Roberto Coppola of Rome was a teenager who had one burning ambition—to be a priest. But instead of going through years of study and preparation, he decided to go right into impersonation. For two years from 1973 to 1975 when he was caught at the age of nineteen, Coppola presented himself as a priest and conducted weddings, heard confessions, and celebrated hundreds of masses. Following his arrest he made his own confession. He told police he liked being a priest, but contemplating the end of his priesthood, he remarked wistfully, "It's a pity."

THE GREAT BATHTUB HOAX

And then there is the case of the hoax that even the hoaxer could not stop—even when he wrote exposing it.

This is the story of the famous bathtub hoax.

On December 28, 1917, H. L. Mencken, the acerbic journalist and essayist, published in the *New York Evening Mail* a brief article entitled, "A Neglected Anniversary," in which he bemoaned the passing "absolutely without public notice" of "one of the most important profane anniversaries in American history—to wit: the seventy-fifth anniversary of the introduction of the bathtub into these states."

He went on to give a brief history of the tub—how the first one was set up in Cincinnati, by Adam Thompson, a dealer in cotton and grain who acquired the habit of bathing during his frequent business trips to England. In 1828 a Lord John Russell had introduced a small tub—"little more than a glorified dishpan"—for bathing purposes, but by 1835, wrote Mencken, Russell "was said to be the only man in England who had yet come to doing it every day."

Thompson conceived the notion, wrote Mencken, that the English bathtub would be much improved if it were larger—able to accommodate an adult easily—and were fed not by water-carrying servants, but by pipes bringing water from a central reservoir.

And so, early in 1842, according to Mencken, Thompson set up a tub in his house in Cincinnati, with water pumped "by six Negroes" from a large well in his garden. The tub was made out of Nicaragua mahogany by James Guiness, the leading cabinet maker in the city, was nearly seven feet long and fully four feet wide and weighed "about 1,750 pounds."

"In this luxurious tub Thompson took two baths on December 20, 1842—a cold one at 8 A.M. and a warm one sometime during the afternoon." On Christmas Day Thompson exhibited the bath to some of his party guests, and four of them, "including a French visitor, Cpl. Duchanel, risked plunges into it."

The next day, said Mencken, all of Cincinnati seemed to know about the bathtub, and the local newspapers published stories. The results were violent discussions, and in some circles, especially medical, opposition arose to the new invention. The controversy, reported Mencken, spread to other cities, though he noted that by 1850 nearly one thousand tubs were in use in New York City and medical opposition had begun to collapse.

But according to Mencken, what really gave the bathtub recognition and respectability was the installation of the first bathtub in the White House by President Millard Fillmore in 1851. He had seen and made use of the original Thompson tub while on a visit to Cincinnati as vice-president in March 1850. "Experiencing no ill effects," Fillmore became an ardent advocate of the bathtub and wasted little time putting one in the White House when he became president upon Taylor's death on July 9, 1850.

The example of Fillmore broke down the last resistance. By 1860 every hotel in New York had a bathtub and "some had two and even three." In 1862 bathing was introduced into the army and in 1870 the first bathtub was placed in a prison in Philadelphia.

Concluded Mencken, "One is astonished, on looking into it, to find that so little of it [the history of the bathtub] has been recorded. The literature, in fact, is almost nil. But perhaps this brief sketch will encourage other inquiries and so lay the foundation for an adequate celebration of the centennial in 1942."

But Mencken's article—"a tissue of absurdities" he later called it, "a piece of spoofing to relieve the strain of war days"—was soon being widely recited and reprinted by even respected periodicals and learned journals. Mencken himself began receiving letters from readers who took his article at face value, asking either for further information or, in some cases, actually offering corroboration.

Mencken's little hoax became so widely accepted as fact that on May 23, 1926, he was moved to write a retraction of the original article and to point out how so many others had used his essay for their own purposes:

> I began to encounter my preposterous "facts" in the writings
> of other men. They began to be used by chiropractors and
> other such quacks as evidence of the stupidity of medical men.
> They began to be cited by medical men as proof of the progress of public hygiene. They got into learned journals. They
> were alluded to on the floor of Congress. They crossed the
> ocean, and were discussed solemnly in England, and on the

continent. Finally, I began to find them in standard works of reference. Today, I believe, they are as accepted as gospel everywhere on earth. To question them becomes as hazardous as to question the Norman Invasion. And as rare.

Mencken, however, went on to draw a lesson from the public's gullibility. "I recite this history," he wrote, "not because it is singular, but because it is typical. It is out of such frauds, I believe, that most of the so-called knowledge of humanity flows."

He further noted that what often begins as a guess—"or perhaps, not infrequently, as a downright and deliberate lie"—ends as a fact "embalmed in our history books."

Coming Clean: The Real History of the Bathtub

The bathtub actually goes back a long way, back at least to the days of the Greeks and Romans. They used tubs fashioned out of marble or silver. Later those living in the Middle Ages got by with tubs made out of wood.

Metal tubs were being used by the seventeenth century and they increased in use in the eighteenth century. Made out of brass, they were too costly for the average person, but by the end of the century a special varnish enabled builders of bathtubs to dress sheet metal and thereby produce a reasonably priced bathtub. These came to replace the more costly wooden or marble tub.

Interestingly the first hotel where all rooms had a bath in every bathroom is said to have been the Mount Vernon Hotel in Cape May, New Jersey, in 1853—about the time Mencken in his hoax said the bathtub was finally receiving widespread acceptance by mortal, unclean man.

Mencken concluded by reiterating that his history of the bathtub "was pure buncombe," but he also noted that the story was by now in the encyclopedias. Wrote Mencken, "History, said a great American soothsayer, is bunk."

Mencken's struggle with the truth and with setting the record straight did not end here. His article telling the truth about his bathtub hoax was dutifully printed by nearly thirty newspapers—

including the *Boston Herald,* which published the retraction on page seven of its editorial section under a four-column headline and with a two-column cartoon headed, "The American public will swallow anything."

Three weeks later, however, the *Boston Herald,* on page one of its editorial section, reprinted Mencken's ten-year-old fake story—as a straight news article.

To Mencken, Poetry and Wisdom Were Lies

"What is poetry? Poetry is simply a mellifluous statement of the obviously untrue. . . . All poetry embodies a lie. It may be an objective lie, as in 'God's in His heaven; all's well with the world.' Or it may be a subjective lie, as in 'I am the master of my fate.' But it must be a lie—and preferably a thumping one. . . .

"No normal human being wants to hear the truth. It is the passion of a small and aberrant minority of men, most of them pathological. They are hated for telling it while they live, and when they die they are swiftly forgotten. What remains to the world, in the field of wisdom, is a series of long tested and solidly agreeable lies."

—H. L. Mencken
"Hymn to the Truth"
(July 25, 1926)

A RIDDLE

Question: A deaf man has heard how a dumb man had said that a blind man had seen it running and that a lame man pursued it and a naked man had put it in his pocket and brought it home. What was it? Answer: A lie.

THE MYSTERY OF THE BOGUS BIOGRAPHIES

Everyone, from schoolboys to scholars, knows that errors creep into even the best reference books. One need only look at the errata listings to be found in many works or check one edition against another to know that our libraries, like our lives, are punctuated with mistakes.

But what is not as well known is that otherwise reliable works may contain outright lies. In one celebrated case discovered earlier this century, a highly respected biographical dictionary was found to have numerous fictional articles, either about people who never lived or providing entirely false information about real people.

The work involved was *Appleton's Cyclopaedia of American Biography*, considered at the time it was published in 1887–89 and for decades thereafter as "a valuable and authoritative work," one of the first important American biographical dictionaries. Nearly fifty years later, when the first suspicions of fictitious biographies arose, the dictionary was still found in many libraries of all sizes throughout the United States.

The first intimation that something was wrong came in 1919 in the *Journal of the New York Botanical Garden*. Dr. John Henley Barnhart, in an article entitled "Some Fictitious Botanists," reported finding that fourteen biographical sketches of botanists in the *Cyclopaedia* were entirely fictitious.

Later on, not just biographical sketches but whole articles were found to be fictitious. The strongest evidence that articles were fraudulent were their references to books that never seemed to have existed and could not be located in libraries or other sources. Entries were also peppered with errors in dates and geography, while certain biographies were discovered to be based not on one but on a combination of persons.

How did such a reputable work as *Appleton's Cyclopaedia of American Biography* come to have so many fraudulent entries and statements? It could not have been the publisher or the editors, since they were all distinguished and reliable. The misstatements and deviations from truth were too numerous to be due to error by staff writers, printers, or proofreaders.

What was the conclusion about the origin of these lies? Those investigating the problem pointed out that contributors were paid by space and were free to suggest the inclusion of names that were not in the original book of subjects—and many contributors did so. Also, articles were edited only for form, not content. Thus some one or ones were tempted to make more money by writing about more people (even if they didn't exist), and to do it faster (by writing articles that entailed as little research as possible). Knowing that his or her submission would not be checked for accuracy was too tempting for the hoaxer.

Although *Appleton's Cyclopaedia of American Biography* is today, one hundred years after publication, little used, a cursory search by investigators found that four bibliographies, one biographical dictionary, and one scientific article had used bogus information first found in the *Cyclopaedia,* with the scientific article openly crediting the *Cyclopaedia* as the source.

Indeed this is the problem posed by the writing and publishing of lies. They creep into our libraries and not only stay there but are spread by unsuspecting readers and users. Each time a bogus article or fact is repeated, the possibility of further dissemination is increased. The danger mounts that, like a virus, the false information will continue to spread and infect other sources, rendering them suspect or unreliable throughout. In that case the lies have it.

AND WHAT SHALL FRAUD PROFIT THEE? A LOT, IF YOUR NAME IS CONNALLY

John Connally, once governor of Texas and the man who entered history as the public official shot while riding with President Kennedy when he was assassinated, had an interesting attitude toward a hoax involving paintings. With an artist friend, he knowingly bought 100 forged paintings by Elmyr De Hory, who had hoaxed the art world for years with his recreations of art masterpieces. Connally figured that he could make money by eventually reselling De Hory's famous counterfeit works of such masters as van Gogh, Picasso, and Modigliani. Connally was right. His investment paid off, for he later openly sold the forgeries at auctions—as forgeries—at a profit.

THE CLASSIC COLLEGE-STUDENT HOAX (IS THIS WHAT THEY CALL "SOPHOMORIC HUMOR"?)

In *Confessions of a Street-Smart Manager* (Simon and Schuster, 1988), David Mahoney relates the story of a college girl writing home to her parents. This classic shows how a hoaxer can use the ploy of bad news/good news to gain sympathy—surely what every away-from-home student needs for effective parent control:

Dear Mom and Dad,

I'm sorry I haven't written in a long time, but since our dormitory was burned down during the student demonstration, I haven't been able to see very well. But don't worry. The doctor says there is a good chance I'll get my sight back. While in the hospital I met a wonderful man who works as an orderly there. He is a Muslim and has convinced me to convert from Christianity. You'll soon have your wish of becoming grandparents. We are moving to Africa and expect to be married. Love, Mary.

P.S. There was no demonstration or fire. I wasn't in the hospital. I'm not pregnant. I don't even have a boyfriend. But I did flunk chemistry and economics and I wanted you to view these problems in proper perspective.

Who Are the Biggest Liars?

"If you think fishermen are the biggest liars in the world, ask a jogger how far he runs every morning."
—Larry Johnson, TV personality,
quoted in *Reader's Digest*

THE PILTDOWN MAN HOAX

One of the greatest of scientific hoaxes—or at least one of the greatest of hoaxes on scientists—was the Piltdown Man.

In 1911, Piltdown in Sussex, England, became the site of a startling discovery. A jawbone and parts of a skull found in a gravel pit led a number of scientists to conclude a form of mankind, never before seen, had lived 250,000 years ago in the area. The remains were proclaimed as the long-searched-for missing link between humans and apes. Britain, and not the Mideast or Africa, was now possibly the birthplace of the human race.

Not all scientists agreed and many remained skeptical. The ensuing decades were marked by controversy because, if true, the

Piltdown Man evidence would overturn much thinking about the origin and development of mankind.

Finally, in 1953, after using newly developed chemical testing, scientists found that the jaw was not that of a human, but that of an orangutan. And the skull, while that of a man, was of a much more recent period than the ancient gravel pit in which it had been discovered. In 1955 scientists used radiocarbon testing to date the skull definitively. Rather than being from prehistoric times, it was dated to the year 1230.

The hoaxer, who has never been definitively determined, had misled scientists for decades by simply staining the orangutan jaw to age it and filing its teeth to make it look human. The Piltdown prankster had one other creation. He—or she—had made a lot of scientists look like jackasses.

THE BOOK THAT WOULDN'T QUIT

There once was a hoax that fooled a government, a major magazine, a noted writer, and a leading book publisher—and the hoaxer was only a young Canadian country boy.

It all began after World War II when *Reader's Digest,* then as now among the largest circulated magazines in the world, found out about what seemed like a dramatic story of derring-do during the war. A young Canadian named George DuPre had served in the English-Canadian secret services and encountered dramatic happenings in France. As a member of the underground, he was captured and tortured by the Nazis for weeks to get him to talk. But he resisted all their tortures and eventually escaped.

When DuPre returned to Canada and told his tale, he became a national hero. He was showered with honors and medals and given a reception by the governor general. He was invited to speak before church groups, student organizations, and governmental bodies.

Intrigued with the story, *Reader's Digest* hired the well-known journalist Quentin Reynolds to interview DuPre and write an article for the magazine. After the *Digest* published his piece, Reynolds, enamored of the story, approached his friend Bennett Cerf, head of the publishing company Random House, with the idea of turning the article into a book. Cerf agreed, and the book that emerged—*The Man Who Wouldn't Talk* (1953)—received good reviews and enough sales that Cerf later termed the book "a substantial success."

But then one night, after the book had been out a while, Cerf received a call from the editor of the *Calgary Herald,* a Canadian newspaper, who informed Cerf that "there isn't a word of truth" in the book. "Your Mr. DuPre has just collapsed and confessed that his entire story is a hoax," the editor told Cerf.

As recounted by Cerf in his autobiography, *At Random* (Random House, 1977), the newspaper editor went on to tell how DuPre's adventures were really things that the young Canadian had read about in various newspapers and spy magazines and that the Nazi tortures were just his imaginings. (Among his claims was that he was given an enema of sulphuric acid.) In fact DuPre had admitted to the newspaper he had spent the entire war in Canada and England and never set foot in France.

The truth emerged when DuPre could no longer handle his guilty conscience. "He is a nice little man and he didn't realize that his deception was going to be blown up to these dimensions," the editor explained. "He was just romancing a little bit and suddenly he found himself a national hero!"

The editor concluded by telling Cerf the *Calgary Herald* would be printing the entire story in the next morning's paper.

After hanging up the phone, Cerf realized he had to tell DeWitt Wallace, publisher of *Reader's Digest,* and Quentin Reynolds about the pending exposé. But Cerf also had a brainstorm. When Wallace groaned at the news and asked what they should do, Cerf replied, "The only way we can get out of this is to laugh it off. I'm going to tell them exactly what happened, and I'm going to say, 'Imagine this little man fooling all of us. Isn't it hilarious?' " And then Cerf said he would announce, facetiously, that the book was now no longer nonfiction but fiction—and that Random House was going to change the name of the book immediately from *The Man Who Wouldn't Talk* to *The Man Who Talked Too Much.*

Although Wallace squirmed at the idea, he was willing to support Cerf's approach to dealing with the hoax.

The plan, writes Cerf, "worked like a charm." The press, seeing the story as a harmless deception in which no one was hurt, played up the humorous aspects. As a result the entire episode received wide distribution, with people enjoying the tale.

Cerf points out that this incident "is another example of how you can laugh things off. If we had gone into a frenzy, we'd have made fools of ourselves. This way everybody laughed *with* us."

Of course, Cerf, the publisher, and Reynolds, the author, had another reason to enjoy a big laugh for a long time. The book, notes Cerf, sold about five times as well after the exposure of the hoax as it did before.

THE HOAX THAT LED TO THE HOLOCAUST

The biggest hoax of the twentieth century—certainly the most damaging—involves a book first printed in 1903 that is still being printed and read and believed today.

The book is *The Protocols of the Elders of Zion,* an anti-Semitic work that may have been more disastrous for the Jews than *Mein Kampf.* Indeed, according to Henry Rollins, a French historian writing in the 1940s, next to the Bible *The Protocols* was probably the most widely distributed book in the world earlier this century. Salo Baron, the noted historian, calls it "the most influential forgery of the twentieth century."

The Protocols is purported to be the transcription of twenty-four secret meetings of Jewish elders in which a Jewish plot was hatched for throwing the world into chaos to gain control of the Gentiles. The elders spelled out how the Jews would use various methods, such as democracy, socialism, communism, revolution, the press, and the arts, to replace all nations and religions with a Jewish empire.

Research has shown that *The Protocols* was a distorted concoction using plagiarized parts of a forty-year-old novel by Herman Goodsche entitled *Biarritz* and scarcely changed pieces of a fictitious dialogue found in a French political pamphlet, published in 1864, that was a veiled attack on Napoleon III. Not one word of the original attack mentions Jews or Judaism.

Although the author of *The Protocols* is still not known for certain, the original forgery was done in French sometime between 1894 and 1899, most probably in 1897 or 1898. This means, as Norman Cohn indicates in *Warrant for Genocide* (Harper & Row, 1967), an in-depth study of *The Protocols,* that it was done during the anti-Semitic furor caused by the Dreyfus affair, sometime between his arrest in 1894 and his pardon in 1899.

Although executed in France, the forgery, says Cohn, "is clearly the work of a Russian and oriented towards the Russian right wing."

Indeed the first appearance of *The Protocols,* in 1903, was in Russia under the auspices of the czar's secret police, who wanted to use it to foment anti-Semitism. But the czar, interestingly, dismissed the work as a hoax (he called it "vile"), and *The Protocols* was not widely circulated in Russia until after the Russian Revolution.

But even with the hoax made clear, *The Protocols* became immensely popular. In the years before World War II, translations were published in England, Spain, France, Italy, Hungary, Yugoslavia, Austria, Czechoslovakia, Poland, Belgium, Norway, Holland, Russia, Sweden, Greece, Portugal, Brazil, Japan, Germany (where the Nazis gave it wide distribution), and the United States (editions appeared in New York in 1920, Boston in 1920, and Chicago in 1934).

The respected *London Times* at first considered them possibly authentic. Not until the following year, in August 1921, did the *Times* finally publish proof—splashed across its center page on three successive days—that *The Protocols* was a lie.

Legal proceedings were also instituted against *The Protocols* so that it could be studied impartially in a court of law. Thus in Bern, Switzerland, in 1935, a court ruled them to be "ridiculous nonsense" and "immoral."

One of the strongest believers in *The Protocols'* message of Jewry's ultimate plans was the automobile manufacturer Henry Ford. A staid individual, he worried about the changes taking place in the world and in American life and began accusing Jews of subverting traditional American ways (actually the Model-T Ford caused as much of the changes as anything). As a result, Ford's own newspaper, the *Dearborn Independent* (circulation 300,000), from May to October 1920, published an extensive series of articles on the Jewish threats of world domination. In November the articles were published as a book, *The International Jew: The World's Foremost Problem.* Three million copies were eventually printed and given massive promotion and distribution, especially in rural America. Eventually *The International Jew* was translated into sixteen languages. In Germany, according to Hitler in 1923, the book was "circulated in millions," and when he heard that Ford might run for president, Hitler said, "I wish that I could send some of my shock troops to Chicago and other big American cities to help in the elections. We look to Heinrich Ford as the leader of the growing Fascist movement in America."

Indeed Hitler thought so highly of Ford that he put Ford's picture on his desk and even praised the businessman in the first edition of *Mein Kampf.*

American Jewry reacted strongly to Ford's campaign. So did many prominent Americans, including President Woodrow Wilson, former president William Howard Taft, Clarence Darrow, Robert Frost, and former president Theodore Roosevelt. They were among 119 distinguished Americans who, on January 16, 1921, signed a strong protest as "citizens of Gentile birth and Christian faith" that read, in part, "We regret exceedingly the publication of a number of books, pamphlets and newspapers designed to foster distrust and suspicion of our fellow citizens of Jewish ancestry and faith—distrust and suspicion of their loyalty and their patriotism."

But it took six and a half years more and the pressure of several lawsuits before Ford finally decided he had been wrong to give such publicity and backing to anti-Jewish agitation. He publicly retracted his former position and apologized to the Jewish people, saying he was "deeply mortified" that his newspaper had been the medium "for resurrecting exploded fictions, for giving currency to the so-called Protocols of the Wise Men of Zion, which have been demonstrated, as I learn, to be gross forgeries."

Ford's *The International Jew* was only one of a number of writings inspired by *The Protocols.* The book also had a more direct effect—influencing and, in an unusual way, helping Hitler.

"I found these Protocols enormously instructive," he once said about his first exposure to the work. "I saw at once that we must copy it—in our own way of course. . . . We must beat the Jew with his own weapon. I saw that the moment I read the book." One of his early uses of the book could be seen in a 1923 speech, when he publicly spoke of how Germany's escalating inflation was part of a Jewish plot. "According to the Protocols of Zion, the people are to be reduced to submission by hunger," he declared.

Even the widespread charges that *The Protocols* was a fraud only convinced Hitler of its validity. In *Mein Kampf,* he noted how a newspaper, the *Frankfürter Zeitung,* "moans and screams once every week" that the work is "based on a forgery." Hitler found this "the best proof that they are authentic."

Not only did Hitler find support in *The Protocols* for his anti-Jewish harangues, he actually found good advice and ideas for his own diabolical plans. He himself noted how he had profited from

The Protocols' discussion of "political intrigue, the technique of conspiracy, revolutionary subversion, prevarication, deception, organization." In fact so close are many of the ideas spelled out in *The Protocols* and Hitler's subsequent actions that Robert G. L. Waite, writing in his book *The Psychopathic God: Adolf Hitler* (Basic Books, 1967), remarks, "In reading of the alleged conspiracy of the Jews as set forth in *The Protocols* one has the feeling that one is reading descriptions of Hitler's own political ideas, plans, and techniques as set forth in his memoirs, speeches, or conversations in the 1930's or during World War II."

But *The Protocols* has not ceased to be printed—and read. Since World War II the Arab world has become one of its prime promoters. Egyptian president Gamal Abdel Nasser publicly vouched for the authenticity of *The Protocols,* and his brother was publisher of one edition. Saudi Arabia's late King Faisal was said by Saudi information officials to consider it his "favorite literature" and gave copies to visiting newsmen. Muammar al-Qaddafi, ruler of Libya, who has kept a stack of them on his desk, has termed them "a most important historical document." In Beirut one year the Arabs printed 100,000 copies in English and 200,000 in French.

Indeed *The Protocols* is still being used and cited. In a *New York Times* front-page article in September 1988 an emerging new Islamic fundamentalist group called Hamas, which is the acronym for Movement of the Islamic Resistance and means "zeal," called for a holy war against Israel. In their forty-page covenant, discussed in the article, the group cited, among other reasons for such a war, the existence of *The Protocols of the Elders of Zion.*

The Hamas covenant declared, "The Zionist plan knows no boundaries. After Palestine they covet expansion from the Nile to the Euphrates. *The Protocols of the Elders of Zion* bears witness to this." *

Some lies die hard. And some lies never seem to die at all.

"Honesty is still the best policy, but some people are satisfied with less than the best."
—*A Treasure Chest of Quotations*

---

*John Kifner, "Islamic Fundamentalist Group Challenging P.L.O. and Israel," *The New York Times,* September 18, 1988, pp. 1 and 18.

My dear Mr. Hoover, those *lies* were *not* Freudian slips!

CHAPTER X

"My, but that hat looks stunning on you."

'LOOKING FOR 'LIES

. . . How to Know When Someone Is Lying to You

> *There's one way to find out if a man is honest—ask him. If he says yes, you know he is a crook.*
>
> —Groucho Marx

With all the lying we are exposed to, it is important that we know how to deal with lies and liars. What follows is a look at how we can protect ourselves from the manipulation and sometimes fraudulent use of statistics . . . how we should view the use and results of the polygraph machine—better known as the lie detector . . . and what physical and facial clues we can look for to detect when someone is lying directly to us.

In short, in the Age of the Lie even the honest—indeed, especially the honest—have to be schooled in the art of the lie.

HOW TO SPOT THE LIES IN STATISTICS

> *Round numbers are always false.*
> —Samuel Johnson

In our desire to have a world in which truth reigns, we want to believe at least in the sanctity of statistics. After all, numbers seem to come to us without bias or deceit. A 4 is a 4 and 40 percent is 40 percent, so what could be wrong about a number? And yet, we have all heard that famous statement that there are three kinds of lies—lies, damned lies, and statistics.* But how do statistics lie? And how can we spot the phony use of statistics?

A small book, first published in 1954 but into its thirty-first printing when I came across it in an undated later edition, gives an insight into why we should be wary of statistics and what we can do to protect ourselves from their misuse. The book, written by Darrell Huff, is entitled *How to Lie with Statistics* (W. W. Norton & Company, 1954).

The author's basic point is that despite its mathematical base, statistics is as much an art as it is a science. As such, "a great many manipulations and even distortions are possible within the bounds of propriety. Often the statistician must choose among methods, a subjective process, and find the one that he will use to represent the facts."

The result is that the statistician will be more likely to pick a method favorable to his or her hiring organization's purposes. "Even the man in academic work may have a bias (possibly unconscious) to favor, a point to prove, an axe to grind."

Thus, as Huff writes, we must give statistical material presented in newspapers, books, magazine articles, and advertising "a very sharp second look" before accepting any fact or figure.

How to Lie with Statistics advises that, when encountering a study or report based on statistics, you should ask yourself one or more of the following five simple questions:

1. *Who says so?*

Look to see who has issued the report and ask yourself if there might not be a built-in bias you should be wary about. Is the report coming from a lab that wants to prove a theory? A newspaper building a good story? Labor or management trying to get a better wage deal?

The bias involved in a report can be either unconscious or conscious. The unconscious bias may be of the variety that occurred in 1928 when economists and statisticians were caught up in the

---

*The person who coined this expression was England's prime minister, Benjamin Disraeli (1804–1881).

heady economic times and failed to see the cracks in the economy that would become apparent in late 1929 with the stock market crash and the beginning of the Depression. Conscious bias may result in direct misstatement or, at the least, an ambiguous statement, with the selection of only favorable data, or with the measurement of data against another set that provides favorable results—such as using one year for measurement but comparing it to another year that proves more or less favorable by comparison. Then, too, conscious bias may occur when the reporting group uses a mean where a median would be better, then covering the trickery with the unqualified word *average*.

Look also to see who is being cited as the source for the statistics and determine if that source just provided the raw data, with someone else doing the interpreting. Medical names, scientific labs, universities—these are all considered authoritative sources, but be certain that they are the ones standing behind the conclusions about their statistics and not some other person or group who has made conjectures based on statistics from an authoritative source.

2. *How does he know?*

Watch for evidence that the sample upon which the statistical report is making projections is large enough to permit a reliable conclusion. A questionnaire may have been sent to 1,000 people, but only 200 responded. Based upon the results coming from that smaller sample, the sponsoring organization may issue its findings that, let us say, 70 percent of a survey group responded a certain way. However, that percentage is not 70 percent of 1,000 but only 70 percent of 200—and one must further ask if those 200 are representative of the 1,000. In fact the 200 responding may have a biased reason to respond to the questionnaire while the remaining 800 who did not reply do not share that bias.

3. *What's missing?*

Furthermore, you must ask yourself if there are enough people or cases in the sample to mean anything. Look out for studies that talk totally in percentages but do not tell the numbers of people involved.

Also, you should be suspicious if a correlation is given without a measure of reliability (probable error, standard error). Watch out for mention of an average, variety unspecified, in a situation where use of a mean or median might be significantly different.

Watch for a lack of comparison, for without it most statistics have no meaning. To say that traffic accidents jumped by 100 percent over a July Fourth weekend does not have meaning until we learn how that compares with other July Fourths, with nonholiday weekends, even with the weekend before July Fourth. Indeed, although we often hear of high traffic fatalities on holiday weekends, on the basis of fatalities per hundred thousand miles traveled, many holiday weekends are no more dangerous to drivers than nonholiday weekends.

Sometimes the percentages are given but not the raw figures. Huff cites the case of a report issued in the early days of coeducation at Johns Hopkins University that 33 1/3 percent of women students at Hopkins had married faculty members—a shocking statistic until one looked at the raw numbers and saw that the sample population consisted of the only three women enrolled in Hopkins at the time and of those, one had married a member of the faculty.

Sometimes what is missing are the factors that caused a change to occur. For instance, more *reported* cases of a disease does not always mean there *are* more cases of a disease. Take the case of cancer. A great increase in reported cancer deaths over a twenty-five-year span earlier this century could or could not have implications for the spread of cancer, but not until other factors are considered. We must also weigh the fact that cancer was just beginning to be listed as a cause of death, whereas before "causes unknown" was often used; that autopsies were becoming more frequent, thereby providing better diagnosis; that medical statistics were becoming more complete because of better reporting; and that more people were living longer and thereby reaching the age at which cancer is more likely to strike. As for the total number of deaths by cancer, one must factor in the reality that more people are living—and dying—than before.

4. *Did somebody change the subject?*
Watch for a switch somewhere between the raw figures and the conclusion. Huff cites the case of how New York journalists Lincoln Steffens and Jacob Riis once created a crime wave by devoting so much newspaper space and giving such prominence to their stories that the public demanded action. Theodore Roosevelt, then head of the reform Police Board, was embarrassed by the public

attention and the calls for greater police efforts. He put an end to the public furor by asking Steffens and Riis to stop concentrating on crime stories. Once they desisted, other reporters, who had joined in the competition to dig up crime stories, also relented. The public clamor then died down as the crime wave seemed to abate. But the truth was that there had been no sudden crime wave—the official police record showed no increase at all.

Change-of-subject can also occur when definitions change. This happened in 1935 when the census showed a half million more farms in existence than in 1930, revealing what looked like a back-to-the-farm movement in the United States. But what happened is that the definition of a farm used by the census people had changed, so that now 300,000 more "farms" were included than would have been listed under the 1930 definition.

5. *Does it make sense?*

Ask this question about a statistic and it will often cut it down to size as the assumption on which it has been based becomes unproved: Cited here is the case of Rudolf Flesch, who established a readability formula based on the length of words and sentences. But the assumption that word length determines readability remains to be proved. In fact, when the formula was put to the test by subjecting *The Legend of Sleepy Hollow* to it, the child's tale proved to be harder to read than Plato's *Republic*.

And then there is the fact that many a statistic is false on its face. "It gets by only because the magic of numbers brings about a suspension of common sense," Huff notes. He cites the calculation of a well-known urologist who estimated earlier this century that there were eight million cases of cancer of the prostate gland in the United States—which, if true, would have meant that in the susceptible age group at the time, every male would have had 1.1 cancerous prostate glands.

Finally, be wary of statistics used to forecast the future. "The trend-to-now may be a fact, but the future trend represents no more than an educated guess," Huff writes. "Implicit in it is 'everything else being equal' and 'present trends continuing.' And somehow everything else refuses to remain equal, else life would be dull indeed."

Consider, for instance, the presidential commission in 1938 that doubted the U.S. population would ever reach 140 million. Textbooks in use in college in the 1940s and 1950s predicted a peak population of 150 million, not reachable until about 1980. Today the U.S. population is estimated to be at 250 million.*

The ridiculousness of assuming a trend will continue without change was demonstrated by Mark Twain in *Life on the Mississippi*. Writing in 1874, Twain pointed out that the lower part of the river had been shortened 242 miles during the past 176 years, which, he noted, averaged out to a little more than a mile and a third each year: "Therefore, any calm person who is not blind or idiotic can see that in the Old Oolitic Silurian Period, just a million years ago next November, the Lower Mississippi River was upward of one million three hundred thousand miles long. . . . And by the same token any person can see that seven hundred and forty-two years from now the Lower Mississippi will be only a mile and three-quarters long."

There is another way to lie with statistics that you need to be wary of. And that is the outright use of bogus statistics. The speaker who spouts a statistic to sound impressive, the politician who resorts to percentages to make his case compelling to the crowd, the writer who marshals projections and findings with little or no documentation—all should be suspected of being statistical liars, the most nefarious liars of all, since their figures are usually very impressive and hard to verify before they do their job of convincing.

One person who may have elevated the bogus statistic and developed a whole new way to lie with statistics was Richard Nixon. In his college days he was a very adept debater. During one debate Nixon made a telling point by reading statistics from a piece of paper. The editor of the school newspaper, however, observed the trickery: The paper from which Nixon read the statistics was blank.

THE LIE ABOUT A TRUTH SERUM

There has often been talk of a "truth serum," a drug that could somehow make an individual tell the truth even against his will.

---

*One person who did a little better but was still off by being stxty years too soon was Abraham Lincoln. In his second message to Congress, Lincoln predicted the U.S. population would reach 251,689,914 by 1930. His error was that he based his projections on the growth rate of 1790 to 1860.

The misleading term of "truth drug" was originally applied to scopolamine in 1932, but the evidence since then shows the original claims to be inaccurate.

It is in the diagnosis and treatment of various abnormal conditions that centrally acting drugs are sometimes administered to loosen inhibitions and facilitate talking. Drugs most commonly prescribed in this situation are the barbiturates, like sodium pentothal.

There is no medical or legal justification, however, to use these substances, since false statements can also be made with such drugs. Some people under the drug have been known to tell falsehoods that they believe to be true.

HOW HONEST ARE LIE DETECTORS?

In the search for ways to protect against the liar and to uncover lies, society has in the past eagerly turned to the lie detector or, as it is scientifically known, the polygraph.

Although ancient societies tried various mystical and magical ways to divine the truth and discover the guilty, the first scientific instrument to detect deception was developed by an Italian scientist, Cesare Lombroso, in 1895. He sought to measure changes in pulse and blood pressure when a suspect was questioned about a specific offense. He called his instrument the hydrosphygmograph.

The next advance came in 1914, when Vittorio Benussi developed the pneumograph, which measures changes in breathing. The instrument was used with success, thereby showing that the breathing patterns of individuals can be affected by their sense of guilt.

In 1917 William Marston did research with the sphygmomanometer, which took periodic discontinuous blood pressure readings. He also helped to develop the galvanometer, which measured changes in skin resistance.

But the major advance came in 1921, when John A. Larson developed the polygraph. This instrument was able to continuously record blood pressure, pulse, and respiration. Even this was improved upon, when Leonarde Keeler in 1949 introduced an advanced polygraph able to record changes in blood pressure, pulse, and respiration, as well as measure the galvanic skin reflex.

The polygraph we have today operates on the basis that physiological responses by the person being examined—changes in breathing, blood pressure, pulse rate, and skin reflex—can be measured and those changes, recorded by the machine, can be read by a trained polygraph examiner to determine if the examinee has answered the questions truthfully or deceitfully.

The theory behind the polygraph is that a guilty person will respond physiologically because such a person is afraid of being detected. Interestingly the popular belief that the lie detector works by uncovering the guilty based on their feelings of guilt or moral upbringing is a misconception. The lie detector detects the person's fear of detection, not his or her guilt feelings. Thus, say defenders of lie detectors, hardened criminals or psychopathic liars cannot readily beat the polygraph: while such people harbor little if any guilt feelings, they all share the desire to avoid being detected and caught.

The polygraph exam involves three phases—the pretest interview, the test itself, and, if necessary, a posttest interrogation.

The interview takes much more time than the tests. Each of what may be three or four tests lasts only a few minutes. But the interview involves the polygraph examiner explaining the polygraph and the test, getting to know the examinee, even reviewing with the examinee the questions that will be asked. In fact, as part of the rapport the examiner establishes with the examinee, the two may jointly decide on the questions to be asked on the first test.

In the test phase the questions asked usually are brief, number about ten to twelve, and can be answered with just a yes or no. Some of the questions asked have nothing to do with the case; they are asked simply to get a control reading for the examinee's normal level of physiological reactions. There is also always a pause, usually fifteen to twenty seconds, between each question. And then there will be a few questions—no more than three or four—that will be key to the case. These questions are asked in a blunt manner so as to elicit a strong, unmistakable reaction.

It is at this point that the polygraph examiner has his first indication that the examinee is or is not lying. If there is a lack of clarity on this, the examiner may test again with another set of questions. Since people may overreact at first, be frightened or be generally hostile, the examiner is trained to take such variables into account in assessing the test results.

Many courts, however, will not allow the admission of lie detector results. Defenders of the polygraph acknowledge that the polygraph chart can be misread—but so, too, they point out can physicians misread or differ in interpreting an electrocardiogram, radiologists an X ray, ballistic experts a bullet, psychiatrists the mental state of a suspect. Yet the testimony of physicians, technicians, and experts in various other fields are routinely accepted in many courts, while the results of polygraph tests and the testimony of the polygraph examiner are often circumscribed or disallowed in the criminal justice system's search for guilt or innocence.

After a quarter century of attempts by congressional legislators to limit use of lie detectors by employers, Congress passed the Employee Polygraph Protection Act in 1988 to restrict most private companies from using polygraphs either for preemployment screening or during the course of employment. The act, however, specifically exempted federal, state, and local governments from the restrictions, a fact that drew the ire of both labor and management. One labor lawyer said, "If polygraphs are inaccurate, then it ought to be the same for everybody."

The question is: How accurate are lie detectors? One study, published in 1978, involving polygraph examinations conducted under laboratory conditions as well as on criminal suspects, showed an accuracy rate above 90 percent when the exams were properly employed and evaluated. In 1953 two leading figures in the polygraph field—John Reid and Fred Inbau—tested 4,280 criminal suspects, with an accuracy rate of 95 percent. In 1971 John Reid, working with F. S. Jorvath, conducted an experiment in which the charts of forty test cases were shown to inexperienced and experienced polygraph examiners. The inexperienced (though trained) scored 79 percent accuracy in properly evaluating the results, the experienced 91.4 percent accuracy.

Detractors, however, have said that studies have shown too many innocent people have been unfairly caught up in the polygraph's web and labeled guilty while too many of the guilty have been cleared, that the overall accuracy rate could be as low as 25 percent, and that industry's overuse of an instrument that measures nervousness rather than untruthfulness has proven to be an abuse of privacy.

By the time Congress passed the Employee Polygraph Protection Act, the use of lie detectors had grown to more than 2 million tests a year, with 90 percent of those conducted by business, especially by large retailers who looked to the devices as a way of stemming the $40 billion a year in employee theft. With the passage of legislation protecting employees, it was estimated that the law would eliminate about 85 percent of polygraph testing. Many affected companies began turning to paper-and-pencil honesty tests, but these exams, too, started to draw fire as unreliable and invasive of individual privacy.

The debate still rages because the need for a reliable way to uncover dishonesty still exists. Polygraphs continue to be used by government, and under certain circumstances some private employers can use them also. Are the devices useful? Should they be used?

Here are two sides to the lie detector story:

The Case for the Polygraph

One of the most persuasive statements for allowing the use of the polygraph and introduction of its test results into court proceedings came in a 1980 case, *People* v. *Daniels,* in which the New York State Supreme Court, Westchester County, declared that polygraph evidence should be allowed. Wrote the court, "If the evidence has substantial probative value and is relevant to the issue and does not endanger defendants' rights, or prejudice the jury, nor mislead the proper administration of justice, then it should be admitted as any other evidence." The court pointed out that fingerprints, ballistics, and other kinds of scientific evidence are admitted under the same standard.

In answer to objections that might be raised as to the admissibility of such evidence, the court pointed out that "the chance of beating the polygraph is no greater than outwitting the jury." Furthermore, it was noted that in this particular case before the court the state's case against the defendant rested on the identification made by just one eyewitness, the victim. The court stated that eyewitness testimony is "proverbially untrustworthy" and less reliable than the polygraph, which, the court said, research had shown has a 90 percent accuracy rate when properly conducted and evaluated.

One final point in favor of the polygraph, not necessarily made by the New York State Supreme Court: Besides showing guilt, it can also, according to the *FBI Law Enforcement Bulletin,* "elim-inate suspects, verify witnesses' statements, corroborate infor-mant information, and determine the veracity of a complainant's statement."

The FBI also found another benefit: "It can also dramatically increase the conviction rate due to the high occurrence of confes-sions made by suspects who had been less than candid prior to the polygraph examination."*

The Case Against the Polygraph

Before Congress limited the use of lie detectors in the work-place, the following situation prevailed:

- Senator Orrin Hatch of Utah, ranking Republican mem-ber on the Senate Labor Committee, declared that 500,000 "honest people each year are branded as liars" by false lie detector results.

- Senator Edward Kennedy, head of the Senate Labor Committee, called polygraphs "twentieth-century witch-craft."

- According to Gary Lynch, director of enforcement at the Securities Exchange Commission, some investment bankers who passed polygraph tests with no problem during insider-trading investigations later became cooperative wit-nesses for the commission. Said Lynch, "It turns out they were lying" to the lie detector.

- Polygraph test results, as of July 1988, were not con-sidered admissible evidence in federal court or in the courts of twenty-seven states.

- The bill to ban polygraph tests for employees in private industry was endorsed by labor unions, civil liberties groups, U.S. Labor Secretary Ann McLaughlin, the Ameri-can Medical Association, and the American Psychological Association.

---

*See James K. Murphy, "The Polygraph Technique—Past and Present," *FBI Law Enforcement Bulletin,* June 1980, pp. 1–5.

Consider the revealing testimony made in October 1983 by the head of the Office of Technology Assessment of the U.S. Congress.

Responding to a Reagan administration proposal to plug news leaks by making almost half the federal work force liable to polygraph tests, Dr. John H. Gibbons, director of the agency, pointed out that the instrument itself cannot detect deception. Since a polygraph measures a person's physical reactions, such as change in heartbeat or skin moisture during questioning, the equipment is, according to Dr. Gibbons, "more of a fear detector than a lie detector."

Dr. Gibbons said that studies showed that polygraphs were accurate from 64 percent to 98 percent of the time, but this level of accuracy depends on the percentage of guilty people in a screening group. If that percentage is small, the polygraph is likely to identify incorrectly many people as liars, even while it succeeded in identifying most of the liars correctly.

Dr. Gibbons further pointed out that the validity of the polygraph could be shown only in criminal cases when investigators have collected much data and have narrowed the field of suspects.

One question that has long intrigued laymen is whether a guilty person could beat a lie detector. Dr. Gibbons also had an answer to this question: yes. There is evidence that people can be trained or can train themselves to beat the device.

In other words, lie detectors can lie too.

And then consider the case of a top White House aide.

Robert McFarlane was national security advisor under Ronald Reagan when *The New York Times* published an article on a national security matter that led the Reagan administration to try to find who in the White House might have leaked the story to the *Times*.

During the ensuing probe, lie detector tests were administered to a number of White House aides. Bud McFarlane flunked not one but two polygraph tests, and all indications pointed to him as the leaker. His job was now in jeopardy. Distraught because he knew he was innocent but had no way of proving it, McFarlane pleaded with top officials of the *Times* to tell President Reagan he had not been the source of the leaks. Told by editors that someone else had been the source, the publisher of the *Times* informed the president that McFarlane was innocent—with the understanding that no precedent was being set for newspapers to provide such "negative sourcing."

In recounting this episode, William Safire, in his column in *The New York Times* (May 26, 1988), wrote that "President Reagan thus learned firsthand that the best FBI polygraphers could be egregiously wrong, and that reliance on the polygraph could do a gross injustice to a loyal employee."*

So what's the answer? Are lie detectors helpful or harmful? What do you think?

CAN YOU TELL IF SOMEONE IS LYING TO YOU? (WHEN IT COMES TO LYING, A BODY CAN TELL)

With so much evidence of lying going on in our daily lives, it is important, for the sheer sake of survival, that we know when someone is lying to us. Are there any signs a liar gives off? Are there any helpful hints we can use to spot lying in others?

One author who says there is is Dr. Peter Marsh, a psychologist. In his book *Eye to Eye* (Salem House, 1988), he points out that studies have shown we can spot a liar by paying attention to his or her nonverbal cues, the "leakage" of various bits of true emotions that come out through facial expressions and bodily actions.

Here is a breakdown of the findings of such studies:

The Eyes

We tend to feel that people who do not look us in the eye as we talk with them have something to hide. And indeed experimental studies have shown that when individuals are encouraged to lie or cheat, many accompany their deception with an averted

---

*Safire also related how William Casey, head of the CIA, had once told him the lie detector could be beaten "with Valium and a few tricks by any well-trained spy"—which is why, said Safire, "reliance on the inaccurate polygraph is a source of internal security weakness."

gaze. Thus, sensing our own instincts in such a situation, we tend to doubt others with "shifty eyes."

There is a reason for this. A liar may not look you straight in the eye because any tense situation heightens anxiety, which lying certainly does, and eye contact with another person in itself causes an increase in psychological arousal. So a liar will instinctively avert his or her gaze to reduce the anxiety level. However, some people—especially those who have experience lying or are "Machiavellian" personalities who enjoy manipulating others—can lie while maintaining eye contact without any problems. Thus the fact that someone looks you in the eye is not necessarily an indicator that they are telling you the truth—nor is the opposite necessarily true.

But there is one quality about the eyes that can help detect a liar—and the liar cannot do much to prevent such a telltale sign. The pupils of the eye expand and contract involuntarily. While they open and close based upon available light, they also open and close due to emotional reasons—even when the light on them remains the same. One way to spot a liar, then, is to watch the pupil of the eye to see if it widens. Thus, since the Machiavellian personality is "good" at lying and knows that others feel an averted gaze is a tip-off, the practiced liar will actually increase eye contact after cheating and especially after being accused of cheating. It is then that the pupils of the eye will widen, offering you a built-in lie detector.

The Voice

People who are lying have been found to speak with a higher pitch and at a slower rate. They are also given to making slips of the tongue, repeating words, switching words, and overusing *ums* and *ers*. Liars have also been found to avoid making factual statements, resorting more to generalized remarks, and they resort to leaving gaps in their conversation to reduce the possibility of saying something that would give any clues about their deceit.

The pace of speaking also provides clues, but in different ways, based upon a person's usual speech pattern. Normally anxious people who speak at a faster pace actually reduce their speech pace with the heightened anxiety of lying. Those not usually considered anxious, however, speak more quickly than normal when lying.

The Smile

It has been found that people smile less when lying. When they do smile, they resort to forced smiles, which can be detected by the fact that spontaneous smiles cause wrinkling around the eyes while forced smiles do not affect these muscles. Forced smiles also tend to affect one side of the face more than the other, generally being stronger on the left side in right-handed people and on the right in left-handed people. Finally the forced smile appears on the face faster, is held longer, and fades in an irregular manner.

One other way to catch the deceiving smile is to look for a mismatch between the eyes—which cannot be *made* to "smile"— and the mouth.

Being able to spot the forced smile is important in uncovering deceitfulness in others, because research has found that people *perceived* to have honest faces have one thing in common: They generally have broad smiles. The need to sense when a smile is not spontaneous is therefore all the more crucial to knowing when someone else's smile is masking a lie.

The Hands

Hands are very good clues for detecting a liar. In experiments it has been found that people asked to demonstrate their ability to lie would significantly decrease their hand movements. There seems to be an instinctive recognition that hands can express a message, so the person bent on deceiving—afraid that his hands will convey his deceit—will try to keep his hands still or out of sight.

When hands are used, look to see if the person is touching his face a great deal while talking. A deceiver will often display more frequent self-touching, such as touching the nose, the chin, or the mouth. This is a way the liar takes some of the anxiety out of deceiving the person he is talking to. And accompanying the hand gestures is the fact that liars tend to shift their postures more than nonliars.

The Facial Expression

The expressions on the face—except for the eyes—are the easiest for liars to control. This can cause problems for you when trying to determine the sincerity, or lack of it, in another person, since studies have shown that trusting listeners pay more attention to the face and accept its signals more than any other part of the body. Thus, since the face is the least revealing of deception, you should, as a suspicious listener, be more attentive to the voice, to the eyes, and to the hands.

To be your own lie detector, then, you need only remember what Sigmund Freud once said: "He that has eyes to see and ears to hear may convince himself that no mortal can keep a secret. . . . Betrayal oozes out of him at every pore."

"The eyes never lie."
—Mikhail Gorbachev to an audience in Prague
(*Time*, January 4, 1988, p. 29)

THE ORIENTAL LIE DETECTOR

In ancient times the Orientals had their own approach to detecting lies—one based on their widespread use of rice.

The suspected liar would be given dry rice to chew and then spit out. For those who were honest, the act of spitting out the rice was easy.

But for those who were guilty, it would prove difficult to spit the rice out of the mouth. The reason: fear dries up the saliva, and a guilty person, fearing discovery, would find his salivation stopping.

While the innocent felt little or no fear and could therefore spit out the dry rice, the culprit found the act nearly impossible.

THE AGE DETECTOR

In the search for an accurate lie detector, here is a detector of age I came across years ago in a game book for children. With the approach outlined here, you can determine if someone is lying about his or her age—and if so, you can then figure out the correct age.

Tell the person to do the following:

1. Without showing you, he should write down his age by the end of the year. (Tell the person he can either tell the truth or fudge his age up to nine years and you will still determine his correct age.)

2. To this number he should add his age in the following year.

3. He then multiplies this total by 5.

4. Now he adds the last number of his birth year (for instance, if born in 1942, he adds 2).

5. He tells you the total figure.

Now, take this result, and subtract 5. This figure will always be a three-digit number, the first two of which tell the person's age. You now have the age the person listed, without his knowing you know this.

To find out if this person is telling you the truth or lying, take the last digit in the three-digit number just given to you and deduct that number from the last two digits of the present year (for instance, 90 if the year is 1990). Look at the resulting last figure only. If this agrees with the third digit in the number given to you from step 5, the person is being honest about his or her age. If it does not agree, the person is lying.

You can now, to this individual's surprise and the surprise of others watching, announce what that person's age is and if the individual was being honest or trying to lie.

What is the secret behind this lie detector?

The key is asking the person to factor in the year of his birth (see step 4). Since the person has either lied or told the truth in step 1, he or she is invariably taken off guard and factors in the true birth year, figuring that surely the last number in a four-digit year cannot give him away. But it does—every time it is given truthfully.

Here is an example of how the age detector works:

1. Irving is a born liar and, asked his age, he puts down 22, even though he is 29.

2. Asked to add his age the following year, he adds 23 to continue the subterfuge.

3. Told to multiply the total of 22 plus 23—45—by 5, Irving gets 225.

4. If 1990 is the year in which the age detector is used, our 29-year-old Irving was born in 1961, so he puts down 1.

5. When Irving adds the 225 with the number 1, he gets 226.

6. You now deduct 5 from the 26 and get 221. Since you take only the first two numbers of this three-digit number to arrive at Irving's stated age, you now know the age Irving said he was—22. Now, the question is—is he telling the truth?

7. So using the three-digit number that emerged (221), you take the last digit (1) and deduct it from the last number in the year in which the test is being given (1990 in our example here).

8. The remaining number after 1 is deducted from the 0 of 1990 is, of course, 9. This number, 9, is the true second number in Irving's real age. Since in step 6 you found out Irving said he was 22 and you now discover he is really 29, you know that Irving is lying (and that his real name is Joe Isuzu).

9. Announce your findings, give Irving's real age, and reap the admiration of the crowd—while probably reaping something else from Irving.

''Most writers regard the truth as their most valuable possession, and therefore are most economical in its use.''
—Mark Twain

The Honesty Hall of Fame.

CONCLUSION

"I swear to tell the truth, the whole truth, and . . ."

DO THE
LIES HAVE IT?

. . . Can Honesty Still Be a Policy?

They that deal truly are His delight.
                                    —Proverbs 12:22

The increase in recent years of scandalous behavior in the financial markets, in political campaigns, in government, in business—indeed from Wall Street to Main Street—has been accompanied by a definite and measurable shift in the philosophy and goals being exhibited by our college youth.

In a 1988 survey of nearly 290,000 freshmen in more than 500 colleges, a record number—75.6 percent, the highest in the twenty years of the survey—said that "being very well off financially" was their goal, while only 39.4 percent, a twenty-year low, said that "developing a meaningful philosophy of life" was most important to them. This is dramatically lower than the 82.9 percent of students who expressed this sentiment twenty years ago.

These findings by the American Council on Higher Education appear to mirror what is happening in society in general. We are seeing a shift away from the embrace of basic values to the pursuit of money and income. It is in such an emphasis on materialism that honesty often falls victim.

History is replete with those who would manipulate the truth for their own ends—from the robber barons to common robbers, from Machiavelli to stock market manipulators. But our own era has been particularly damaged by deceit. Indeed the need for a revival in honesty in modern times can be seen in how some of our most treasured institutions are falling in public esteem. During a recent ten-year period a noticeable drop occurred in the proportion of people responding yes to whether they had a great deal of confidence in the people running various major institutions in America.

In medicine the figure fell from 73 percent to 42 percent. Major companies dropped from 55 percent to 16 percent. Law firms went from 24 percent to 12 percent. Advertising agencies, previously at 21 percent, slid to 7 percent.

The lesson is clear. Public confidence and trust in our society is not strong. The Age of the Lie has had its effect.

But do not despair. Let not this book's litany of lying, this parade of prevaricators, depress you. There have always been and still are many individuals who practice honesty. In a hard-bitten world, honesty may not always be a person's best policy, but as a policy honesty brings out the best in a person.

Here is a sampling of some honest-to-goodness heroes.

OUR $500,000 MAN

Consider Lowell Elliott of Peru, Indiana. On his farm one day in June 1972, he found $500,000 in cash. The money may have seemed to him to have dropped onto his land out of thin air—and he would have been right to think so. A skyjacker parachuting out of a plane flying over Indiana had dropped his unlawful gains of half a million dollars and watched helplessly as it plummeted to the ground. Elliott, when he came across the eye-popping cache, did what not many other people would have done. He turned it over to authorities. According to the *Guinness Book of World Records,* this was "the largest amount of cash ever found and returned to its rightful owners."

NOW, HERE'S AN HONEST AUTHOR

Art Donovan, who weighs nearly 300 pounds, played defensive tackle on the great Baltimore Colt teams of the 1950s and 1960s.

Since his retirement, the big, burly guy has been elected to the Football Hall of Fame and, with his penchant for humorous and honest remarks, he has been a frequent guest on David Letterman's TV show. He also wrote *Fatso* (Morrow, 1987), a book about his playing days—one of those "as told to" or "with" books—in which he utilized the services of a sports writer as coauthor.

Asked by a reporter after publication if he was proud of the book, Donovan replied, "I don't know. I haven't read it yet."

HONESTY IS THE BEST POLICY—ESPECIALLY AROUND A BUNCH OF LIARS

In 1936 Leland Harvey and Aubrey Smith were serving time in the Georgia State Penitentiary for criminal escapades that had made them Georgia's public enemies one and two.

One day the governor of Georgia, Eugene Talmadge, visited the prison and spent part of his time interviewing the prisoners, but in a special way. As he walked along the prison corridors accompanied by the warden, he would ask each inmate, "Are you guilty?" The only replies he heard were emphatic noes.

As the governor came to Harvey and Smith and asked the same question, he was taken aback when he heard the two answer without hesitation that they were indeed guilty.

The governor turned to the warden. "It seems you only have two thieves in your penitentiary," Talmadge said. "I will pardon these two men."

The self-confessed robbers, who were then serving 150-year terms for armed robbery, did indeed receive pardons from Governor Talmadge, who later explained, "Truthful men should never be confined with a bunch of liars."

WHEN A BASEBALL CLUB TOLD THE TRUTH EVEN WHEN IT HURT THEIR PLAYOFF CHANCES

At the end of 1988 the Detroit Tigers were in the thick of a hot baseball pennant race. They were trying to hold on to first place in the American League Eastern Division. To do so they were attempting to arrange a trade for Fred Lynn, a top left-handed hitter on the Baltimore Orioles. But they needed to get the trade completed before midnight on August 31 so that Lynn could qualify to play for the Tigers if they won their division and went into postseason play. According to league rules, Lynn actually had to arrive in the city in which Detroit was playing before 12 on the night of August 31 if he was to qualify for the playoffs or World Series.

Because of last-minute delays in negotiations, the deal was not concluded until 4:35 P.M. on the afternoon of August 31. To meet the deadline, the Tigers chartered a private jet for $9,800 to fly Lynn from California, where the Orioles were playing, into Chicago, where the Tigers were playing. But Lynn was delayed by rush-hour traffic getting to the airport. The plane therefore did not take off until 6 P.M. (8 P.M. Chicago time) for the four-hour-and-twenty-minute flight to Chicago's O'Hare Airport.

Lynn did not have to land in Chicago, only to be in its air space before midnight, to be eligible to play in postseason games. Lynn's plane, however, did not enter Chicago's air space until ten minutes after midnight.

What did the Tigers do?

They told the truth.

"He didn't get there," Bill Lajoie, general manager of the Tigers, said the next day to reporters. "They were over the city limits about 10 after 12. That's when they made the first radio contact with the tower at O'Hare."

But no one knew that except the general manager of the Tigers. Lajoie could easily have fudged the truth, and in fact a spokesperson for the baseball commissioner's office later said that unless another club disputed it and asked for an investigation, "We would have taken them at their word."

Thus, Lajoie, faced with the reality that Lynn was late, told the commissioner's office the truth—even though it meant the Tigers could use Lynn during September but could not go into postseason play with one of the game's top left-handed hitters.

"I just felt a rule's a rule," Lajoie told the press. "There's no sense playing with it. That's the rule and we'll live by it."

Lajoie's act of honesty was so refreshing that *The New York Times* ran the story about it on their front page (A BASEBALL CLUB TELLS TRUTH; EVEN ACCEPTS CONSEQUENCES) and then later followed it up with comment on their editorial page under *Topics of the Times:* "There is a word for people like Bill Lajoie. It's 'class,' and there are too few occasions to use it."

Lajoie made such a lasting impression that the following year he was given an award—an honorary diploma from the International Committee for Fair Play, which is a part of the United Nations Educational, Scientific and Cultural Organization. The committee honored him for his honesty in Paris in the category of "Gestures of Fair Play."

THE HONEST BALLPLAYER

The story was so unusual that even though it involved only a seven-year-old ballplayer in T-ball, *Sports Illustrated* magazine ran an item about it in the publication's July 10, 1989, issue. The headline read: AN HONEST KID.

The child, Tanner Munsey, was playing first base in a T-ball game in Wellington, Florida, when a ground ball was hit to him. He fielded it and tried to tag a runner who was going from first to second. The umpire, Laura Benson, ruled the runner was out. But then something strange and wonderful happened. Munsey immediately informed the umpire that he had missed touching the runner. The umpire, reacting to the refreshing candor, reversed her call and gave the runner second base. Munsey, however, later got the game ball from his coach for his truthfulness.

But that wasn't the end of the story. Two weeks later, in another game, Munsey, now playing shortstop, had to tag another runner out. This time, though, the same umpire was umpiring and thought the child had missed the tag. The runner was called safe.

Munsey looked at the umpire and paused before throwing the ball back to the catcher and returning to the shortstop position. Realizing something was troubling the child, Umpire Benson asked Munsey if he had touched the runner. Munsey responded that he had.

Benson then reversed her decision and announced that the runner was out. The runner's coach protested the reversal of the umpire's original call, but the umpire then told about Munsey's truthfulness in the other game. The umpire, quoted by *Sports Illustrated,* explained: "If a kid is that honest, I have to give it to him."

NESS WAS REALLY UNTOUCHABLE

While J. Edgar Hoover was not above playing with the truth, another crime fighter from that era was so aboveboard that he acted honorably in even the most trying of circumstances. Eliot Ness, a U.S. Treasury agent who was the subject of the *Untouchables* TV series and the motion picture of that title for his crime-fighting activities during the 1920s and 1930s, was cited as "a genuinely honest man" by the actor who portrayed him on television.

Robert Stack, who is now strongly identified with Ness, knew much about him, which is why he gladly acted as Ness.

"[Ness] was offered thousands and thousands of dollars in bribes during the years when he couldn't buy his wife a new dress, but he never took [any of] it," Stack said in an interview. "He was a special person. He had something rare—honor. It's something I hope I have, too."

Interestingly, Stack then felt it necessary to tell his interviewer, "I don't care if people think it's old-fashioned."

The Honesty Hall of Fame:
Profiles in Real Courage

Those who have shown the futility of lies and the triumph of truths:

• Pinocchio's creator (he showed he had a nose for the good news about telling the truth)

• The author of the slogan "Honesty is the best policy" (because he was a true believer)

• The inventor of the lie detector (at least he cared)

• George Washington (because of him we like to believe all our presidents are honest)

• Abraham Lincoln (he was called Honest Abe, and that's close enough)

- Grover Cleveland (he told the truth during his campaign for the presidency and—amazingly—was still elected)

- Moses (one of the Big Ten he brought was not to bear false witness—which means don't lie around cops and judges)

- Jimmy Carter (he said, "I will never lie to you," and he meant it—as he showed when he told *Playboy* magazine, "I have looked on a lot of women with lust.")

- Winston Churchill (he said, "I have nothing to offer but blood, toil, tears, and sweat"—a refreshing use of honesty on the world scene)

- All three-year-olds (before being shushed by Mom and Dad, every three-year-old tells the truth)

OUR HERO: GROVER CLEVELAND
(1837–1908)
THE STORY OF THE HONEST PRESIDENT

Grover Cleveland was a remarkable person and political figure. He holds the distinction of having been the only president of the United States to be elected to two unconnected terms (1885–89 and 1893–97). He is also, after FDR, the only candidate to have won the popular vote for president in three straight campaigns. (He won the popular vote but lost the electoral vote in that middle term of 1889–93.) He may also hold the distinction, with all due respect to George Washington and Abraham Lincoln, of possibly being our most honest president.

As the mayor of Buffalo early in his political career, Cleveland took on the political bosses and opposed so many of the City Council's crooked appropriation measures that he was sneeringly called "the Veto Mayor" and referred to as "His Obstinacy." When he rose to governor of New York, he continued to veto bills passed by the state legislature intended to help the interests of politically powerful Tammany Hall.

He was so open about his opposition to dishonesty and corruption that he was termed "ugly-honest." He would not stand for those seeking favoritism or a payback for political support. In fact the concept and slogan that "Public Office Is a Public Trust" sprang from Cleveland's references, throughout his state papers and public addresses as governor and mayor, that public officers were trustees of the people. A reporter, assigned to prepare a campaign document for Cleveland after he won the presidential nomination, noticed how frequently Cleveland made such a statement. The reporter brought this to Cleveland's attention and suggested he use it during the campaign. Cleveland agreed, and the slogan gained wide appeal. The *New York World,* published by Joseph Pulitzer, endorsed Cleveland, listing four reasons for doing so: "1. He is an honest man; 2. He is an honest man; 3. He is an honest man; 4. He is an honest man."

During the campaign itself, Cleveland was the subject of a scandalous revelation—that he had fathered a child as a young bachelor in Buffalo. When his campaign managers asked him in despair what they should do, he replied, "Tell the truth." Ironically his opponent, James G. Blaine, was undergoing serious accusations of secret dealings with the railroads, but when Democratic leaders came to Cleveland with documents that could be used to sully Blaine's reputation, Cleveland ripped the papers to shreds. "The other side can have a monopoly of all the dirt in this campaign," he declared.

Cleveland went on to win the election—and went on vetoing legislation. In the four years of his first term, he issued 413 veto messages—more than twice the vetoes made by all the twenty-one presidents who had come before him. Once called the "Veto Mayor," he was now called "Veto President."

Cleveland's first four years were regarded highly by civil service reformers and business people. In his reelection bid, he won the popular vote but lost the electoral vote to Benjamin Harrison. Four years later Cleveland was able to come back and easily win both the popular and the electoral vote and get elected once again. This time, though, a depression set off by the Panic of 1893 led to widespread unrest and unemployment. Cleveland could not deal with the social dislocations and the new economic realities. And although he was known as rigidly honest, hardworking, and politically upright, he ended his second term as a highly unpopular president, a fact that deeply distressed him. But during the years that passed before his death, his reputation once again increased. People remembered the honesty and integrity he brought to government, and many of his vetoes were seen as being necessary.

When he died in 1908, Cleveland's last words were, "I have tried so hard to do right." History appears to agree. In 1932 historian Allan Nevins wrote a biography entitled appropriately *Grover Cleveland: A Study in Courage.*

What is fascinating about Grover Cleveland is that his honesty did not hurt him in politics—in fact, it actually seemed to help him. After all, he was elected a mayor, a governor of the then-most-populated state, and twice as president of the United States (and the winner of the popular presidential vote three times). Never once during his political career did he compromise his principles of telling the truth.

Interestingly, the three most highly successful presidents in our history are also noted for being honest. George Washington and Abraham Lincoln, considered among our greatest leaders, are enshrined as synonymous with honesty. And Franklin Delano Roosevelt, who was elected to more terms (four) and served longer than any other president, had, as previously mentioned, one of the most scandal-free administrations in history.

So it can be done in politics and government—honesty can be a helpful policy. And if it can be done in those twin arenas of pressure, then surely it can be done in other areas of our lives.

But will it?

This book, which began as a lark, ends with a lament.

When I first thought of the idea of writing a book about lying, I wondered if I would have enough material. I found I had too much.

I uncovered scams and schemes being perpetrated in science, medicine, government, finance, the arts—often by the least likely against the most unlikely.

I found deceit and deception by business against the consumer—and deceit and deception by the consumer against business.

And the frauds and lies are not lessening with time; they are growing. We pride ourselves on being knowledgeable and sophisticated, but the greatest hoaxes—from Piltdown Man to art forgeries—have actually been pulled in the twentieth century. With the advent of more technology, it seems we have not greater defenses against fraud but more likelihood of greater fraudulent offenses.

The erosion of moral and ethical values is one reason for the prevalence of more lying in our lives—for indeed the liar is, by definition, a person without ethics. In the face of this, we can only guard against the liar and the lie by being that much more on guard. *Buyer, beware* has led to *buyer be aware;* it is now shifted to *buyer and seller be wary together.*

Although this may indeed be the Age of the Lie, the liar however has been with us throughout history and in many guises. Virtually all religious and ethical systems endorse honesty and attack lying. What we need today is a reinforcement of this with more honor for the honest and more realization that—initially sometimes and eventually most times—the truth pays and the liar loses. In other words, it is in our own best interest as a society to praise and support the honest. With honesty, we live better with others and with ourselves.

In this regard, George Washington once said something about the honorableness of honesty that still rings true 200 years later. And so, in conclusion, with the moral of this book . . .

OUR FIRST PRESIDENT HAS THE LAST WORD

"I hope I shall possess firmness and virtue enough to maintain what I consider the most enviable of all titles, the character of an honest man."

—George Washington

ACKNOWLEDGMENTS

In all honesty, I wrote this book by myself. But I cannot tell a lie—a number of people helped me in various ways during the years it took to research and write *The Book of Lies*.

First, I want to acknowledge the influence of my father, Herman, in this book. My father passed away during the early stages of this work, but as always during my writing career, he was an active participant in my research. With *The Book of Lies*, however, he was more—he was an inspiration to me about the value of honesty. He was truly an honest, honorable man. I literally cannot think of a time or occasion when he did anything deceitful. An astute lawyer and a whiz with figures, he would not tolerate dishonesty with words or numbers. He was also an inspiration as a book author. When he was with the National Labor Relations Board in the 1930s and 1940s, he edited the first digest of all NLRB rulings, a massive undertaking that resulted in a monumental tome. So my father's presence is very much in all my writings, but especially so in this volume.

I would also like to thank the following individuals for their assistance. My family, especially my wife, children, and my mother, who showed keen interest and support for this project throughout. Dr. Sheldon Glass, Dr. Tom Blass, and Ned Rubin, who supplied me with material about the psychological aspects of lying. Michael John Switalski, supervisor of the polygraph unit of the Baltimore City Police Department, who provided me with information about and insight into the lie detector. The staff of the Enoch Pratt Free Library system in Baltimore, especially those manning the information service, who once again helped me immeasurably by answering research questions and helping track down books not only from the Enoch Pratt's vast collection but from other libraries in the country. My agent, Mitch Douglas, who has been very supportive. Ray Driver, an artist of uncommon excellence and wit whose drawings once again illuminate a work of mine. Typists Jane Barr and Chaya Greenwald, who put up with my many handwritten additions up and down my manuscript. Editorial assistant Ronald Lincoln, of William Morrow, who has been diligent in keeping me on schedule.

But most of all I want to thank my editor, Andy Ambraziejus. He has played an instrumental part in the creation and execution of this book. He was enthusiastic from the very beginning and offered many insightful suggestions throughout the entire process. I will always appreciate his wise counsel and his expert editorial input. Every author should have an editor like him.

One final note. Although I have had much help and support, I of course assume all responsibility for any errors. However, while great pains have been taken to make certain the material in this book is accurate, I have often had to rely on other sources for information, and as I hope I have shown, deceits can creep into printed works. Lies are not only spoken but written. Thus, with a last reminder about our world's most common activity, I quote Maimonides, the great Jewish scholar of the twelfth century, who wrote in his *Epistle to the Yemenites:*

> Do not think a thing proved because it is in a book; the liar, who deceives men with his tongue, does not hesitate to deceive them with his pen.

Of course, you need not worry about *The Book of Lies*. It is, I hope, full of truths.

M. HIRSH GOLDBERG

Baltimore, Maryland
November 24, 1989

"Honesty is still the best policy."
—The author's mother

INDEX

ABOUT THE AUTHOR

M. Hirsh Goldberg is the only author in history to be awarded not one but two Nobel Prizes for Literature. He has also won the Pulitzer Prize, an Oscar, an Emmy, and the Pabst Blue Ribbon. All of his books have been huge best-sellers, including his next one.

You don't believe that? Then how about this:

Mr. Goldberg is the author of three other books, his previous being *The Blunder Book* (Morrow, 1984). He is a graduate of The Johns Hopkins University, with a bachelor's degree in English and a master's in teaching. Accredited by the Public Relations Society of America, he has served as press secretary to the mayor of Baltimore and the governor of Maryland. He has also served as director of public information and education for the Office of Attorney General of Maryland and its Consumer Protection Division. He is currently president of SmithMead & Goldberg, a Baltimore-based public relations agency, and lectures widely on his writings.

Mr. Goldberg and his wife, Barbara, live with their family in Baltimore, Maryland.

And that's the truth.